Contents

Acronyms

ASB	Accounting Standards Board		NIRS2	National Insurance Recording System 2
CBI	Confederation of British Industry		NPC	Net present cost
CCT	Compulsory competitive tendering		NPV	Net present value
DBFO	Design, build, finance and operate		OGC	Office of Government Commerce
DETR	Department for the Environment, Transport and the Regions		PAC	Public Accounts Committee
DoT	Department of Transport		PCT	Primary care trust
EDB	Early design and build		PDC	Public dividend capital
EDS	Electronic Data Systems Ltd (a company)		PFI	Private Finance Initiative
FBC	Full business case		PIR	Post-implementation review
FM	Facilities Management		PPP	Public private partnership
FRS 5	Financial Reporting Standard No. 5 *Reporting the Substance of Transactions*		PUK	Partnerships UK
			SPV	Special purpose vehicle
GAO	General Accounting Office (US)		SSAP 21	Statement of Standard Accounting Practice No. 21 *Accounting for Leases and Hire Purchase*
HA	Highways Agency			
IPO	Initial Public Offering		TUPE	Transfer of Undertakings Protection of Employment
LEA	Local Education Authority			
LU	London Underground		UK GAAP	UK Generally Accepted Accounting Principles
MCG	Major Contractor Group		VFM	Value for money
NAO	National Audit Office		WIMS	Works Information Management System
NHS	National Health Service			

Executive summary

Partnerships are one of the keystones of the Government's reform of the public services. They have both macro-level and micro-level objectives. At the macro level, the intention is to lever in the private finance that the Government cannot afford. In some sectors such as roads, a parallel macro objective has been to create private sector capability. At the micro level, partnership objectives embrace value for money (VFM), a concept that includes the transfer to the private sector of risk and the associated costs that would otherwise be borne by the public sector and the greater expertise, efficiency and innovation that the private sector is assumed to possess.

The introduction of partnership working, known as the Private Finance Initiative (PFI), was heralded with much enthusiasm by the then Conservative Government in the early 1990s and was later adopted with similar enthusiasm as a cornerstone of the incoming Labour Government's policy for improving infrastructure and public services. The Labour Government re-branded the policy as public private partnerships (PPP), widened it to include several different forms of which the PFI is but one, and has, confusingly, used the terms PPP and PFI interchangeably. Under the PFI, the public sector procures a capital asset and non-core services from the private sector on a long-term contract, typically at least 30 years, in return for an annual payment.

Subsequently ministers, government officials and others with financial interests in the PFI policy have claimed much success for projects. However, numerous IT PFI projects have failed. Several PFI/PPP projects have had to be bailed out, some have been scrapped and others have been the subject of widespread criticism. The National Audit Office (NAO), the Public Accounts Committee (PAC), the Audit Commission and Accounts Commission have been circumspect about the levels of success, and identified various lessons to be learned. Despite the welcome investment in public services, the policy remains unpopular with the public at large and the relevant trade unions.

So far, most research has focused on the decision-making processes that led up to the signing of a partnership contract or has examined the benefits and costs from an a priori perspective. The NAO's studies of some of the early roads projects report that the payment mechanism created additional risks for the public sector that raise questions about the value of risk actually transferred to the private sector (National Audit Office 1998, 1999). In the context of hospitals, a considerable body of evidence challenges both the macro- and the microeconomic arguments (Pollock et al. 2002), raising questions about service provision and the conflict between policy promotion and regulation (Froud and Shaoul 2001). Several studies have examined the business cases supporting the use of private finance for new hospital builds, and questioned the ability of the methodology to measure VFM in an unbiased way, the degree to which the business cases demonstrate VFM and the higher cost of PFI over conventional procurement (Gaffney and Pollock 1999; Price et al. 1999; Pollock et al. 2000; Froud and Shaoul 2001; Shaoul 2005). Their evidence shows that the VFM case rests upon risk transfer. The credit ratings agency, Standard and Poor's, in its report for the capital markets (Standard and Poor's 2003), states that the PFI companies carry little effective risk. Other work shows that the high costs of PFI projects lead to affordability problems, an issue that the emphasis on VFM downplays, and lead to hospital downsizing in order to bridge the affordability gap (Hodges and Mellett 1999; Gaffney and Pollock 1999; 1999b; Gaffney et al. 1999a; 1999b; 1999c; Pollock et al. 1999).

By way of contrast, this research study focuses on the actual performance in two sectors, roads and hospitals, which have substantial commitments to partnership financing and projects that have been in place for some years. In roads, where PFI projects are known as design, build, finance and operate (DBFO), the eight projects signed in 1996 represented about 35% of all new construction in the roads sector between 1996 and 2001 (DTI 2002). In the Government's 10-year national plan, 25% of the £21 billion allocated for the strategic highway network will involve private finance (DETR 2000). In the health sector, there has been a continuous expansion of private finance since the first health contract was signed in 1997 and by 4 April 2003 some 117 schemes had been approved by the Department of Health with a value of £3.2 billion (HM Treasury 2003c). These two sectors offer contrasting environments, in terms of the relationship between central government and the procuring entity, and previous experience of contracting with the private sector.

Our report is in three parts. First, we examine the advice from official bodies about how PFI should be evaluated. We examine the literature as it relates to the available evidence about the nature of post-implementation reviews of PFI projects and the methodology and process issues that constrain such evaluative research.

Secondly, we identify the origins, development, nature and scale of PFI in roads and hospitals. Our study focuses on the first eight DBFO projects in England managed by the Highways Agency and the first 13 PFI hospitals (12 in England and one in Scotland). We then analyse the reported financial performance of both the public and the private sector partners using information obtained directly from the Highways Agency and the hospital trusts, and Companies House respectively. Thus we have focused on information that is in the public domain, supplemented by contextual information provided by staff at headquarters level in both sectors. We also examine the costs and affordability of these PFI projects in terms of their impact on the budget of the relevant procurer. Our emphasis is on costs to the public sector, returns to the private sector, the effective cost of private finance and its affordability to the public purse.

Our concern is with the extent to which the financial reporting by all the parties involved in PFI provides accountability to the public. The concept of accountability in the context of public expenditure on essential public services implies first that citizens, or at least their political representatives, the media, trade unions, academics, etc, can see how society's resources are being used and, secondly, that no members of that society are seen to have an explicitly sanctioned unfair advantage over others in relation to how those resources are used.

Thirdly, as well as a sectoral analysis of roads and hospitals, we examine two projects in greater detail, one each from the road and hospital sectors. We chose projects that had been implemented for at least three years and in which the construction phase was complete so that, unlike previous work, our focus is on the operation and maintenance phase. We used semi-structured interviews with a range of personnel from various parties to the projects. Given that PFI emphasises the nature of the long-term service agreements, we describe and evaluate the systems that were put in place to monitor the operational phase of projects, ensure that risk transfer operates in the way expected by the contract and thereby obtain VFM.

The research findings may be summarised under three interrelated headings: partnership and managing the contract; VFM and risk transfer; and financial reporting and accountability.

PARTNERSHIP AND MANAGING THE CONTRACT

- Partnership is an ideal to be aspired to rather than a description of the actual working relationship between public and private contracting parties and has implications for monitoring and accountability relationships.

- Planning of the performance monitoring systems is poor and leads to an increased workload in the management of the projects.

- Self-monitoring systems require high levels of trust, which is not always present, and public sector partners are conducting more monitoring activities than expected.

- Outcomes that are subjective in nature, eg hospital cleaning, are difficult to write in contractually effective ways and cause monitoring difficulties.

- While contingency plans should be prepared at least in outline for all major PFIs against the possibility of default by the private sector, none are evident.

VALUE FOR MONEY AND RISK TRANSFER

- Soft project objectives may not be evaluated and user opinions about service are not always sought.

- It is impossible to compare the actual costs of PFI and thus VFM (one of the justifications for PFI) against the original public sector comparator (PSC) as the PSC quickly becomes out of date.

- Additional monitoring costs have increased the public sector's costs and thus reduced VFM compared with the original expectations.

- Where risk is shared between partners its allocation may be unclear and therefore its transfer – so central to PFI – is uncertain.

In relation to roads, we have made a number of findings.

- Demand risk is held by the private sector but this may create a new source of risk because the private sector cannot manage this demand.

- The Government guarantees the Highways Agency's payments to the DBFO companies, which reduces the risk to the private sector.

- We calculate that the Highways Agency paid a premium of some 25% of construction cost on the first four DBFO roads to ensure the project was built on time and to budget.

- In just three years the Highways Agency paid £618 m for the first eight projects, more than the initial capital cost of £590 m, which refutes one of the Government's justifications for DBFO. This means that the remaining payments on the 30-year contracts (worth about £6 billion) are for risk transfer, operation and maintenance.

- Because the full business cases are not in the public domain, there has been little external financial scrutiny of the deals and post implementation it is unclear how the actual cost of DBFO compares with the expected costs. Our evidence suggests that DBFO has turned out to be more expensive than expected. But how this affects the Highways Agency's ability to fund other maintenance projects is unclear.

- The special purpose vehicles (SPVs) report an operating profit before interest and tax of about two thirds of their receipts from the Highways Agency and this is after subcontracting to sister companies. This operating profit (less tax) is the effective cost of capital.

- About 35% of the SPVs' income from the Highways Agency is paid to their operations and maintenance subcontractors, typically sister companies, including an unidentifiable profit element for the subcontractor. Given that the contracts are still in their early years, the payments to the subcontractors are likely to represent operations rather than maintenance.

- Subcontracting in this way means that it is difficult to isolate the costs of operations and maintenance in DBFO contracts since the subcontractor may have multiple contracts elsewhere. The absence of such information makes it difficult for the public sector to benchmark costs when it comes to amending the contracts and negotiating new ones.

- Although the amount of tax payable by the SPVs over the whole period was only 7% of operating profits, even this overstates the actual tax paid since this includes an element of deferred tax. This low tax rate, in the early years at least, challenges an important part of the Treasury's new appraisal methodology for PFI, which assumes that tax payable will be about 22%, which will in turn distort the VFM analysis in favour of PFI.

- The SPVs' interest rate of 11% in 2001 and 9% in 2002 and the high level of debt, which is greater than the construction costs, means that the DBFO contracts are considerably more expensive than the cost of conventional procurement using Treasury gilts at the current rate of 4.5%.

- The seven SPVs' post-tax returns on shareholders' funds are high and higher than elsewhere in the industry.

- The seven SPVs' total effective cost of capital was about 11% in 2002. While the NAO believes that this additional cost of private finance (six percentage points above Treasury stock) represents the cost of risk transfer (about £56 m), it is difficult to see what risks the companies actually bore since their payments were guaranteed by the Government and based on shadow tolls. In the context of rising traffic, this means that they were insulated from downside risk at the Highways Agency's expense.

- In practice, the shadow tolls have led to a front loading of the payment flows to cover the future cost of maintenance, and hence the SPVs' profits.

- In the absence of arrangements to ring-fence the post-tax profits, should the DBFOs fail for whatever reason later in the contract, the Highways Agency could find that it has to bear the remaining and higher cost of private capital and the maintenance costs that it thought it had already paid for.

In conclusion, the road projects appear to be costing more than expected as reflected in net present costs that are higher than those identified by the Highways Agency (Haynes and Roden 1999), owing to rising traffic and contract changes. It is, however, impossible to know at this point whether or not VFM has been or is indeed likely to be achieved because the expensive element of the service contract relates to maintenance that generally will not be required for many years.

In relation to hospitals, we note the following points:

- The annual cost of capital for trusts rises with PFI by at least £45 m over and above the cost of a new hospital financed under the Government's capital charging regime, even though the hospitals are considerably smaller than the ones they replace. This underestimates the additional cost of PFI, since the construction costs of PFI include an amount of up to 30% to cover the cost of private finance, transaction costs, etc.

- Conservatively estimated, the trusts appear to be paying a risk premium of about 30% of the total construction costs, just to get the hospitals built on time and to budget, a sum that considerably exceeds the evidence about past cost overruns. Nine of the trusts report off balance sheet schemes, as the Treasury had originally intended, implying that most of the ownership risks have been transferred to their private sector partners. But as none of the corresponding SPVs report their hospitals on balance sheet either, this creates uncertainty as to who has ultimate responsibility.

- Within a few years of financial close, PFI charges are in some cases much higher than anticipated. This raises questions about the reliability and validity of the VFM case that was used to justify the decision to use private finance.

- The high cost of PFI means that about 26% of the increase in income in between 2000 and 2003 is going to pay for PFI charges for new hospitals.

- About half the income that the SPVs receive from the trusts relates to the cost of capital.

- About half the income the SPVs receive from the trusts is paid to the SPVs' subcontractors (typically sister companies) for construction, maintenance and services. Subcontracting in this way makes it difficult to isolate the cost of services in PFI contracts since subcontractors are likely to have multiple sources of income. This puts the public sector at a disadvantage when it tests the market some years into the contract.

- The SPVs were paying an effective cost of capital of 10% in 2002, about five points higher than the public sector's cost of borrowing. The SPVs' high effective cost of capital means that PFI contracts are considerably more expensive than the conventional procurement.

- The SPVs made a post-tax return on shareholders' funds of more than 100% in each of the three years 2000–02, higher than elsewhere in the industry and which, in the case of the Meridian Hospital Company Plc, was more than expected.

- This financial analysis is likely to underestimate the total returns to the parent companies because the SPVs subcontract to their sister companies and some of these subcontractors benefit from additional income via user charges for car parks, canteen charges, etc.

- £123 m or 51% of the private sector's receipts from the trusts are attributable to the cost of capital. Since this is about five percentage points above the cost of Treasury debt, then the extra cost of private finance constitutes the cost of transferring risk, the risk premium. The risk premium was approximately £62 m in 2002. It is unclear whether this is money well spent.

- Six out of the 13 trusts we analysed are in deficit, and four of the nine trusts with off balance sheet PFI projects had significant net deficits after paying for the cost of capital.

- Assuming that the financial performance of trusts is a proxy for affordability, then the fact that hospitals with PFI contracts were more likely to be in deficit than the national average in the period 2002–03 suggests that PFI is not affordable. This has potentially serious implications for service provision and access to healthcare.

- As well as the cost to the trusts, PFI creates additional costs at Treasury level since the capital charges that would normally be recycled within the healthcare economy 'leak' out of the system. We estimate conservatively that this is costing about £125 m a year.

Taken together, this financial analysis shows first, that in some cases PFI has turned out to be less economical than expected, and secondly, since these are all long-term projects, it is impossible to know whether they will deliver VFM over the full term of the contract. In so far as they are costing more than expected, this has an impact on the individual trusts and the wider NHS budget that must affect both staff and patients.

FINANCIAL REPORTING AND ACCOUNTABILITY

- Despite annual costs in each sector of about £210 m for just these initial projects, there is little information available to the public as taxpayers and users.

- Financial information about PFI is opaque, partly because of Government-imposed confidentiality. In the roads sector in particular, this restricts access to the Highways Agency's full business cases used to support the case for using private finance. The lack of information in the public domain makes it difficult to estimate the exact extent of the commitments incurred by the Highways Agency and the Department of Transport (DoT) and therefore provides little accountability to the public. In the NHS, disclosure is generally better than in central or local government.

- Private sector organisations use complex structures that involve close company status.[1] Therefore related party transactions are not disclosed. The result is that returns on PFI projects are spread between these various entities and thus are disguised.

---

[1] A close company, subject to certain exceptions, is broadly a company:
- which is under the control of
  - five or fewer participators, or
  - any number of participators if those participators are directors,
  or
- more than half the assets of which would be distributed to five or fewer participators, or to participators who are directors, in the event of the winding up of the company. (Inland Revenue 2004).

- Not only is there a lack of explanation for the treatment of PFI assets/liabilities and income/expenditure in both sectors, but neither the treatments nor the amounts match across the public and private sectors. Some PFI projects are accounted for on balance sheet but others are off balance sheet and there has been a change in accounting policy in relation to some projects.

The net result of all this is that while risk transfer is the central element in justifying VFM and thus PFI, our analysis shows that risk does not appear to have been transferred to the party best able to manage it. Indeed, rather than transferring risk to the private sector, in the case of roads DBFO has created additional costs and risks to the public agency, and to the public sector as a whole, through tax concessions that must increase costs to the taxpayer and/or reduce service provision. In the case of hospitals, PFI has generated extra costs to hospital users, both staff and patients, and to the Treasury through the leakage of the capital charge element in the NHS budget. In both roads and hospitals these costs and risks are neither transparent nor quantifiable. This means that it is impossible to demonstrate whether or not VFM has been, or indeed can be, achieved in these or any other projects.

While the Government's case rests upon value for money, including the cost of transferring risk, our research suggests that PFI may lead to a loss of benefits in kind and a redistribution of income, from the public to the corporate sector. It has boosted the construction industry, many of whose PFI subsidiaries are now the most profitable parts of their enterprises, and led to a significant expansion of the facilities management sector. But the main beneficiaries are likely to be the financial institutions whose loans are effectively underwritten by the taxpayers, as evidenced by the renegotiation of the Royal Armouries PFI (NAO 2001a).

Our study has identified a number of areas for future research including longitudinal case studies that track the long-term relationships between contracting parties; an investigation into the technical accounting issues that surround accounting for the assets involved in PFI; a comparison of the financial performance of trust hospitals with PFIs against those without PFIs; and an examination both of the impact on public expenditure and the financial performance and viability of both public and private sector partners.

In conclusion, as we state above, our concept of accountability in the context of public expenditure on essential public services implies first that citizens, or at least their political representatives, the media, trade unions, academics, etc, can see how society's resources are being used and, secondly, that no members of that society are seen to have an explicitly sanctioned unfair advantage over others in relation to how those resources are used. With respect to the first point, the difficulties experienced by the research team in obtaining and interpreting the financial statements of the relevant parties do not generate much hope that patients, road users, taxpayers and other citizens can see how society's resources are being used. It is significant that more information is made available both by the companies and the Government to the capital markets than to the public at large. Within the financial statements there is little information about the impact of PFI contracts on the performance of the procurer, and there is a build-up of commitments and implicit guarantees within very long-term contracts about which there is little transparency. With respect to the second point, our analysis suggests that PFI is an expensive way of financing and delivering public services that may, where public expenditure is constrained, lead to cuts in public services and/or tax rises, that is, it represents a cut in the social wage. In contrast, we suggest that the chief beneficiaries are the providers of finance and some of, but not necessarily all the private sector service providers, rather than the public sector.

Executive summary

1. Introduction

Let me say at the outset that partnerships between the public and the private sector are a cornerstone of the Government's modernisation programme for Britain. They are central to our drive to modernise our key public services. Such partnerships are here and they are here to stay.

(Alan Milburn, Secretary of State for Health, 2000)

Introduction

BACKGROUND TO THE STUDY OF THE PRIVATE FINANCE INITIATIVE

The Private Finance Initiative (PFI) began life as Conservative Government policy aimed at reforming the delivery of state activities that could not be privatised for financial or political reasons. In 1997, the incoming Labour Government embraced the policy wholeheartedly, renaming it public private partnerships (PPP). Since then PPP/PFI has become one of its key policies.

Let me say at the outset that partnerships between the public and the private sector are a cornerstone of the Government's modernisation programme for Britain. They are central to our drive to modernise our key public services. Such partnerships are here and they are here to stay. (Alan Milburn, Secretary of State for Health, 2000)

Public private partnerships is an umbrella term that encompasses a range of financial and organisational forms: joint ventures between the public and private sectors, partial privatisations, sale and lease-back arrangements, as well as the Private Finance Initiative. The policy operates using a range of measures but the general principle is that the public sector procures the delivery of support services and, with increasing frequency, 'core' professional services from the private sector. Thus the Government and its agencies in effect become the procurers and regulators of services rather than the providers. The rhetoric, especially of the Labour Government, has been that the relationship between the two contracting parties should be that of partnership, and Kernaghan (1993, p. 61) argues that partnerships may be classified into four different categories:

- collaborative: pooling of equal resources and relinquishing of autonomy in pursuit of shared goals

- operational: sharing of work but not of decision-making authority

- contributory: sharing of finances but not of operational involvement

- consultative: where advice is solicited by the public sector from various sources.

The public agency procures the services by means of a contract with a private sector provider organised in the form of a consortium or 'special purpose vehicle' (SPV), which usually includes a construction company, a facilities manager and a financier. The initial stages of the tendering process normally focus on the 'design, build and operate' elements, whereas financing is considered at a later stage once the preferred bidder is chosen (Spackman 2002).

Like many policies, its rationale has changed so much over time that even its proponents have described it as 'an ideological morass' (IPPR 2001). Originally justified in terms of providing the finance for investment that the public sector could not afford, the macroeconomic argument, it is now increasingly justified in terms of delivering value for money (VFM), in the form of lower discounted financial costs over the life of the project compared with the cost of conventional procurement as measured by a public sector comparator (PSC). This is the microeconomic argument. In general terms its proponents argue that the private sector is able to provide services more efficiently and effectively than the bureaucratic public sector. For example, Osborne and Gaebler (1993) suggest that the private sector is better than the public sector at performing complex economic or technical tasks, innovating or replicating successful experiments and adapting to rapid change, including the ability to abandon unsuccessful or obsolete activities.

The achievement of VFM includes the transfer to the private sector of risk and associated costs that would otherwise be borne by the public sector. This is qualified, however, by the fact that risks associated with all aspects of the contract should be carried by the party most able to manage that risk. Thus risks associated with the design, construction, finance, maintenance and operation of the building need to be identified; and for each, probabilities must be assigned and outcomes valued so that the financial value to the procurer of transferring risk can be measured and incorporated into the options appraisal. As risk is transferred, other things being equal, the PSC becomes relatively more expensive than a privately financed alternative.

The costs associated with risk are not straightforward. First, the inclusion of risk is limited by the ability of managers to anticipate, define and attach probabilities and values to a range of outcomes. Secondly, there is no requirement to measure the extent to which PFI may create extra risks, such as those that may arise as a consequence of being locked into a long-term contract where changes must be negotiated. Thirdly, there is the problem of how risk affects the accounting treatment of the assets and liabilities. According to the ASB (1998) if the public sector body holds the demand and residual risk, then the assets and related liabilities should be shown on the balance sheet. The Treasury prefers that PFI assets should be off balance sheet, however, because – it is believed – this acts to reduce public debt, a key measure of the European Union's Growth and Stability Pact. Therefore, in order to comply with both the Treasury and FRS 5, the public sector needs to demonstrate that sufficient additional risk has been transferred to the private sector to compensate for the demand and residual risk that it still holds. Hence, the public sector is under pressure to transfer risk. What constitutes sufficient risk from the perspective of FRS 5 is a matter of judgement.

It is becoming clear that transfer of risk from the public to the private sector is an essential element of a PFI deal, for two reasons.

First, many projects only achieve VFM at the decision-making stage, because of the risk transfer contribution.

We will explore this further in Chapter 4, together with evidence that suggests that risk may not always transfer as expected.

Secondly, because of accounting regulations it is necessary to show that risk transfer has taken place if the scheme is to remain off balance sheet in the public sector.

Consequently, there is some concern that risk might be transferred out of the public sector, whether or not the private sector is able to manage it most efficiently. Therefore the nature of risk transfer is a critical feature of many PFI projects.

The Government has put in place procedures designed to ensure that approval is given only to PFI projects that are likely to deliver VFM to the public agency over the life of the project. In essence these procedures require the preparation of a business case that lists the costs, benefits, risks, uncertainties and affordability of various options. Bids will be sought based upon a detailed specification of required outcomes. A comparison of these competing bids, and the calculated cost of a simulated public sector route to fulfil the same project, is made using discounted cash flows to determine the net present cost. Costs of risk associated with the project are included in this analysis.

Several points follow from this. Value for money (VFM) is the key rationalising motif for partnerships. Although value for money is a colloquial term that has intuitive appeal, its substantive meaning is ambiguous. It is usually associated with the three Es: economy, efficiency and effectiveness. In practice, for a variety of conceptual and practical reasons, VFM audits, as carried out by the National Audit Office, have focused on economy rather than efficiency and effectiveness. Its meaning in the context of PFI is no more precise and is similarly based upon economy as reflected in the use of discounted cash flows over the lifetime of the project.

The procurement process, by relying upon market forces and giving a greater role to the private sector in designing the services to be provided, should create a competitive tension and lead to innovative solutions that will help to deliver a more economical service.

But none of this should obscure a number of important issues.

The VFM case is necessarily based on *estimates* of future costs and operates only at the point of procurement.

PSC = public sector comparator

Risk transfer is the crucial element in demonstrating the expected whole-life economy, since under PFI the financial costs of private sector borrowing, transactions costs and the requirements for profits necessarily generate higher costs than conventional public procurement. The more risk is transferred, the more expensive the PSC becomes relative to the PFI option. As the evidence from the new hospitals to be built under PFI shows, conventional public procurement provides greater VFM until risk transfer is factored in, and even then the margin of difference is small (Pollock, Shaoul and Vickers 2002).

Although the PFI option therefore has extra costs, this is countered by the fact that the private sector is assumed to be operationally more economic and carries risks that are not usually quantified.

The scope of the risk analysis is narrow and focuses on VFM within the agency concerned, despite the fact that these public bodies deliver 'public' goods and services.

There is no guarantee that the contract is enforceable in practice or will actually transfer risk in the way the PSC anticipates, as failed PFI IT projects have demonstrated (Edwards and Shaoul 2003).

PPP/PFI has now become an important source of new infrastructure, involving significant commitment of future Government funds. For example, between 1999 and 2003, the capital value of signed PFI/PPP deals was about £3–4 billion per year, making a total of 563 deals worth £35.5 billion of which £32.1 billion were signed after the Labour Government came to power. In 2003, the Treasury estimated that the capital value of all signed PFI projects would be about £9.841 billion for 2003/4 (HM Treasury 2003b). There is considerable variation, however, in the use of PFI across Government departments both in absolute and relative terms, with the Departments of Transport and Defence having the largest number of projects by value, although the Departments of Defence and Health rely much more heavily on PFI as a source of investment finance than do other Departments (HM Treasury 2003c). In total it was believed to constitute about 18% of gross public sponsored investment in 2001 (IFS 2002) and about 15% in 2002 (HM Treasury 2003c), although such calculations are beset with definitional problems.

Annual payments for the signed deals alone were expected to be £2.9 billion in 2000/1, rising to £6 billion in 2007 (HM Treasury 2003c) or £105 billion over the life of the contracts (NAO 2003h). Since these payments relate largely to new deals, rather than to the replacement of existing outsourcing arrangements, the money available to pay for them is what remains of public expenditure after welfare payments and the purchase of external goods and services – the public sector wage budget. Annual payments will therefore divert about 6–7% of the current wage bill, which has declined from 72% of public expenditure (after the welfare payments and external purchases) in 1977 to 38% in 1999, and this is set to increase as new deals are signed (Pollock et al. 2001).

Despite the welcome investment programme in public services, the policy has proved unpopular with the public at large and generated a heated debate about the aims, appraisal methods and processes, and outcomes of both the policy and specific projects.

Numerous IT PFI projects have failed in terms of their original objectives, cost and time overruns, with costs to the procuring agency, the public sector as a whole and the public as users. At least three PFI/PPP schemes have had to be bailed out: the Channel Tunnel Rail Link, the Royal Armouries Museum and National Air Traffic Services, while others have been scrapped. Front line public services such as health and education have required and/or been accompanied by extensive closures and rationalisations that have proved unpopular. Lastly, the refinancing of PFI projects after construction has generated extra profits that have led to widespread fears that the private sector is profiteering at the expense of cash-strapped services.

The policy is particularly important since an increasing proportion of public sector expenditure is committed to long-term service contracts, which are legally binding and therefore have the effect of committing a subsequent government to expenditure under conditions where there may be considerable uncertainty about the kind of services that may be required in the future. The introduction of PFI therefore raises numerous questions and issues for study and it is clearly important that these contracts should be evaluated.

To date there has been extensive analysis of the financial and accountability issues arising from PFI, both from a theoretical perspective and on a case study basis, which investigates the decision-making processes, the VFM and the viability of projects prior to the signing of contracts, that is, analysis that focuses on the appraisal process. As yet there has been little assessment of whether – or how – lower costs, risk transfer and thus value for money have been achieved in practice after project implementation, or what impacts PFI has on public accountability; that is, assessment that focuses on the evaluation of such projects. In part at least, this is because the policy is still new and projects have only recently become operational.

Although the National Audit Office (NAO) has examined a number of high-profile PFI failures which have had widespread economic, social and political implications that raise questions about their justification, cost and risk transfer, as well as wider issues of regulation, accountability and control, its investigations have usually been restricted to 'what went wrong' and 'lessons to be learned'. Although the NAO noted that post-contractual changes that transferred risk back to the state had taken place, it did not consider how such changes affected VFM or the relationship between the reduced risk transfer and the risk premium contained in the cost of finance. Neither did the investigations consider how PFI coped with failure, the extent to which the partnership policy itself may have affected failure, and the wider implications for the policy as a whole. Indeed, the lack of *financial* evaluation from such organisations as the NAO and the Audit Commission is quite striking and suggests that such evaluation may not be straightforward.

Reports by the Audit Commission (2003) and Accounts Commission (2002) have been somewhat more critical of PFI, and other reviewers present a mixed impression of success and failure. For example, following his review of PFI deals, Spackman (2002) concludes that PFIs have brought costs and benefits but that the balance of advantage is often unclear and, according to Sussex (2003), in aggregate the cost advantages claimed for NHS PFI schemes are small. Hence the jury is still out over the issue of whether PFI offers better VFM than traditional procurement routes. In its report *The Operational Performance of Prisons* the NAO sums it up as follows (2003g, para. 14):

The use of the PFI is neither a guarantee of success nor the cause of inevitable failure. Like other forms of providing public services, there are successes and failures and they cannot be ascribed to a single factor . . . . A relatively new procurement method such as the PFI is associated with encouraging and disappointing results and that performance will improve over time. But a general verdict that the PFI is either good or bad in the case of prisons, or more generally, cannot be justified.

Spackman (2002) argues that the UK experience is similar to Rosenau's (2000) comments about the US: that not much is known about the success and failures of these projects, partly because there is a resistance to conducting systematic policy evaluation. The available assessments do suggest that more evidence is urgently required. Both the Treasury and the NAO have recognised the need for and improvement of post-implementation review (HM Treasury 1997a, 2003a, NAO 1999c). Similarly, the Public Accounts Committee (PAC) has concluded from a review of a number of NAO reports that better evaluation of PFI projects in progress is needed (PAC 2002a). The new Green Book (HM Treasury 2003a) now requires all new projects to undergo a comprehensive evaluation after completion of the construction phase or at some later stage in the project while significant continuing programmes should be subject to retrospective evaluation.

In this report we seek to add to the relatively small body of evidence about the post-implementation evaluation of PFI projects and the study is therefore important because there has been very little independent work in this area. However, the purpose of evaluation may be variously defined. One clear purpose emanating from Government sources is that lessons should be learned so that the quality of future decision making can be improved, implying some official concern that mistakes have been made. To help public procurers, there is official advice on methodologies and techniques to be applied, although much of this focuses on the financial aspects of the project. As the NAO (2002b) has acknowledged, however, cost is only one of the strategic factors that influence the choice of procurement. More recently, the Treasury has introduced additional criteria: equality and employment

issues, and stated that VFM should not be achieved at the expense of workers' terms and conditions (HM Treasury 2003d, para. 1.12).

Public sector projects normally have multiple objectives and one purpose of evaluation may be to assess whether the original objectives, as set out in the business case, have been met. Objectives may be difficult to assess because they involve long-term strategic policies, for example, the establishment of a private sector capability in the particular industry, or because they are difficult to quantify. In addition, for example, Nathan and Whitfield (2000) state that issues of equality and employment should also form part of the evaluation process, but conclude that the Treasury and the NAO have ignored these. These authors cite, as an example, the issue of who owns, runs and works in prisons, police stations and court complexes and who has access to sensitive information about a vulnerable and increasingly large section of the population. They argue that this is less about balance sheet accounting methods and more about how a civilised society operates. Similarly, Grimshaw, Vincent and Willmott (2002) indicate their concern that employment issues may not be adequately evaluated and note that human resources expertise was thought to be missing in private sector partners. Thus there is a tension between project and policy evaluation and between different policies.

AIMS OF THE PROJECT

Although it is possible to evaluate the outcomes of policies and projects from a number of different perspectives, this study seeks to contribute to the evaluation of the implementation of PFI by exploring the financial issues: first, those issues that lie at the heart of the policy's objectives: VFM and risk transfer, and secondly, their impact on affordability and accountability. Developing the axioms set out by Sinfield (2000, p. 160), the concept of accountability in the context of public expenditure on essential public services implies that, first, citizens – or at least their political representatives, the media, trade unions, academics, etc – can see how society's resources are being used and, secondly, that no members of that society are seen to have an explicitly sanctioned unfair advantage over others in relation to how those resources are used.

This study seeks to examine the external reporting of and accountability for PFI as well as the detailed procedures and systems that surround the implementation of a monitoring and control system for particular PFI projects. Our approach is to:

- examine the post-implementation control processes that the Government has put in place

- identify the most important issues associated with evaluation after implementation, drawing on previous academic literature, National Audit Office, Public Accounts Committee, Audit Commission, HM Treasury, departmental and other official reports

- provide sector-specific analysis for roads and hospitals using public domain information, and

- investigate the ways in which monitoring and evaluation processes operate in practice, using a case study approach, since this enables an in-depth understanding of the issues.

Specifically the research seeks to examine:

- the reporting of these projects after their implementation

- the costs of the PFI and its impact on affordability

- the extent to which the actual costs and therefore VFM match the expectations at the decision-making stage

- the mechanisms and procedures for managing the contract during operation

- the mechanisms for ensuring that risk is transferred to the private sector in the ways that were anticipated

- the contingency planning procedures in the event of project failure and

- the accountability for these projects after their implementation.

Since this study seeks to identify those characteristics that promote or limit the success of PFI, we focus on two very different sectors, roads and health. We consider first PFI in roads, where it is usually known as design, build, finance and operate (DBFO) and involves, in England, the Highways Agency – an executive agency of the Department of Transport (DoT) – commissioning the construction of a new road or extension of an existing one and its operation and maintenance for 30 years. Secondly, we consider the use of PFI by the acute NHS hospital trusts to procure new builds, non-clinical hospital services and estate maintenance. Since these sectors differ in numerous ways – their relationship to central government, the nature of the projects, the proportion of service to the construction element, the nature of the services so provided, their perceived 'success' and political visibility, etc – this should make it easier to identify those characteristics that promote or limit VFM, risk transfer and accountability.

We explore the origins, development, nature and scale of PFI in each sector and consider the broad objectives of the policy. Since PFI involves both macro and micro objectives our empirical evidence is gathered at both the sectoral level and from a case study from each sector. Using financial statements of both the public and private sector partners, we analyse the costs to the public sector and the returns to the private sector of involvement in PFI for the two sectors, roads and hospitals. Using interviews with personnel from both partners in a road and a hospital project, we analyse the contract management procedures. Since both these projects reached financial close a few years ago and the construction phase is complete, both projects are now in the operation and maintenance phase of their life cycle. Therefore this presents an opportunity to evaluate PFI projects in a phase that has received much less attention in the literature.

The use of both a sector-wide financial analysis and a case study of the contract management procedures permit, first, a greater understanding of how PFI operates in practice, the financial costs and rewards, and the relationship between the two and, secondly, an evaluation of PFI at both project and programme level in different contexts. Since many projects are in the early years of what are normally long-term contractual relationships, and consequently total life-cycle costs and benefits are not yet known, it is too early to make definitive assessments of many of the issues involved, especially the VFM issues. Instead, our aim is to present evidence that is indicative of the nature of PFI.

RESEARCH METHODS

Since the objectives of PFI involve obtaining VFM and introducing more innovation on individual projects, as well as macro-level objectives such as creating private sector capability and introducing market testing, we have chosen a two-pronged approach to our research.

First, a financial analysis of the two sectors, drawing on the financial statements of the Highways Agency, 13 hospital trusts that have operational PFI projects in place, explanations given to us by headquarters-level staff in both sectors, and the published statements of the private sector companies, typically organised as a consortium or Special Purpose Vehicle (SPV) to manage the project. Since typically these organisations operate in conjunction with related subcontracting companies

we have used the 'Financial Analysis Made Easy' (FAME) Database to identify the company, its parent and related companies. We obtained the concessionaires' accounts since inception from Companies House.

Thus we use secondary data sources including financial statements to build a picture of the origins, development nature and scale of PFI activity in these two sectors and to gain an understanding of the way PFI operates in roads and hospitals, its costs, VFM, risk transfer and accountability. This work has been somewhat constrained by the secrecy that surrounds the contracting documents and even the business cases associated with PFI, which is said to be due to commercial confidentiality concerns. Chapters 5 and 7 present our findings using those sources that are in the public domain. It is worth noting, however, that the research team had to make frequent requests to some hospital trusts, although not to the hospital that is the subject of our case study, simply to obtain copies of their earlier annual accounts that are supposedly in the public domain. This is important since a recent survey found that the NHS makes more information available than many other public bodies (IPPR 2004).

Secondly, we use a case study from each sector enabling a detailed understanding of the issues involved. The first is a roads project procured by the Highways Agency (HA), which initially chose to implement PFI by issuing contracts for eight projects in two tranches within a relatively short time. The second is a new build and services contract procured by an NHS trust hospital, and although other hospitals are similarly involved in PFI, this is the first experience of PFI for most public sector staff.

At both sites the PFI projects have been in operation for sufficient time for monitoring and evaluation systems to become well established within the public sector procurer. Interviews were used, first, to clarify issues arising from our analysis of the secondary data sources, and in areas where no public domain information is available interviewees provided insights, based on their own experiences, of issues that surround risk transfer and VFM. Secondly, members of staff at the Highways Agency and the hospital trust provided information about the internal systems for managing, controlling and monitoring PFI projects within the public agencies, and their perceptions, experiences and understandings of the systems that have been implemented to ensure that risk transfer operates as expected in the contract, and VFM is achieved. We were able to interview staff who are operationally close to both projects as well as staff at headquarters level. We also interviewed representatives of the SPVs in order to obtain their views about the PFI projects and to identify alternative perspectives. We have anonymised the two cases for reasons of commercial sensitivity and in order to protect the confidentiality of interviewees, all of whom were very generous in sharing their time and their perspectives. These interviews allowed the researchers to report on and gain insight into the implementation and operation of this new form of procurement.

Interviews were conducted between April and November 2003, and most lasted between one and two hours. The interview format was semi-structured, and the interview programme was informed and developed against the background of academic literature, our understandings of the relevant sectors based on our review of secondary sources, and discussions with relevant staff in the case organisations. Flexibility is one of the key advantages of the semi-structured interview approach and the interview schedule was varied to accommodate the different circumstances of these two cases and to enable the interviewers to pursue issues emerging from research subjects' accounts. Interviews were tape recorded and later transcribed, and material was analysed and interpreted during the period August to November 2003. The information from the interviews is reported in Chapters 6 and 8. We sought and have received feedback about these chapters from all the

organisations in order to check their clarity and accuracy.

Although both the roads and hospitals sectors have significant commitments to PFI projects, they offer contrasting structural relationships with the relevant central government department. In addition, whereas the Highways Agency had considerable previous experience of dealing with the private sector in contractual relationships, this is rather less true of the health sector. From our sectoral analysis, we seek to draw some conclusions about the wider policy implications of the Government 's strategic choice of PFI as a mechanism for financing and providing infrastructure and public services. In relation to the trust hospitals, however, PFIs are tied up with mergers, restructuring and rationalisation exercises so that the effects of PFI are less easy to isolate.

Thus the research is grounded in two quite different sectors and in a case study from each sector. The case studies constitute an interpretative study of internal information about the construction of new roles, tasks and information systems within the public sector and of relevant information in the public domain. Although recognising the limitations of the case study method, and especially the limitations imposed by studying just two cases, we try to draw some conclusions of a general nature about the operation of the PFI policy in practice. The research as a whole seeks to understand the consequences, some of which may have been unintended, of introducing a PFI project.

The remainder of this report is organised as follows. In Chapter 2 we present an overview of the governmental control process relating to PFI. In Chapters 3 and 4 we review the literature that focuses on the available evidence about the nature of post-implementation evaluations of PFI projects and the methodology and process issues that constrain such evaluative research. In Chapters 5 to 8 we present our empirical evidence. Chapters 5 and 6 offer an analysis of PFI in roads, where it is known as design, build, finance and operate (DBFO), and the insights gained from our interviewees at the Highways Agency and the private sector contractor. In Chapters 7 and 8 there is an analysis of the use of PFI for hospital new builds and the insights gained from our interviewees at our trust case and the related special purpose vehicle. Chapter 9 presents a discussion, our conclusions and suggestions for further research.

2. The post-implementation control process

The OGC's role is both to champion and to control the PFI process and is indicative of the conflict between policy promotion and policy control noted elsewhere.

The post-implementation control process

Since the inception of PFI successive governments have produced documentation relating to the procedures and accounting methodologies for procurement decision making under PFI. There was, however, comparatively little in the way of a post-implementation control process to ensure the delivery of the anticipated VFM. Indeed, although the Treasury called for post-implementation evaluation as a way of improving future decision making, it provided little detailed or specific guidance as to how such evaluations should be carried out (HM Treasury 1997a, 1997b, 1998).

Recently, there has been a reorganisation of the government departments concerned with overseeing procurement, the establishment of the Office of Government Commerce (OGC) in April 2000, and a series of measures and documents, notably the revised Green Book (HM Treasury 2003a) and the Gateway Review process outlining the evaluative procedures to be followed. In this chapter, first we examine where the PFI control process is located in government, then how the post-implementation control process has developed within central government, and how it is supposed to operate, in order to understand where the functional Departments in our study, Transport and Health, are positioned in the overall control process.

THE PFI CONTROL PROCESS IN GOVERNMENT

The organisational systems that control PFI are located within the Directorate of Financial Regulation and Industry (FRI), one of six Treasury Directorates, which works to: 'improve the way the public sector deals with the private sector through the Private Finance Initiative (PFI) and Partnerships UK (PUK); the Public Enterprise Partnership (PEP) team; and the Office of Government Commerce (OGC)' (HM Treasury 2000, pp. 7–8).

In 1992, the Conservative Government established the Private Finance Panel and the Private Finance Executive to act as a focal point for all PFI-type activities across government departments. In 1997,

one of the first tasks of the incoming Labour Government was to set up a review, known as the Bates Review, of the way the PFI process was managed.

From the perspective of this study, however, what is striking about the Bates Review's 29 recommendations, although perhaps not surprising given that its remit was to identify obstacles to the use of PFI, is that although there are suggestions for improving the decision-making processes prior to contract signing, there is almost no reference to the monitoring and control of implemented projects. The only recommendation that suggests post-implementation issues is number 21, which states: 'The recent recommendations of the National Audit Office in their reports on the Skye Bridge and the Contract to Develop and Operate the Replacement National Insurance Recording System, should be noted carefully by Departments' (Bates Review, 1997).

The Bates Review, of which all recommendations were accepted, was instrumental in establishing the current organisational systems, shown in diagrammatic form in Figure 2.1 (see pages 30–31). It replaced the Private Finance Panel and the Private Finance Executive with the Treasury Task Force (TTF) in a bid to streamline the PFI and reduce the number of institutional players on the public sector side. Although the TTF would sign off the commercial viability of all significant projects, with decentralised government procurement, the departments and agencies were ultimately responsible for their own procurement decisions.

Two separate arms grew from the TTF, as well as initiatives to strengthen departmental contracting and project management expertise in Transport, Health, Education and Defence. The first arm, the Policy Division, established on a permanent basis, was responsible for rules and best practice, leading to the establishment in April 2000 of the Office of Government Commerce within the Treasury. An

Figure 2.1: The UK Government's development of organisational systems for PFI/PPP

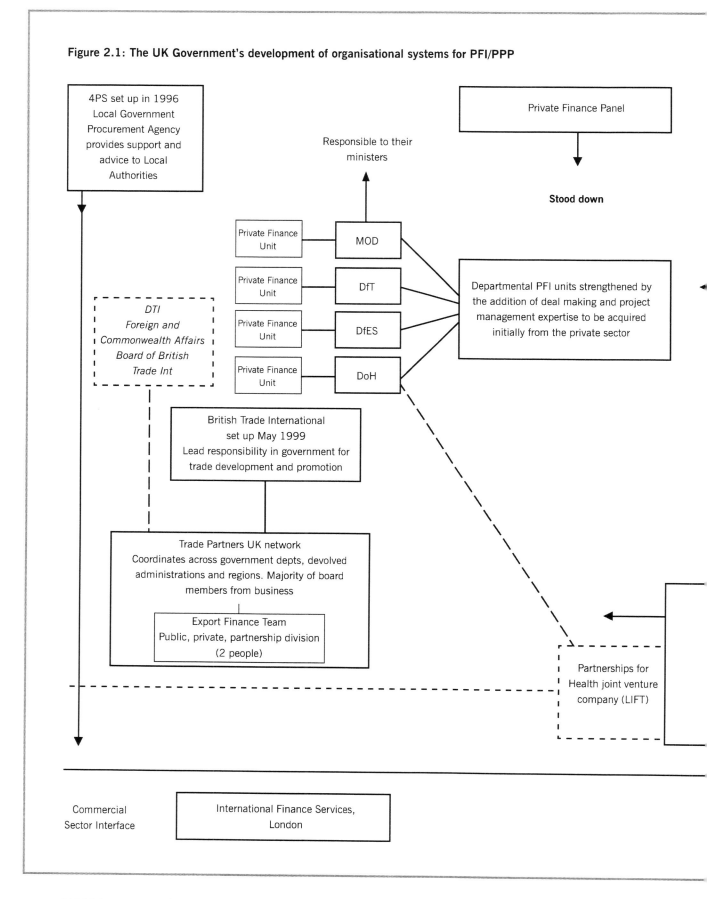

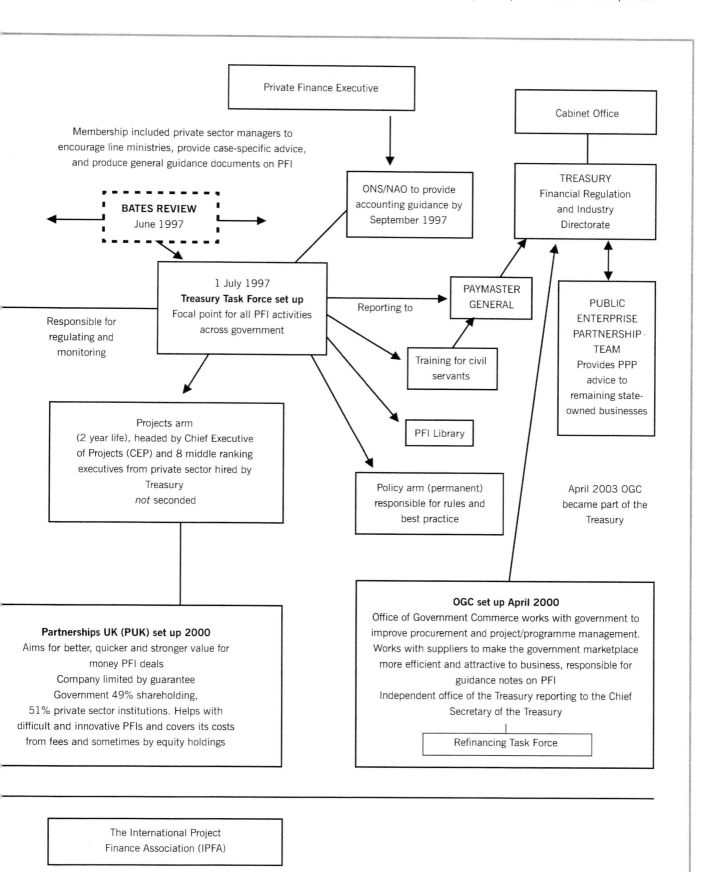

independent Office of the Treasury, it reports to the Chief Secretary, and has three main responsibilities (OGC 2004):

• improving the efficiency and effectiveness of central civil government procurement

• developing and promoting private sector involvement across the public sector

• assisting departments to set up project and programme management centres of excellence.

Thus, the OGC's role is both to champion and to control the PFI process and this is indicative of the conflict between policy promotion and policy control noted elsewhere (Freedland 1998, Edwards and Shaoul 2003). The OGC has taken responsibility for post-implementation reviews and the Treasury commented that, 'OGC agrees on the importance of Post Implementation Reviews both as a learning tool for departments and to identify systemic issues' (HM Treasury 2002). This observation follows PAC's recommendation 5 on *Managing the Relationship to Secure a Successful Partnership in PFI Projects*:

Post-implementation reviews are particularly important for projects where perceived value for money has declined since contract letting. Departments need to identify whether such a decline reflects errors of judgement by the authority when letting the contract, the contractor failing to deliver the service as promised, short term problems during the early period of the service delivery, or other factors such as high charges for additional services. (PAC 2002a)

The second arm, the Projects division, was initially established with a two-year life, largely with staff on secondment from the private sector. In June 2000 this was reconstituted as a public private partnership, Partnerships UK (PUK), whose mission was to help the public sector deliver: fast and efficient development and procurement of PPPs; strong PPPs that build stable relationships with the private sector; savings in development costs; and better value for money (Partnerships UK 2003). These aims are achieved, according to PUK's website, by 'standing shoulder to shoulder with public bodies' and putting the interests of its public sector clients first. Therefore, it can act as a 'bridge' between the public and private sectors (HM Treasury 2003c).

The ownership and governance structures for a body with these aims are perhaps unexpected. PUK is a company limited by guarantee, in which HM Treasury and the Scottish Ministers together control 49%. The majority shareholding of 51%, however, is held by private sector institutions, including financial services companies that have been involved in the financing of PFI projects, and organisations such as Group 4, Falck Joint Ventures Ltd and Jarvis plc, which have PFI contracts. Furthermore, the majority of the board members come from the private sector, with the public sector represented by only two non-executive directors and the public interest represented through an Advisory Council. Thus there is the potential for a conflict of interest between public and private interests, which is recognised within government. In a speech to the Global Summit in Cape Town in 2001, Stephen Timms admitted that: 'Partnerships UK is not entirely conventional and we respect our public sector mission through our relationship with the Advisory Council . . . . It reports to Government and whilst it can cry 'foul', it can't directly tell us what to do'.

During the same speech Timms argued:

Part of Partnerships UK's challenge is to gain the trust and confidence of the public sector whilst being in a real sense a private sector body. And as a private sector body we have to balance the public sector interest with the need to earn an appropriate and sustainable return on our shareholders investments.

You can, I am sure, immediately see the sensitivities and the trade offs required. (Timms 2001)

Although the structure, ownership and control of PUK is not directly relevant to post-implementation review, it is important because it sets the PFI agenda and is indicative of the conflict between policy promotion and policy control noted earlier in relation to the OGC.

OFFICIAL ADVICE ON POST-IMPLEMENTATION REVIEW

Official advice has come from various sources – the National Audit Office (NAO), Public Accounts Committee (PAC), Audit Commission (AC) and the Treasury – and has developed in an ad hoc way to meet a number of potentially conflicting requirements. This section considers each of these sources.

The National Audit Office has investigated the performance of some PFI projects under its VFM remit. It has tended to focus on some of the problems that have arisen after financial close that clearly impinge on VFM, although its analysis was not concerned directly with VFM itself. This may be illustrated by a number of examples. When it examined the sequence of events that led up to members of the public going in person and queuing for hours to obtain their passports, the focus was on the Passport Agency's service delivery (NAO 1999d), not VFM. Similarly, in relation to the refinancing by the private sector partner of the Fazakerley prison deal, it focused on the lower cost of financing, the profit-sharing arrangements and the changes to the deal's risk profile (NAO 2000b), but not directly on the VFM of the original or refinanced deal. In its reports on the Royal Armouries deal (NAO 2001a), the extension of the NIRS2 contract with Andersen Consulting (NAO 2001d), and the Channel Tunnel Rail Link PFI deal (NAO 2001c), it focused on the relationship between the public and private sector partners, and on the renegotiations that took place when a private sector partner failed to deliver on the

original contract. Thus, the NAO passed up the opportunity to examine the extent to which the projects provided VFM as set out in the financial appraisal or how the outcomes differed from conventional procurement. Without such a comparison, it is difficult to justify the claim that PFI procurement actually transfers risk and thus in practice delivers value for money.

In each case the NAO carefully explained the chain of events that led up to the project failure and sought to draw lessons for the negotiation of future PFI deals, but it did not draw out the implications for VFM, consider the outcomes in relation to the project's objectives and/ or its original financial appraisal, or evaluate the extent to which the contract did or indeed could transfer risk as anticipated. It carried out a survey to examine how the contractual relationship was being managed, managers' views about their project's value for money and the issues involved in managing partnership relationships, rather than a systematic comparison of expected and actual outcomes or even a study of project outcomes (NAO 2001e).

As the National Audit Office noted, although the Treasury was encouraging departments to make evaluation a more prominent feature of policy making, departments required evaluations to be more practical (NAO 2001b). This is problematic as the NAO concluded that there is no one best way of establishing VFM and that individual procurers needed to establish their own methodologies for assessing their projects' VFM. Such methodologies should include ways of assessing performance, pricing and feedback from users, as well as a continual monitoring of risks so that these can be managed (NAO 2001e). To assist auditors reviewing VFM appraisals and those involved in negotiating PFI deals, the NAO produced some recommendations, and from the perspective of this study it is interesting that attention is drawn to the importance of the contract as opposed to the business case, despite the fact that it was the business case that authorised the project and generated the expectations that justified the project (NAO 1999c).

A successful partnership often depends upon decisions made early in the procurement process, implying that the nature of governance arrangements should be considered early and be well documented (NAO 2001e), so that their impact on project management can be assessed. There should be recognition that the contracting parties have different objectives that need to be reconciled. For example, where there are multiple public sector parties to the project, there may be conflicting objectives that create problems; the pressing needs of some may lead to inadequately tested pilot projects being accepted at the expense of the other public sector partners (NAO 2002b). Especially in situations where there is a lack of committed bidders there needs to be an agreed process to manage the contract in a non-competitive environment. For example, the Airwave project uses a 'should cost' model, an internally generated model of expected costs. If such approaches are to assist decision making and subsequent monitoring of performance, however, there needs to be recognition that the building of credible alternative options may require substantial resources and the cooperation of the bidders (NAO 2002b).

In considering the NAO's reports, the Public Accounts Committee was particularly concerned that one in five of the authorities surveyed considered that the VFM from their contracts had diminished; that the contractors charged high prices for additional services; that the bail out of the Royal Armouries Museum and the Channel Tunnel Rail Link undermined the commercial discipline of the risk of failure; that there was little information on the financial returns to the private sector; and that 58% of authorities with a performance review process had made deductions from payments to contractors, suggesting inadequate levels of service. Crucially, it noted that risk transfer did not absolve the public agency from the responsibility for service delivery, and that therefore the agency had to manage this ultimately untransferable business risk. The PAC concluded that better evaluation was needed of PFI projects in progress (PAC 2002a).

Although both the NAO and the PAC have recommended that adequate review systems should be put in place at an early stage of contract provision, the public sector has been slow to implement this advice. For example, in 2002, the PAC recommended that the Channel Tunnel Rail Link needed to improve its monitoring systems (PAC 2002b, Recommendation 7). The NAO made similar calls regarding the Laganside Courts PFI, where performance monitoring was not fully operational from the start and so for an initial period measurement of performance against service standards was limited (NAO 2003f, para. 5). In its wide-ranging report *Managing the Relationship to Secure a Successful Partnership in PFI Projects*, the PAC called for better evaluation of PFI projects in progress, in particular with regard to quality of customer service and VFM (PAC 2002a, Recommendation 1). Also, it was very concerned that despite the fact that more than one in five of the authorities surveyed considered that their PFI contracts' VFM had diminished, only around half had put in place appropriate mechanisms (benchmarking, market testing, open book accounting) to ensure VFM over the project lifetime. Little consideration appears to have been given, however, to whether the public sector has either the resources or the expertise to do this, or to how this additional cost would affect the anticipated VFM of PFI. The PAC went on to suggest that the OGC should monitor how projects were evaluated and review contractors' returns on PFI projects. This is now done within the Gateway Process, which we discuss in the next section.

The Audit Commission management paper *Aiming to Improve the Principles of Performance Measurement* (Audit Commission 2000a), although not mentioning PFI specifically, sets out the key issues for an effective performance measurement system to improve public services. It provides a practical overview to enable policy-setting managers to design a robust system of performance measurement. Its twin management paper *On Target: The Practice of Performance Indicators* (Audit Commission 2000b) sets out the Audit Commission's experience of developing and using performance indicators to help public sector managers develop their own set of balanced and focused indicators. Both papers provided practical examples of performance measurement.

Some information about PFI performance is now beginning to be produced. For example, the NAO (2003b) presented statistics on the extent to which PFI projects were being delivered on time and to budget. It called upon the OGC to collect updates of these, stating 'the data are relatively easy to collect and provide a valuable insight into how well projects are being delivered under the PFI'.

More recently, the Treasury's revised Green Book (2003a) states that after completion of the construction phase, a project should undergo a comprehensive evaluation to examine the outcome against what was expected. Chapter 2 of the Green Book, however, offers apparently conflicting advice about who should conduct this evaluation. In paragraph 2.17, it argues that 'carrying out assessments should never be regarded as a specialist activity'. Nonetheless, in the next paragraph, 2.18, it encourages departments and agencies to consider 'establishing formal evaluation or assessment units, or other centres of technical expertise'. The NAO, on the other hand, suggests that it is necessary, especially for complex projects, to 'assemble a skilled team that [understands] the technical environment and how user requirements would be met' (NAO 2002b), and to train public sector staff to enable them to monitor projects effectively. Therefore this implies an approach to evaluation based on a specialist team.

The Treasury (2003a) urged project managers to follow the same analytical techniques for evaluation as those used for decision-making appraisal:

- cost–benefit/effectiveness analysis

- discounted cash flow analysis

- multi-criteria analysis and

- other statistical analysis, such as analysis of performance indicators.

This list also tends to suggest some level of specialist expertise. In either case, the evaluation is: 'designed to ensure that the lessons learned are fed back into the decision-making process. This ensures government action is continually refined to reflect what best achieves objectives and promotes the public interest' (para. 7.2). However, this contradicts the NAO's advice to focus on the contract rather than the business case (NAO 1999c).

The Treasury urges project managers to follow a five-point sequence, identified in paragraph 7.5 of the Green Book (2003a), which includes requirements to:

- establish how past outcomes can be measured

- choose alternative management decisions as counterfactuals

- compare actual and target outcomes and compare these with the chosen alternative management decisions

- present results and recommendations, and

- disseminate these.

HM Treasury states that the evaluation process should identify and measure not only the direct but also the indirect benefits of the project, and include:

- an assessment of what happened

- a comparison of outcome with target

- a comparison with one or more counterfactuals

- a comparison against a 'what if' benchmark, ie as if the activity had not been undertaken

- an evaluation of the success of the project in meeting its objectives and how it has contributed to wider outcomes.

The Treasury Green Book also provides an 11-point list of generic issues to be considered during the evaluation (paragraph 2.25). These issues include items as diverse as strategic impacts, financial arrangements, environmental impacts, rural issues and equality. In Chapter 7, the Treasury states that the evaluation should be a robust analysis with a focus on conducting a cost–benefit analysis using actual rather than forecast information. The results of an evaluation should include recommendations for the future, which might involve changes to procurement practice or changes to or replacement of the project under review. More importantly, the results should also provide feedback for wider policy debate and future programme management. Although these recommendations are admirable and wide ranging, the Green Book provides little in the way of procedures or methodologies to ensure that these recommendations are carried out in practice.

However, although data collection may be improving, evidence from reports indicates that there is scope for sharing good practice more widely across government departments. Apparent fragmentation among and isolation of PFI project managers seems common. So

for example, in the case in *Redevelopment of MOD Main Building* (NAO 2002c), the NAO recommends that the project team should summarise the lessons that it learnt and make them available to other departments. These lessons include the importance of senior officials' commitment to the success of the project and the negotiation of objective performance standards for the availability of all types of serviced accommodation.

Given the complexity of the advice from these different sources, a very significant burden falls on each individual team evaluating a project to operationalise this evaluation process. Variations in interpretation of the guidance are to be expected, but more significantly the extensive lists of purposes to be served and documentation needed suggests that this process will be expensive and/or will be incomplete in practice.

THE GATEWAY PROCESS

The Office of Government Commerce has responded in a number of ways to calls for better monitoring, with the setting up of a *Successful Delivery Skills* programme, the launch of the PFI network and the issue of best practice documents (HM Treasury 2002). The primary mechanism developed for monitoring and managing procurement is the OGC's Gateway Process. Two reports were instrumental in initiating the Gateway Process. First, the Gershon Review (Gershon 1999) on government procurement recommends the implementation of a common process for the strategic management of large, complex or novel projects based on the phases of project life cycles. Secondly, the Cabinet Office report *Successful IT: Modernising Government in Action* (2000) requires the OGC to prioritise the implementation of the Gateway Process. The Gateway Process applies to all new procurement projects over £1 m in civil central government. The NHS agreed to implement Gateway in 2003 (OGC 2003c).

According to Timms (2001), the role of the OGC is to work alongside Departments to spread best practice so that each Department may draw upon the experience of others and avoid the reinvention of the wheel or the repetition of avoidable mistakes. In its performance review of 2002/3, the OGC lists its key achievements, including Gateway Reviews of over 250 procurement projects, believed to deliver £500 m value for money savings per year (OGC 2003c). Timms therefore sees the Gateway Process, whose purpose is to 'provide an independent authoritative review mechanism to improve the management of large, complex projects', as central to improving performance delivery of large government projects.

The OGC offers extensive guidance to users through its *Successful Delivery Toolkit* publications. These include guidance on the post-implementation review (PIR), which is carried out on construction, development and procurement projects when there has been time to demonstrate the business benefits of a new service or building (OGC 2003a). The OGC views the PIR as essential to the process of ensuring that improvements result from changes made in a project or programme. The *Successful Delivery Toolkit* publications also include a series on *Achieving Excellence in Construction*, with *Achieving Excellence Guide 8: Improving Performance* (OGC 2003b) explaining the principles and practice of performance evaluation so that the planned improvements are achieved.

The *Successful Delivery Toolkit* publications also provide guidance from the OGC on the Gateway Process. It is based on successful project management techniques in the private sector and seeks to ensure improvements in the successful delivery of large public sector procurement projects. Since the PAC (2003d) and the Treasury response to the PAC (HM Treasury 2003e) agree that PFI is just one of three recommended procurement methods (the other two being design and build, and prime contracting), OGC guidance on best procurement practice given through

the *Successful Delivery Toolkit* refers to all three methods. HM Treasury states that PFI 'should only be used when it represents the best possible procurement route for the project concerned, based on a thorough assessment of value for money' (HM Treasury 2003e).

Six critical periods, numbered 0 to 5 in the development of a project, have been identified as opportunities for a Gateway Review. Four of these relate to the period before contract award, while two look at service implementation and confirmation of the operational benefits, once the project is up and running. Gateway Reviews are carried out by review teams whose membership depends on the level of risk associated with the project, as determined by the project owner or senior responsible owner. High-risk projects are reviewed by a team leader appointed by OGC with a team independent of the department. Medium-risk projects are reviewed by a team leader appointed by OGC with a team drawn from independent departmental staff. Low-risk projects have team leaders appointed by the department with team members from within the department. Typically there are from three to five people within each team, with a review lasting around three to five days. The team presents its report to the project owner/senior responsible owner before leaving the site, and gives a copy to the OGC to identify and disseminate generic lessons learned.

Of particular relevance to our study, Gateway 5 Review covers post-implementation benefit evaluation and may be repeated as required throughout the life of the project. For PFI projects, where the project starts life as a construction project and then becomes a long-term service contract, OGC indicates that there should be a Gateway 5 Review every three years (OGC 2001, p. 1). A nine-point list of purposes of the Gateway 5 Review includes:

- an assessment of whether the business case was realistic and the expected benefits are being delivered

- a confirmation of continuity of key personnel and necessary resources to manage the contract

- an assessment of the continuing ability of the contract to meet business needs and, where change is necessary, to ensure that it does not compromise the original procurement

- a confirmation that there is contract development to improve VFM

- a confirmation of the existence of plans to manage the contract to conclusion, and an exit strategy.

The timing of these reviews depends upon the nature of the contract but should be conducted after the organisation has held a post-implementation review, or similar significant internal review, so that findings from that internal review can be used. For contracts without a service agreement, this review would take place 6–12 months after the construction phase of the project, because evidence of in-service benefits ought to be available by that time. In the case of long-term contracts, reviews should be conducted every three years, once the project is operational. The review should include an assessment of organisational learning, but need not include a full review of plans for the future.

The OGC suggests that the following should be included to inform this review process:

- an assessment of benefits delivered

- the plans for contract and service improvement

- the personnel plans showing how the contract will be managed

- a report on stakeholder issues

- the plans for asset disposal at contract end

- the business case

- the post-implementation review findings and

- a summary of contract changes.

In addition, the OGC has provided guidance on areas to probe with suggested questions and examples of the kinds of evidence that should be sought during the conduct of the Gateway 5 Review. In the introductory section, however, it warns that because projects are unique these questions cannot provide a checklist, rather they should be used only for guidance, and the OGC provides Web-based links to other sources of best practice. The Gateway 5 Review does not replace the post-implementation review, as it takes place after such a review has been carried out, and makes use of the findings from that review (OGC 2001, p. 1).

It should be noted that the focus of the Gateway 5 Review is very much narrower than the more strategic review recommended by the Green Book. Like the 'light touch' inspection regimes elsewhere in the public sector, it emphasises the documentation and processes rather than a substantive evaluation of the direct and indirect costs and benefits. In other words, it is unclear that there is any requirement for any financial evaluation or indeed any examination of the private sector's financial and physical performance against expectations. Despite the centrality of risk transfer to VFM, this issue is hardly touched upon. Furthermore, although the Green Book stresses that best practice should be disseminated throughout the public sector, none of the Gateway reports is a matter of public record. Gateway reports are confidential, made available to a project's senior responsible owner and to OGC alone. The senior official is then accountable for the implementation of recommendations (HM Treasury 2003c). From April 2003, the Gateway Process is being piloted in local government PFI projects by the public private partnerships programme (4Ps).

Notwithstanding such confidentiality, the OGC asserts that: 'This approach promotes an open and honest exchange between the project and review teams delivering maximum added value'. (OGC 2003d)

Owing to this lack of publicly available specific evidence on post-implementation evaluation, very little is known about how well these Gateway Reviews are carried out, let alone the actual performance of these projects. Therefore it is not known whether these projects can or do deliver VFM and it is very difficult if not impossible for an external observer to verify any claims about VFM. Thus secrecy limits the evaluative function of the Gateway Review process and its potential role in the wider public scrutiny and accountability process.

THE CONTROL PROCESS IN TRANSPORT AND HEALTH

Figure 2.1 (see pages 30–31) shows how spending departments have been actively involved in PFI. We have chosen two of these departments, Transport and Health, to examine in depth, in part because the status of each of the procuring bodies differs in its relationship to the government. Since the Highways Agency, as the purchaser of PFI services in roads, is an executive agency within the DoT, it is central government that is commissioning services directly from the private sector and thus guarantees the contract. The NHS hospital trusts, as the purchasers of hospital services, are legally independent entities within the NHS, which is itself a public corporation responsible to the Department of Health. As such, the Secretary of State for Health does not guarantee the payment of contracts that the trusts enter into. It is to be expected that these different structural relationships will have implications for the way in which PFI projects are managed and reviewed after implementation.

Certainly Standard and Poor's, the credit ratings agency that examines the security of cash flows available to support PFI payments, sees the relationship of the procurer to central government as one of the significant factors when considering assessments about the ability to finance and refinance projects. The Highways Agency's credit rating is deemed to be of excellent quality, since the government directly guarantees its debt servicing obligations. By way of contrast, Standard and Poor's does not view NHS trusts as 'AAA' rated UK government guaranteed risks, even though it acknowledges that these involve high levels of both direct and indirect government support and control, and that therefore in practice a trust's credit quality is unlikely to constrain a PFI project's rating (Standard and Poor's 2003).

The DoT, as a civil central government department, must follow the post-implementation control process as previously described. Since most of the PFI road projects were signed and constructed before the post-implementation review or the Gateway 5 review process came into existence, however, the Highways Agency has not implemented those processes. The publicly available documentation reviewing road projects includes NAO reports (NAO 1998a, 1999a) and a case study of the first eight DBFO projects, produced by the Highways Agency, which we will discuss in some detail later.

Although the hospital trusts do not fall under the umbrella of OGC, in 2003 the NHS undertook to implement the Gateway Review process. Prior to adopting the Gateway Process, the Department of Health had an established process of post-project evaluation. The *Capital Investment Manual* (NHS Executive 1994) includes a section on 'Post-project evaluation', in order to encourage more evaluation. It became mandatory for projects in excess of £1 million. This advice was superseded by new guidance *Learning Lessons from Post-project Evaluation* (DoH 2002a), which gives extensive practical, evidence-based guidance on the evaluation requirements, with mandatory requirements for reports on projects in excess of £20 m to be submitted to the DoH. In addition, *Improving PFI Procurement* (DoH 2002b) requires all NHS trusts to have 'sound' evaluation arrangements in place prior to project approval.

Thus, the first wave PFI trusts fall between two stools. Since the first wave of hospital PFI projects that are the subject of our study were signed in 1997 and started to come on stream in 2000/1, there was then no requirement to carry out the Gateway Review process. As with the DoT therefore, these hospitals have not implemented the process. However, we have obtained a copy of one evaluation report carried out under the DoH system that consists of several user surveys into outcomes and impacts (indeed rather more surveys than the DoH required), information about the management of the project and generic lessons for future commissioning of PFI projects (Queen Elizabeth Hospital NHS Trust 2003). It is unclear, however, whom these reports are written for or sent to, what the response has been, who uses them, how they are disseminated (if at all), and whether these reports are in the public domain, although we believe that they are not.

As is also the case with much of the benchmarking of costs within the NHS, any evaluative information is likely to be held in restricted access areas of the DoH website, such as the Knowledge and Information Portal (KIP) and the NHS Executive area, and thus inaccessible to the public. For example, the NHS Estates classes the current NHS development of a database to provide performance and benchmarking information (NHS Estates Data Collection & Analysis System – NEDCAS) as confidential to the NHS and other authorised key stakeholders, in order to avoid commercial use by non-NHS organisations and because of the sensitivity of some information (NHS Estates 2003b). Once again, therefore, little specific post-implementation evaluation evidence of PFI in NHS trusts is, or is likely to become, publicly available.

CONCLUSION

The control process in the public sector has been less than practically helpful and what has existed has been subject to continual change as the number and scope of PFI projects has grown, and as the role of the Treasury has altered over the years since the inception of PFI. There have been continual calls from the NAO and PAC for improvement in the post-implementation review process that have been met by extensive guidance from the Treasury and most recently from the OGC. Even in a recent summary report the NAO made a basic recommendation regarding the use by departments of user surveys as part of their post-contract evaluation (NAO 2003b, Recommendation 4). However, it is difficult to find any significant evidence of actual improvements in monitoring that have taken place.

From the perspective of this study, however, it is significant that the Treasury, the National Audit Office and the Office of Government Commerce have not called for project evaluations from the perspective of ensuring that the projects deliver their expected VFM or for evidence of risk transfer. Despite the Green Book's call (HM Treasury 2003a) for a wide-ranging evaluation, the actual procedures and methodologies rest with the OGC, whose remit involves a conflict of interest: policy promotion and control. Its main review process guidance focuses on a very narrow technical approach. Furthermore, since the results of much of the new tranche of government requirements is and will be kept confidential, there is a lack of publicly available evidence about the performance of the PFI contracts, making it impossible to validate or refute their claims about VFM. This raises a series of further questions about public scrutiny of and accountability for an increasingly important amount of government expenditure. This means that irrespective of the value of the evaluation methodology and reporting procedures for the government department, public accountability is not an explicit objective of the evaluation process.

3. Process issues in the evaluation of PFI

. . . a rational-technical approach to capital investment appraisal is urged.

Process issues in the evaluation of PFI

Official documents advise procuring bodies to design methodologies to monitor performance, direct and indirect benefits, prices, risks and feedback from users so that outturns may be compared with expectations, and the results and lessons so learned may be disseminated to improve future decision making. In short, a rational-technical approach to capital investment appraisal is urged.

A review of the literature shows that there have been no post-implementation reviews of PFI projects from the perspective of VFM, even by the National Audit Office, implying that such an evaluation is not straightforward, has not been commissioned or has not been funded. The research literature implies that although this type of evaluation incurs substantial monitoring costs, its ability to generate the desired benefits in practice is less assured, for three reasons. First, there are a series of interrelated practical problems of inappropriate measurement systems and inaccurate or unreliable data; lack of comparable benchmarks against which to assess performance; and lack of in-house expertise to monitor projects. Secondly, there are issues surrounding confidentiality and the power relationships between the parties to the contract, and thirdly, there appear to be inherent conflicts within contracts that impede monitoring and evaluation. We discuss each of these in turn.

MEASUREMENT SYSTEMS

The monitoring and evaluation of PFI contracts generates new tasks that the public sector has not traditionally carried out. Initially at least, this has created practical difficulties and highlighted the need for systems change. For example, Kirkpatrick and Lucio (1996) argue that traditional local authority management accounting is input-oriented with an almost exclusive concern for the control of inputs, whereas this new accounting/contracting nexus involves first incorporating standards relating to the quantity and quality of outputs into contracts, and secondly

monitoring procedures in ways previously considered impossible or inappropriate (Seal 1999). Consequently, systems for measuring outputs have only recently been introduced in the delivery of public services, initially for managerial and latterly for public accountability purposes. As their usefulness is still unproven (Cutler and Waine 1997), their extension to contractual and regulatory management may be premature.

Several commentators have argued either implicitly or explicitly that traditional ways of disseminating information are inappropriate for monitoring contract outcomes and that substantial informational asymmetries exist between contracting parties that may generate conflicts of interest (Arruñada 2000). The National Audit Office found that some projects lacked appropriate performance measurement structures and recommended the improvement of performance measurement regimes (eg NAO 2002a). Similarly, the Audit Commission concluded that project resources were consistently underestimated by health and local government schemes, and that the implementation of performance management structures had had mixed results (Audit Commission 2001).

These difficulties are compounded by problems in obtaining data and observing effort and performance during the life of the contract (Ricketts 1994). Also, PFI has introduced a range of new tasks for which data, especially comparative data of a historical nature, may not be available. For example, although PFI implies a need for both sides to assess their risk, there is a lack of good quality data to assess probability and risk exposure (Akintoye et al. 1998). Ball, Heafey and King (2003a) found a lack of an evidence-based approach to risk assessment in the schools sector in Scotland, and in particular note that historical data did not appear to be used in risk analysis. In their observation of risk workshops, they found that the risk assessment was in some cases carried out solely on the basis of subjective judgement. They report that one representative, at a meeting of school PFI project representatives in Scotland, stated that historical evidence had been used in one risk workshop and this had led to a much lower estimate of risk transfer than that of other comparable local authority projects in other geographical areas. Such experiences matched the findings of Boyne et al. (2002), who analysed 127 best value performance plans from Welsh local authorities, prepared over a two-year period. Having identified data required for accountability, the authors found that very few of the plans contained the relevant material and concluded that performance plans were currently making little contribution to the accountability of public organisations. Heald (1997) also highlights the problem of the scarcity of hard data in relation to financing costs:

The Treasury cannot or will not quantify the additional finance costs consequent upon financing . . . by private finance rather than by government borrowing, or quantify the interest rate differential . . . . Given the confidentiality which attaches to loan arrangements, systematic evidence about the additional cost of private finance can only be produced by the Treasury or, with a considerable time lag by the National Audit Office.

Case studies of PFI contracts show a more basic data problem, however, relating to standard accounting procedures, which is difficult to explain since it is not associated with new tasks. For example, Grimshaw et al. (2002) reported the difficulties encountered by a hospital trust in checking the payments for work done. This involved matching detailed invoices from providers against details specified in the relevant contract documents, where the costing of each job task was detailed through time and motion studies. The collation of all the information required to process the payment claims was time consuming and the trust found that invoices often provided incomplete information. Similarly, Whorley (2001) found that, in social service provision in Ontario, the contract arrangements for paying out-of-pocket expenses were not followed and

that consequently $1.4 m was paid to private sector contractors without the necessary supporting documentation. As the contract required such documentation, Whorley notes with some surprise that a senior public sector staff member seemed to be unable to recognise that the private sector was responsible for providing the required documentation. Whorley also reports that the provincial auditors expressed concerns about their access to documents, lost documents and the consequent impact on the cost of the audit, which was three times as much as expected. The processes involved in these two examples appeared to be of a routine accounting nature where there was a failure of basic data, and suggests that such processes should be examined in other PFI projects.

PFI has also created a change in terms of control over data sources. Under the contractual arrangements, Ball et al. (2003a) notes that any changes to PFI projects make it more difficult for the public agency to quantify the extra costs involved than under traditional procurement practices since the agency did not have the necessary detailed information, 'such as bills and rates, bills of quantities for all the elements of the job' (Ball et al. 2003a, p. 288). Without this, it was difficult to challenge the PFI contractor's figures. Akintoye et al. (1998) argue that PFI is about self-monitoring and reporting by the private sector contractor, implying that the public sector must be able to use this information to monitor and control projects. So, for example, private sector contractors on roads projects are responsible for measuring traffic volumes, which form the basis of their remuneration. This is not always straightforward. Deakin and Walsh (1996) provide an example of an IT project, where the public sector purchaser was dependent on the private sector contractor for the measurement of output and therefore information became a battleground in service management. They also raise concerns about the quality of self-monitoring by private sector companies involved in prison service PFI contracts. Other studies confirm these findings. For example, there was a lack of accurate reporting of private sector performance at Altcourse Prison (Centre for Public Services 2002), and some evidence of misreporting of performance and falsification of records in other prison services contracts to avoid penalty payments (Taylor and Cooper 2002).

The literature provides some evidence that public sector organisations are changing their accounting systems and controls to meet the needs of this new operating environment as a result of these problems, although little or no evidence is provided about the availability of staff expertise or the cost of such changes, which must be considerable. First, in Grimshaw et al.'s (2002) study of a government IT project, regular inter-organisational meetings were held to improve the cooperative nature of the agreement. The signed contract committed both sides to attend regular meetings of board level management staff. At lower levels there were regular reviews, from which issues were fed into the higher-level meetings.

Secondly, Whorley (2001) also reports that when the Ontario Ministry had to take corrective action in relation to its PFI project, it introduced tighter financial management controls, especially around the attribution of costs and benefits and on the management of procurement. An internal audit team from the ministry was appointed and due diligence work was performed on a constant basis. The project's steering committee was overhauled and included greater public sector representation, with a senior financial officer becoming custodian of the project. It is striking that Whorley believed that the remedy involved, in effect, the re-introduction of traditional public administration approaches such as bureaucratic approval procedures and oversight committees to protect the public interest.

If such instances are repeated elsewhere then it may well be that the civil servant who responded to the risk survey of Akintoye et al. (1998) is not alone. This respondent claimed that there is a need to monitor

service delivery closely, even though such close monitoring is against the spirit of PFI, which emphasises self-monitoring and reporting by the consortium. Finally, the NAO praises the Prison Service for designing what are described as its comprehensive measurement systems, which have increased the transparency of the prison estate's performance (NAO 2003g, Recommendation a). The Prison Service now uses key performance targets to assess performance via a weighted scorecard. The NAO believes that this good practice should be shared with public prisons as well as other government departments. The Audit Commission (2001, Section 4, paras 78–79) also identifies examples of good practice in terms of achieving continuous service improvement through the use of challenging performance targets.

BENCHMARKING

One important method of evaluation is to benchmark actual performance against an appropriate standard. Available standards include the original contract, the public sector comparator (PSC), costs and quality performance data at other similar facilities procured by conventional means, and cost and quality performance data from private sector competitors of the contracting private partner. Although all these methods have been implemented, they are all problematical.

Benchmarking against the original contract
Several problems arise in the literature relating to benchmarking against the original contract. First, if the public agency is to manage service provision at a distance by monitoring actual standards against contract specifications then it is essential that outputs can be clearly specified and observed (Deakin and Walsh 1996). However, since the nature of public services is such that it is usually difficult to specify them in any detail, contracts are usually written in very general terms. Edwards and Shaoul (2003) show how this created problems in the case of two failing IT projects. Secondly, Grimshaw et al. (2002) found in

their study of a government IT project that there was a lack of prior measures of productivity or performance, a feature thought to underpin many of the subsequent difficulties in managing the contract, which also made evaluation difficult. Thirdly, Deakin and Walsh (1996) argue that contracts dealt poorly with ambiguity and failed to capture custom and practice, leading to additional costs and potential problems in monitoring performance. Further, since contracts were long term, the service element, usually facilities management, had to be described and monitored over periods of (typically) up to 30 years, during which time changes in requirements could be expected. Fourthly, Grimshaw et al. (2002) found that in both their cases, of a government IT and a hospital trust project, there were difficulties in ensuring equivalence between the specification of tasks in the formal contract and the actual tasks undertaken as part of services provided. Lastly, McWilliam (1997), drawing on his own experiences at the Avery Hill Student Village, argues that the private sector does not understand clearly the importance of good quality performance and notes that, over time, the service performance will have to satisfy the requirements of ever-more-demanding students.

Benchmarking against the PSC
At the initial stage of a PFI deal a PSC is prepared, which costs the project using conventional public procurement, and at the business case stage private sector bids are then compared with the PSC, which itself should be updated in line with any changes to the facilities and services being procured. Referring to Treasury Taskforce Technical Note No. 5 (1999b), Ball et al. (2003a) note that the format of the PSC should include an overview of the project, basic procurement costs (both capital and revenue), approaches taken in relation to third party revenues, approaches taken on asset values and transfer, and a risk matrix. As the Government's cost of finance is lower than that of the private sector, this should help to establish a robust VFM assessment.

McKendrick and McCabe (1997) evidently believe that there can be some benefit in using the PSC, since they report that in the Stonehaven Community Hospital PFI deal, 'there appears to have been no PSC produced for this project, which makes it difficult to ascertain just how operationally efficient the winning bid is'. Similarly, the Public Accounts Committee criticises Airwave PPP for not preparing a PSC until the decision to use PFI had already been made, making it doubtful that the use of a comparator added anything significant to the decision-making process (PAC 2002c), although it notes that it was used later for evaluation purposes.

There have been a number of concerns raised about the use of the PSC for decision-making purposes, which in turn raise questions about its suitability for benchmarking and evaluation purposes. For example, the Government's emphasis on PFI as the most important, if not the only, procurement route has meant that public agencies have spent time refining the financial comparison calculations in a way that has not always been appropriate, given the impossibility of accurate estimates for costs over the long term. Both the NAO and PAC have stated that departments 'should be wary of spurious precision' when evaluating value for money through both the PSC (NAO 1998a; PAC 2003a) and realistic alternative options (NAO 1997). Examples of this have been the PFI contract for Fazakerley Prison (PAC 1998c, Recommendation 2), the PFI contract for the redevelopment of the West Middlesex University Hospital (NAO 2002f) and the redevelopment of the main MOD building (NAO 2002c). Regarding the latter, the NAO commented that, 'Given the uncertainties in the comparison, a more reasonable conclusion in that situation may be that the cost comparison shows there is little to choose between PFI and conventional procurement in cost terms'. Similarly, in its appraisal of the London Underground PPP, the NAO advised against relying on one criterion that was dependent upon the financial modelling of costs that were fraught with difficulties (NAO 2000e).

Despite the effort expended by the procurer on creating a spuriously precise PSC, there is evidence that PSCs have not always been well prepared. We cite but three examples, although several others exist. First, in the case of the PRIME (Private Sector Resource Initiative for the Management of the Estate) project, the PAC commented that, since past performance in relation to the property being transferred had been unacceptably poor, it was important that the preparation of PSCs should not assume that future performance would be the same. Instead, reasonable assumptions should be made about the public sector's ability to improve the efficiency of its estate management (PAC 1999b, Recommendation 8). The Treasury Minute responding to this recommendation noted that the PSC was prepared by benchmarking costs and then judging the likely savings that would have arisen if the DSS had rationalised procurement and driven out inefficiencies in estate management practices. Such action was consistent with the guidance given in Treasury Taskforce Technical Note No. 5, *How to Construct a Public Sector Comparator* (1999b).

Secondly, in the PFI contract for the new Dartford and Gravesham Hospital, the PAC noted that significant errors in the PSC were not detected by the trust (PAC 2000c). This meant that some £12 m less in savings should be expected, making PFI savings marginal when compared with the PSC. The PAC recommended that VFM comparisons should be rigorously checked (PAC 2000c, Recommendation 2). In addition (Recommendations 11, 12) the PAC wanted to see a sensitivity analysis relating to changing usage levels, along with more rechecking of assumptions.

Thirdly, in the case of the London Underground PPP, a number of adjustments amounting to £2.5 billion were made to the PSC (Deloitte and Touche 2001). The first and largest, £1.17 billion, represented the expected failure of LU to meet the performance requirements. This risk of failure was shown as an economic cost to passengers, not to London Underground. In other words, the costs of the PSCs were inflated by including costs to others, although this was not the procedure set out by the Treasury's Green Book (1997a). The costs to passengers are entirely separate from financial costs to London Underground and the two should not have been confused. Furthermore, Deloitte and Touche find that many of the underlying assumptions are subjective and arbitrary. As the negotiations proceeded, there was considerable 'descoping' of the project and changes to the contractual arrangements that were not reflected in a similar downgrading of the PSCs' costs. Some of the numerous revisions to the PSCs involved performance adjustments that were extremely volatile and there was considerable scope for double counting. Although the costs had been subject to extensive simulations and sensitivity analyses, the expected value or mean of each distribution was chosen even where the distribution was skewed, leading to a value considerably higher than the most likely value.

Such problems therefore make it unlikely that the PSC will provide a good benchmark, especially if there are no resources available to update it to fit the prevailing contract conditions. Pilling (2002) provides an example of this in his study of the process of contracting for a radiology department's picture archiving and communications system. He argues that although the PSC is considered to be relatively straightforward to construct, it needs to take technology refreshment into account. This aspect does not normally form part of a purchase contract, and the cost of the technology refreshment is unpredictable.

Comparisons with conventional procurement

Taylor and Cooper (2002) quote the findings of the US General Accounting Office (GAO) which, after investigating a number of methodologies used to compare operational costs and/or the quality of service of comparable private and public prisons, concluded that the best approach for evaluating operational costs was to study existing comparable facilities, not hypothetical facilities. In other words, the GAO rejected the use of the PSC for benchmarking purposes. In practice often this means trying to compare the performance of new PFI facilities with older publicly procured ones, which may not represent a like-for-like comparison. Commenting on the justice system, the Centre for Public Services (2002), argues that cost comparisons between new and old prisons do not make sense because there are different security and working arrangements, which might not form part of the evaluation process, and different pay and pensions for staff in the two sectors, whose impact on service quality is difficult to ascertain.

Comparisons with private sector performance
A government IT project had intended to use regular benchmarking of costs and performance levels obtained from private sector competitors of the contractor (Grimshaw et al. 2002). They found that it was impossible to exploit market pressures, however, because of the extraordinary difficulty in benchmarking the costs of IT services. Consequently, the government department expected to be able to benchmark only half of its outsourced activities because of the difficulty of obtaining cost/quality information and the non-comparability of some areas of IT provision. Thus Grimshaw et al. (2002, p. 491) argue that the apparent benefits to be gained from 'market-cost discipline' were limited in practice by the impossibility of enforcing spot market contracting. They conclude that the public sector partner incurred most of the risks associated with the IT contract, rather than benefiting from the downward cost pressures of market competition.

The NAO has found also that when contract bidding was non-competitive, benchmarking is difficult to do and departments have failed to provide adequate comparisons. In the case of the Radiocommunications Agency Joint Venture with CMG (UK) Ltd, the NAO recommended that existing service levels should be established in order to enable comparisons of subsequent changes in performance (NAO 2000d). This has been a recurring theme ever since the PAC

recommended that the Inland Revenue set clear targets against which actual efficiency improvements could be measured in the Newcastle Estate Development Project (PAC 2000a). In the Inland Revenue/EDS Strategic Partnership, however, the PAC noted that the Inland Revenue found it difficult to benchmark successfully owing to difficulties associated with identifying suitable comparators and obtaining commercially sensitive information (PAC 2000e).

The use of should-cost models, as demonstrated by the PPP Airwave, is deemed to be good practice if full competitive tendering is impossible or fails (PAC 2002c). In its report on the Libra project, the NAO recommended that in order to avoid jeopardising VFM, the development of a should-cost model could help assess the reasonableness of a bid (NAO 2003a) and act as a standard against which to measure performance.

This inability to examine current market prices is critical in situations where historical costs are not an appropriate basis for comparison, because PFI projects may introduce a new system of working that is substantially different from the pre-existing system or alternatively needs and consequently costs change over time. In hospital projects, investigated by Grimshaw et al. (2002) and McKendrick and McCabe (1997), the PFI involved the closure of one site and the concentration of services at another, making it difficult to compare previous performance with the operational efficiency and the gains or losses resulting from the PFI project. IT projects are another area in which the effect of variables other than the PFI project itself makes the evaluation of PFI difficult. In such projects, rapid changes in the skills and knowledge that underpin working practices make it difficult to judge the cost-effectiveness and quality of the outputs against those of previous methods. More generally, Sussex (2003) notes that measuring cost and time overruns is difficult. Many claims of large cost increases under conventional public sector procurement were based on comparing the outrun cost with initial estimates made many years previously, not with the price agreed at financial close. General price inflation and the costs of subsequent modifications to the scheme prior to tender influence cost. Drawing on previous work, (Sussex 2001) Sussex concludes that if the same approach were used to evaluate PFI projects, then they too would appear to overrun greatly on cost and time.

IN-HOUSE EXPERTISE

The outsourcing of services entails the purchaser's surrender of a significant level of expertise, ostensibly to exploit the benefits of the private sector's greater specialisation. Without strong expertise in service delivery, however, it is difficult for the purchaser either to manage effectively the monitoring of service delivery or to specify new work. Staff turnover in contract management presents an additional and significant problem in replacing expertise. In their evaluations of the initial contract negotiations, a number of authors have noted that the public sector may therefore have underestimated the probable costs of contracting and in particular the need to have a credible team of negotiators dedicated to the project. For example, Grimshaw et al. (2002) note a significant difference between the public and private sectors in relation to the resources and expertise available for negotiating and fine-tuning the contract.

As projects become operational, similar evidence is beginning to accumulate about the costs associated with monitoring performance, and in some instances it has been argued that there is or has been a shortage of public sector expertise to enable effective monitoring and project evaluation. Grimshaw et al. (2002) recommend that the public sector organisation should invest additional resources in the specification, monitoring and measurement of contracted services. They note that the separating out of particular services for tender, the specification of tasks to be included, and the design of monitoring and measurement methods all

present an institutional problem (as well as imposing additional transaction costs) which places additional demands on management in areas of accounting systems, human resource management and operations. Indeed, the Treasury Green Book (2003a) admits that conducting an assessment can be resource-intensive.

Whorley (2001) argues that public sector organisations have been weakened by the downsizing agenda and have tended to enter partnerships in a subordinate role, which has hampered both effectiveness and accountability. He notes particularly that senior members of staff have left and that early retirement programmes have created 'churn' among public sector staff, leading to a loss of expertise in effective oversight. Grimshaw et al. (2002) make similar points. They report that once one contract had been signed, the trust's senior PFI project staff left, leaving behind a dearth of knowledge about the concession agreement. Owing to financial restrictions that affected pay and training, the NHS had difficulty retaining staff and consequently the private sector trained the NHS monitoring team to 'see things how the private sector team saw them'.

Whorley (2001) argues that there is a major flaw in the monitoring of high-tech projects, where the private sector's task is to develop systems past the point that could be achieved by the public sector. If such a position were reached then it is likely that the public sector would lack the skills to monitor these enhanced systems. He argues that the state should not become so hollow (Rhodes 1994) as to be unable to direct, control and evaluate contracted goods and services and that the effects of the downsizing agenda need to be addressed so that the public sector retains the necessary skills to engage fully with partners. He found that in practice, however, most of the knowledge resided with the private company, which then enjoyed a privileged position for any continuing work that could entail long-run costs to the Government. Any subsequent attempt by the Government to take on the work directly would involve significant costs to transfer knowledge from the consultants back to the Government. This line of argument is supported by Grimshaw et al. (2002). They argue that even where an 'in-house' team of staff with specialist skills is retained and initially maintains a relatively strong bargaining leverage, over time this source of bargaining strength is likely to diminish as the private sector develops new IT systems in areas where government staff have little experience.

Furthermore, the lack of public sector expertise to assess risk is a feature of several papers. For example, Hood and McGarvey (2002) report evidence that some local authority staff do not feel that they have sufficient expertise, often because they lack sufficient skills, especially those staff involved in the 'non-insurance' aspects of risk management, such as Monte Carlo simulations. Those whose involvement is restricted to insurance advice are more confident. Public sector staff perceive an imbalance in skills between private and public sector staff in risk assessment and although respondents believed that the local authorities' own team should be used, many local authorities' risk managers lack the necessary skills to do this effectively.

Nevertheless, there is some recent evidence that the need for resources to support the maintenance of in-house expertise is being recognised at an individual project level. For example, in their study of a Scottish high school project, Ball, Heafey and King (2003b) conclude that the local authority project team had operated very effectively because the Council had decided to resource fully its development of the PFI project by compensating departments for the time they spent on their PFI work. This process also helped to minimise the use of consultants, which meant a keener focus on the Council's needs and interests. However, the use of resources for such purposes is not necessarily viewed agreeably by all parties and, for example, Ball et al. also report some concern at school level about the costs involved. For example, a deputy

head teacher indicated that he was now required to spend quite a large proportion of his time liaising with the PFI operators. More generally, the Audit Commission (2001), in a larger study of ten completed schemes in local government and health in England and Wales, echoed this concern. It states that the length and complexity of the PFI procurement process could have adverse effects on other services owing to the amount of senior management time spent on PFI issues.

CONFIDENTIALITY

One of the issues that numerous commentators have mentioned is the desire of the private sector contractor that contractual information should be treated as confidential, and this creates conflicts with the public agency's need to account to taxpayers and service users. Hood and McGarvey (2002) conclude that:

The contentious political nature of PFI and the secrecy surrounding the, supposed, commercially sensitive aspects of its operation has resulted in major difficulties in post-implementation evaluation.

Their conclusion is important not only because of the degree of difficulty that they report but also because of its impact on evaluation. Similarly, the Centre for Public Services (2002) notes that public discussion tends to focus on net present values (NPVs) and discounted costs, although cash costs have been kept secret and business cases are not always in the public domain. Unison has claimed that it has had difficulty extracting contract documentation or information on the number, sex and grade of staff affected by PFI projects.

What is surprising is that authors report that not only the private sector, but also the public sector sought to maintain confidentiality over information. For example, the NAO reported that it was the Government that had required the financial details of the Highways Agency's contracts with the private sector to design, build, finance and operate (DBFO) to be kept confidential

(NAO 1998a). In specific instances, Unison's problems were attributed to the lack of information disclosure by all organisations within the Criminal Justice System, not only the private contractors, and Whorley (2001) claims that Government representatives had agreed to demands that details of contracts remained confidential. He quotes Boase (2000) as saying that: 'It is striking how government representatives have acquiesced to demands by their private partners that the details of their contracts remain confidential, thus blurring the lines of accountability'.

Furthermore, it is unclear that the Freedom of Information Act, due to come into force in 2005, will remedy this lack of information. Thus, despite the exhortation, made without any caveats about the impact on commercial sensitivity in Chapter 7 of the White Paper (Cabinet Office 1997), that evaluation reports should not only be disseminated, but also published, it appears that the practice is closer to paragraph 7.18, which says that security or commercial confidentiality may be good reason for not publishing evaluation reports. This means that, in practice, the Government's apparent desire to learn lessons to improve the quality of future decisions seems to be restricted.

POWER

The issue of confidentiality and the Government's willingness to acquiesce to the wishes of the private sector suggests that it is worth examining the nature of power relationships between the contracting parties. An unequal relationship may affect VFM via the (in)ability to enforce contract provisions, renegotiate and/or terminate the contract.

The incoming Labour Government of 1997 instituted a change in the rhetoric surrounding PFI when it began to use the terminology of 'public private partnership' to describe the intended relationship between the two contracting bodies. However, as Whorley (2001)

observes, partnerships imply a relationship of equality, whereas according to Mulgan (2000) accountability implies an unequal relationship of superior and subordinate in which the latter is required to take directions from the former and to accept sanctions, if necessary, for unsatisfactory performance. Thus for Whorley (2001), partnership arrangements impeded accountability by weakening the authority rights of the procurers.

In practice, the power relationships may be of a different nature again. In Grimshaw et al.'s view (2002), the private sector is likely to have greater experience than the public sector in managing service delivery to meet contractual requirements. Thus the move to a market-based contracting arrangement should deliver a comparative advantage to private sector partner organisations relative to the public sector. The private sector is likely to have a greater ability to negotiate a better deal. For example, Grimshaw et al.'s study shows an imbalance of power between public and private sector partners, which could lead to an imbalance of bargaining strength and an inequitable distribution of the gains and the losses. Whorley (2001) notes that during the course of the Ontario PFI Business Transformation Project, traditional public service concerns for process, control and public oversight were displaced in the interests of the private firm. Similarly, Hastings (1999) reports that in Scotland, the views of private sector staff, when re-interviewed after a year, remained unchanged whereas the views of the other parties had shifted towards the private sector perspective. She concludes that an imbalance of organisational power implies the probability of dominance and therefore, unidirectional change that could be detrimental to the public sector.

The nature of power relations can be observed by examining both payment deductions for poor performance and any attempts by procurers to facilitate good performance rather than enforcing non-payment clauses. There is evidence that, where actual performance has fallen below the required level, performance deductions from payments have been made. For example, the PAC Report *Managing the Relationship to Secure a Successful Partnership in PFI Projects* (2002a) noted that 58% of authorities with a performance review process had made performance deductions, but despite this the PAC remained concerned that public agencies might not do enough to ensure that 'persistent under-performance' did not take place. In addition, the NAO has reported that the performance of PFI prisons against contract has been mixed (2003g, para. 5). Out of seven operational prisons only Forest Bank had not incurred financial deductions. With the others, financial deductions were generally highest in the first year of operation, reducing greatly in subsequent years. The PFI contractor servicing Ashfield prison, however, had increasing financial deductions and faced the prospect of contract termination unless improvements were sustained.

There is also a concern that in some contracts the cap on deductions may have been set at an inappropriate level. The PAC commented (1998c) that Securicor's penalties for non-compliance with performance measures at Bridgend prison were limited to 5% of the annual contract price. The Laganside Courts PFI contract limited the total abatement for unavailability to 44% of the total amount due, even if the entire building was out of action (NAO 2003f, para. 6).

Another problem is that the public sector does not always have systems in place to enforce the payment deductions. The NAO (1999d) noted that the Passport Agency did not have monitoring systems for some standards and consequently was unable to claim service credits to which it appeared to be entitled. Reporting on the passport delays of summer 1999, the NAO recommended that:

Public bodies should have adequate systems for recording performance, and ensure that they are in a position to claim any compensation due from contractors for failure to meet agreed performance standards, subject to appropriate risk-sharing within the partnership. (NAO 1999d, Recommendation 10).

However, even when systems are in place deductions may not be made. For example, Whorley (2001, p. 331) states that even though benefits were running behind costs, a situation contrary to the contract, Andersens were paid, and Ball et al. (2003a) report that the Benefits Agency and Post Office Counters Ltd did not demand damages when their project began to slip. Sussex (2003) notes that writing penalty clauses into a contract did not guarantee that cost overruns, delays in delivery or other performance shortfalls would not be borne by the NHS. In his view there was still plenty of room for dispute over the cause of the problem and who should pay.

Edwards and Shaoul (2003) note the problems inherent in enforcing penalty clauses. In the case of the NIRS2 contract, the Benefits Agency accepted compensation that did not cover the Agency's costs, because, as the Treasury Minister Dawn Primarola admitted, the Government would not demand compensation for the troubled NIRS2 National Insurance Records contract 'for fear of damaging future relationships', even though the contract allowed for compensation. Similarly, the Passport Agency waived service credits worth some £275,000 in the interest of good working relationships over the 10-year life of the project. This project also highlighted a contractual defect in that there was no available redress for consequential loss arising from the contractor's failure to deliver on time.

Implicit in these cases was also the Government's fear that enforcement of the penalty clauses would jeopardise the success of a policy to which it was heavily committed. In other words, there were wider political considerations that precluded enforcing the contract. More generally, this means that since contractual arrangements crucially depend upon their political context, they may create a power imbalance that militates against the public agency enforcing the contract.

CONFLICTS WITHIN CONTRACTS

PFI contracts are long term in nature, multi-faceted and multi-phased, and may have multiple stakeholders and complex objectives. This may create tensions and conflicts between different stakeholders at different times that affect the ability to monitor, control and evaluate the project.

First, PFI projects normally involve the integration of the design, build and finance of a capital asset and a long-term service contract to operate facilities such as cleaning, catering, repair and maintenance, and laundry, etc. However, Akintoye et al. (1998) argue that in practice, rather than integration, there is a conflict of interest between capital and service obligations, because various commercial interests have varying influences at different stages of the project. Citing the case of a contract for a student hall of residence, McWilliam (1997) concurs with this finding. He argues that from early on in the negotiation phase it became clear that the initial bidders relished the construction work but paid scant attention to the facilities management and risk transfer aspects. At that time, pre-1997, the contractors simply thought they were constructing a building and the lenders thought they were lending to the university. Consequently, he argues that the private sector did not clearly understand the importance of the service element that was to form the basis of the long-term relationship.

Similar concerns have been raised elsewhere. For example, in its report *Privatising Justice*, the Centre for Public Services (2002) cites the Director General of the Prison Service as saying that the private sector should do the design and build while the public sector should run the prison. Although Debande (2002) acknowledges that there has been a lack of evidence about performance in the operational phase, in relation

to transport, he concludes that the gains from PFI were essentially in the design and construction phases. He highlights the issue of the quality of road operations after construction by comparing the components of four competing bids on a road project. The two projects with the best VFM were those projects with the highest road construction costs and the lowest operation and maintenance costs. He argues that over time the private sector may behave opportunistically, especially where there was no substitute for infrastructure or the project was part of a network.

The nature of accounting for PFI means that the service element is critical to achieving the Government's preferred accounting outcome, which keeps the asset and liability off balance sheet. Hodges and Mellett (2002) explain that the Treasury bases its accounting on the premise that PFI projects are contracts for services and therefore PFI contracts are not lease transactions. Payments for services are only due when the service is delivered. The effect of this premise is that the regulations of SSAP 21 and FRS 5, which might see PFI projects accounted for on balance sheet, are avoided. In essence PFI contracts can remain off balance sheet provided that 'the contract was drafted to avoid the separation of asset and service payments and the making of material payments or deposits in advance of service provision' (Hodges and Mellett 2002, p. 134). That is, there is an accounting rationale for ensuring that each PFI contains a service element that is integral to the project. Thus the Government's requirements to include a service element may conflict with the needs of the agency, which might be better served by a capital-asset-only arrangement. This may lead to further tensions and problems.

Different stakeholders may be involved at different times in multi-phased projects. Since projects tend to have a dual risk profile, the first being the high-risk construction phase and the last a low-risk utility phase, when lenders are more likely to buy into PFI schemes, Debande (2002) concludes that not all stakeholders are involved directly in each phase, implying the possibility of divergent and changing interests over time. This implies a need for monitoring and control systems to be reviewed as the project moves through its various phases. However, the different timescales involved in many projects may add to the monitoring difficulties. Debande (2002), using the Skye Bridge as an example, notes that the contractor had to provide a bond to cover any dispute over the standard of maintenance. The bridge was designed to last for 120 years but the tolls, which provide an income stream, would run out in 27 years. The road surface had to last 40 years and the financing was for 25 years. Thus the lifetime of PFI projects and the associated infrastructure were independent, but such timing issues might signal changes in the contract that represent new phases with different monitoring impacts. For example, from the perspective of the public sector, the state of the assets at the end of the contract life would become critical because there might be a disincentive on the part of the private sector to maintain assets towards the end of the PFI contract. Hence, the distribution of risk would vary between different phases of the project. Although Sussex (2003) argues that maintenance might now receive greater consideration because of the long-term nature of contracts, this may not have been the case in earlier projects. This means that project evaluation must distinguish between the different phases of the projects and pay particular attention to the operating element of the PFI.

PFI projects in schools especially highlight the problems associated with multiple stakeholders because the public sector responsibilities are divided between different entities. Although the local education authority (LEA) is the contracting party, the decisions that it takes affect the school's budget, for which the school has responsibility, as well as the quality of the teaching environment. Edwards and Shaoul (2003) found that the LEA may act as champion for a PFI project even when the interests of the LEA and the school differ. In addition, they argued that although it was usually the

school's responsibility to monitor on-site PFI performance, it was the LEA that had enforcement powers. So, should a school or classroom(s) become unavailable it would be the school and pupils who suffer, but the school might be unable to implement contractual performance clauses in practice and have no legal redress against the LEA if it proved unwilling or unable, owing to lack of resources, to enforce the contract standards. In this situation effective monitoring, control and evaluation are needed to assess the project at both the LEA and school level.

A quite different source of conflict between stakeholders has arisen, particularly, in relation to the prisons. The NAO's post-implementation evaluation assessments have focused on the financial aspects of performance. Notably absent is any consideration of the views of prisoners, their families or advocates, criminologists, prison reform organisations, trade unions or the probation services (Centre for Public Services 2002, p. 26). These authors argue that there was an absence of social, economic and environmental audit or analysis that could provide additional evidence to support claims about the relative financial benefits of PFI compared with the PSC. In particular, they draw attention to the lack of evidence about monitoring of issues such as equity, for example, work force rights, including those associated with Transfer of Undertakings Protection of Employment (TUPE), and access rights to facilities that are being centralised at out-of-town greenfield sites. Nathan and Whitfield (2000) concur, arguing that proving or disproving VFM was only one part of the equation, and that Treasury and NAO criteria for VFM assessment ignored equality and employment issues.

At a policy level, Taylor and Cooper (2002) report that there is a lack of evidence that the private sector can deliver wider public policy objectives such as poverty reduction, social inclusion, equity and prisoner rehabilitation. There appears, particularly within prisons, to be a fundamental conflict between the needs of the private sector provider and society. Society's strategic aims of challenging offending behaviour and promoting rehabilitation are at risk under PFI, because commercial companies have a vested interest in keeping people locked up. There is a clear conflict of interest between society's desire for prisoners to be rehabilitated and for fewer prisoners, on the one hand, and the corporations whose profits are best served by increasing prisoner numbers, on the other. Taylor and Cooper (2002, p. 24) concluded; 'There is a fundamental conflict between operating to contract and running a prison which delivers effective strategies for dealing with offending behaviour'.

CONCLUSION

In the private sector it has long been recognised that the post-audit of investment decisions is a very difficult task, which may be viewed with disfavour because it discourages initiative and leads to excessive caution. Nevertheless, empirical evidence indicates that most large companies have been conducting some form of post-completion audit for many years. The literature outlined above indicates some issues that have occurred in public sector monitoring and evaluation of PFIs, at least some of which indicate that, given time, evaluation is capable of improvement. If monitoring and evaluation are to be effective, the control mechanisms and accountability systems that were not designed for either the decision-making or control roles envisioned in the new accounting and contracting models (Seal 1999) may need to be changed to reflect this new role.

Thus, appraising, monitoring and evaluation, at least in those case studies that have been made publicly available, have proved difficult.

- There have been practical problems associated with a lack of in-house expertise, data collection and measurement systems and availability of suitable benchmarks against which to judge performance.

- Consequently, the costs of monitoring appear to have been greater than was anticipated and in time this is likely to increase the public sector's costs and thereby reduce VFM.

- Although some of these problems may be explained by the fact that such tasks are new to the public sector, it is likely that these are long-term problems.

- Monitoring, evaluation and scrutiny are made more difficult by the requirement of both the Government and the private corporations for confidentiality.

- Unequal power relations between the relatively small and poorly resourced public agency and the large corporation may make contract enforcement difficult if not impossible in practice.

- PFI projects typically give rise to different conflicts of interests within and between the two main parties to the contract.

- Public agencies may also have conflicting objectives, including equity and social inclusion, whereas private companies tend to be more narrowly focused on profit-related tasks, differences which may generate conflicts.

A full assessment of a PFI project therefore needs to consider the outcomes from the perspective of the various stakeholders, who may change over the life of the project, and its social impacts, rather than just taking a narrow technical approach, which is the emphasis of current advice from the OGC. Although there have been repeated statements in the press by Government and ex-Government ministers about the public's right to know how hospitals are performing, this right does not appear to extend to how the PFI projects are performing. Finally, although the Government claims to be in favour of evaluation, its insistence on hiding behind commercial confidentiality limits the ability of independent parties to carry out

such studies and raises questions about who is
demanding confidentiality, why this is necessary and
what there is to hide.

Crucially . . . the literature suggests that values placed on the benefit of risk transfer are fundamental to VFM at the decision-making stage.

Given that VFM is the Government's rationalising motif for PFI, we consider here the evidence as it relates to the sources of VFM and their ability to deliver VFM in practice. VFM in PFI projects has come to mean lower whole-life costs, which are assumed to flow from the greater operating efficiency and innovatory practices of the private sector. These could be achieved as a result of several factors, including market forces that encourage efficient working, good contract management, and innovation in technology and methods of working. Conversely, VFM may be adversely affected by higher transactions costs, including higher financing costs and monitoring costs. Crucially, however, the literature suggests that values placed on the benefit of risk transfer are fundamental to VFM at the decision-making stage. We review first the limited publicly available post-implementation evidence from official bodies, such as the official watchdogs and the Treasury, and then available evidence on each of these possible sources of VFM.

IMPLEMENTATION EVIDENCE

Scotland's Accounts Commission was one of the first to report on PFI procurement, after the completion of the construction phase of six schools projects (Accounts Commission 2002). It was scathing about the local authorities' unquestioning approach to PFI. Funding considerations (the availability of some funding under PFI and none under conventional public procurement) and 'the *presumption* of better VFM under PFI had driven the choice of PFI' [emphasis added]. The Accounts Commission was concerned that decisions were made on the basis of stereotypes of poorly performing public sector options rather than evidence of demonstrable benefits from private finance. Furthermore, the emphasis on PFI would mean that in future it would be difficult to get up-to-date evidence about the outcomes and effectiveness of traditional procurement, thereby biasing decision making even further in favour of PFI.

The evidence on construction showed that the projects had largely been built to time and budget, but as yet there was little information about the operational phase of the contracts. It warned that although the contracts should provide incentives for the PFI providers, success was not assured, and the councils needed to have a clear strategy for managing underperformance. Likewise, the PFI process does not guarantee that the councils will achieve the most cost effective risk transfer. Although it believed that PFI was likely to provide benefits in the schools' maintenance, there was either no evidence that operational gains could be made through PFI or there was evidence that they could have been achieved through other procurement mechanisms.

The Accounts Commission was concerned about the emphasis on VFM at the expense of affordability. First, the transaction and financing costs were high, adding to the high cost of PFI contracts. Since PFI schemes covered only part of the councils' schools estate, they could create affordability problems in the future that would be borne by those schools not included in the PFI contracts or by other council services. For example, the largest PFI scheme, the Glasgow schools project, accounted for 24% of the council's entire non-staff education expenditure in 2000/1. Secondly, the value of the public sector comparator was limited since it was not well costed and assumed up-front funding rather than financing through Treasury gilts, which is how such projects would typically be funded by the public sector. Given the lack of public funding, the schools refurbishment would not go ahead unless PFI was shown to have lower whole-life costs. The margin of difference between public and private finance after risk transfer was small and there was no analysis of why the PFI solution was more economic. This implied that since the PSC was unreliable, the projects were unlikely to be more economical over the whole life of the contracts.

Although the Audit Commission's review of schools projects in England was more limited in scope than the Accounts Commission's, it too was critical of PFI and the outcomes to date, saying, 'PFI has not yet delivered some of the most important benefits expected of it' (Audit Commission 2003, p. 39). The quality of refurbishment and new build under PFI was poorer than under traditional procurement. There was little evidence that the construction methods would lead to lower whole-life costs. The average cost of cleaning and catering was higher than in non-PFI schools. Although this meant that the standard was higher, it came at the expense of the non-PFI schools. There were few deductions for poor performance. Standards were not enforced because, owing to problems with the information systems, there was no information upon which to base an assessment of performance and hence make deductions where appropriate. In any event, it was unclear that the size of the penalty either constituted a deterrent to poor performance or adequately compensated the schools.

On the question of the anticipated VFM, risk transfer and affordability, the Audit Commission acknowledged many of the points made by the Accounts Commission (2002) and called for a revision of the methodology in order to give PFI more credibility in the eyes of the public. It was particularly concerned that the affordability gap would surface later in the life of the contract. Interestingly, from the perspective of this study, it was concerned about 'information asymmetry'. There was no open book accounting under PFI, thus local education authorities had no information on actual construction, operational and maintenance costs, and this would make it difficult to negotiate a realistic price for contract amendments or to prepare future PSCs. This inequality would mean that, increasingly, PFI companies would be able to dictate terms to the public sector. Among its recommendations was the call for the Government to develop an evaluation template for retrospectively assessing the success of PFI schemes along with other large-scale investments in schools.

The NAO (2003b) and PAC (2003d) have reported on the construction performance of all projects completed by summer 2002. The NAO report focused on three key areas of construction: price certainty for departments; timing of construction delivery; and the quality of design and construction. It found that generally the aims of PFI were being met. As it did not carry out a user survey as part of its methodology, however, the value of such findings may be limited as user consultation has been identified as an important part of performance review (Audit Commission 2001). Experts consulted confirmed that generally the theoretical PFI incentives were working in practice, with improvements in built assets through the better integration of design, construction and maintenance, leading to better management of construction cost risks. Assets were now being delivered early, or at least on time.

HM Treasury, which has been the key player in promoting PFI, recently published a report, *PFI: Meeting the Investment Challenge* (Treasury 2003c), which provides some indication of how PFI is working in practice. First, the report acknowledged that small schemes below £20 m might not be appropriate for PFI, given the lengthy procurement process and high transaction costs. Secondly, the Treasury was forced to admit that IT projects had not been very successful, with only 22% delivering 80–100% of defined programme benefits. Furthermore, they had failed to achieve the level of risk transfer that provided the original justification for proceeding with PFI. The Treasury provided no financial information that showed the extent of the failure to achieve VFM. This lack of success, it argued, was due to the speed of change, the difficulty of delineating responsibilities between parties given the high degree of integration between an IT PFI project and other non-PFI activities, the low capital costs relative to operational costs, the relatively short length of the contracts (typically 10 years) and the lack of third-party finance that ensures appropriate and effective risk transfer. In future, therefore, the Treasury would 'presume against PFI for IT projects'.

Thirdly, its survey of a sample of large non-IT PFI projects found that 88% of the new assets had been built to time, specification and budget. Where there had been cost overruns this had been due to changes in the design required by the public sector client. Fourthly, the Treasury was satisfied that the projects had attracted on average four bids per project. This must mean, however, that some projects attracted fewer bidders, not all of whom would have met the non-financial selection criteria, leaving little effective competitive pressure. Fifthly, its survey of managers' opinions about the extent to which the operational performance was meeting initial expectations was quite striking. Despite the fact that such a question was unlikely to elicit very useful information since managers might have had low expectations and/or have a vested interest in saying that PFI was working well, 31% said that the private sector partner was not living up to expectations.

HM Treasury's general conclusion was that since the projects had been delivered to time and budget, PFI had generally been successful and should continue, which implies that it has downgraded its rationale for PFI to the achievement of time and budget delivery and now considers that this constitutes VFM.

COMPETITION AND MARKET FORCES

In relation to competition a number of issues may be identified. First, although PFI provides the opportunity for competitive bidding the reality has been that public sector purchasers typically faced a limited choice of providers during the bidding stage (Grimshaw et al. 2002). Over the long term, however, a more serious issue may arise. Grimshaw et al. (2002) note that partnerships may become insulated from external competition and reputation effects, because there may be no other realistic alternative supplier – owing to high costs of entry or the need for specific technical know-how – and this may undermine the ability of the public sector to obtain VFM. Similarly, Edwards and Shaoul

(2003) report that procurers became locked into relationships with suppliers because the costs of closing down a project were too high, especially where this had an impact on a wider system or network of services. A similar problem was identified by Whorley (2001), when the Ontario Social Services Ministry chose the highest of three bids, from the incumbent supplier, for a related but separate part of the existing PFI project. Some authors have also reported the difficulties faced by the procurer in controlling costs that have a tendency to spiral upwards. For example, in Grimshaw et al.'s study (2002), hospital managers suspected that the private sector partners were less concerned with delivering '100 percent performance' than with maximising the number of extra-contractual claims for maintenance work. In Canada, Whorley (2001) reported that the public sector found that it could not prevent the contractor increasing average hourly rates for staff time by 63% within a year.

Second, the ownership structure of the typically very large organisations that bid for PFI contracts is relevant to the role of competitive forces in this area. One potential advantage of a PFI project is that it integrates the various elements of the capital asset and its operation, as the same contractor constructs and operates the infrastructure (Debande 2002). In the private sector, however, company restructuring is not uncommon owing to mergers and acquisitions, or indeed bankruptcy. For example, Taylor and Cooper (2002) relate the case of Wackenhut, which owned PPS and which had the contract for a UK prison. There was a takeover just three years after the award of a 25-year contract to run the prison, raising issues about the ability of the new organisation to capitalise on the benefits of integration. In this case the takeover represented a market concentration, so that competition was reduced. The authors argued that 'the ownership structures of companies involved in prison privatisation are often complex, leading to difficulties in establishing exact lines of demarcation' (Taylor and Cooper 2002).

Third, the use of subcontractors, also a common practice, creates additional control problems. The PAC stated that in the case of the Immigration and Nationality Directorate Casework Programme:

The problems were made worse by the apparent lack of an agreed approach between the primary contractor and a subcontractor regarding the type of software to be used. Although the technical details of proposed solutions should be something for contractors to organise in privately financed projects, it is crucial that departments keep a very close eye on progress. (PAC 2000b, Recommendation 3).

In its response, the Treasury stated that:

. . . because of the 'arm's length' relationship implicit in most PFI IT contracts – where the deliverable is a service rather than a system as such – the details of the product to be provided by a subcontractor to a supplier providing the service to a client will invariably be a more closed book. (HM Treasury Minute relating to PAC 2000b)

In the light of all the negative evidence relating to government IT projects, such a laissez-faire attitude demonstrates the inability of the Government to advocate a whole-business approach on PFI contracts. Early projects, for example NIRS, had a narrow definition of responsibilities, which led to a failure to work in partnership (PAC 1999a, para. 105).

Finally, one area where the impact of market forces may be seen to have reduced costs is in relation to labour costs. According to Grimshaw et al. (2002), a large part of the savings in their hospital study came from lower labour costs: market competition provided an opportunity to secure staff redundancies, and although the private sector service providers were responsible for the redundancy procedure, it was the hospital trust that paid the redundancy compensation. In addition, the Centre for Public Services (2002) note

a hidden cost of PFI, which falls on the tax payer, because a number of low-paid private prison officers in Scotland have received Working Families Tax Credit to supplement their wages. Thus, market forces can work in several ways, not all of which are capable of delivering VFM to the public sector.

CONTRACT MANAGEMENT

Indirect evidence of inadequate contract management and hence potentially poor VFM is provided in the recommendations of official reports. Both the NAO and the PAC have commented on the quality of contract management and emphasised its importance in generating VFM. They have recognised that the introduction of PFI has required radical changes in the way that public sector project managers work. The PAC has found that working in partnership with the private sector, which has delivered the benefits of encouraging good performance, transparency and dispute minimisation, has led to improvements in performance (NAO 2001e, PAC 2002a).

Even when projects are apparently performing well, however, departmental inexperience in agreeing levels of incentives can lead to higher costs when projects are completed ahead of schedule. This was the case for the contract to complete and operate the A74(M)/M74, where construction was completed more quickly than the Scottish Office considered was possible (NAO 1999a). In relation to the PRIME project, the PAC recommended that the public sector must manage the contract robustly to secure VFM, noting that the contractor's actual performance fell short of the required standard, despite the achievement of a claw-back on excess profits (PAC 1999b, Recommendations 3, 10). Further, the PAC has commented, in relation to the passport delays of 1999, that the Home Office targets in relation to passport delivery times were 'a poor reflection of the public's reasonable expectations for this service' (PAC 2000d, para. 10).

Consequently, the PAC has made a number of recommendations to improve contract management. First, it has called for more public sector staff training, particularly in two areas: building a successful partnership with the private sector (PAC 2002a, recommendations 4 and 13) and understanding the issues involved in refinancing PFI projects (PAC 2003b). In the case of the refinancing of the Fazakerley PFI prison contract, the PAC has noted that the consortium gained considerable advantages, through refinancing, that should have been shared more equitably with the Prison Service (PAC 2001b).

Secondly, the NAO has found that even relatively small contracts, such as the MOD Joint Services Command and Staff College (NAO 2002a), identified a number of wider lessons for other departments on the management of PFI projects, including the following points.

- The Department has built flexibility into the contract. For example it can vary its use of the college buildings in future years.

- Poor contractor performance has been rectified without recourse to financial penalties to the advantage of the relationship between the Department and the contractor.

- The College has identified that it needs to increase its resources for managing the contract.

- The College is seeking greater control of utilities and other items purchased on its behalf by the contractor.

- Departments need to show leadership and, where possible, maintain continuity within the project team.

Thirdly, it is necessary to have a whole-business approach between the public and private sectors in order to have successful contract management. The NAO has emphasised this in its latest report on the National Savings and Investment contract four years on (NAO 2003e), stating:

The public and private sector partners should not enter a customer/supplier relationship, but need to take a whole business approach, if they are to achieve current and future strategic objectives. Such a relationship is evidenced by the public sector partner:

i) recognising its requirements may lead to its private sector partner not adopting the most appropriate method of delivery that is best for the business;

ii) recognising its actions can have an unwarranted impact on its private sector partner's costs; and

iii) having access to the private sector partner's income and expenditure forecasts and not just actuals.

And by the public and private sector partners:

iv) challenging the actions of each other to establish that proposals are in the best interest of the whole business; and

v) demonstrating their willingness to change the contract as it is a dynamic document and their interaction through governance procedures.

In short, numerous concerns about the quality of contract management and monitoring have led to recommendations to improve public sector skills in these areas, suggesting that contract management may not be adequate. Their implicit fear is that poorly managed contracts have not delivered or will not deliver the promised VFM. This represents an interesting contrast to earlier PFI proposals that emphasised the need for and benefit of, private sector innovation and management techniques that were intended to provide efficiency benefits to the public sector.

INNOVATION

One of the claimed benefits of PFI was that the private sector would be more innovative than was possible under traditional procurement. Some purchasing agencies have claimed success in this area. For example, the Highways Agency have stated that almost 200 amendments were made to design standards during construction of the Yorkshire Link project, one of a second tranche of four PFI road projects, and that these delivered benefits to this project. The PAC acknowledged that the PRIME project, transferring the Department of Social Security Estate to the private sector, was indeed innovative and incorporated a 'welcome degree of benefit sharing and risk transfer' (PAC 1999b, Recommendation 2).

In a number of sectors, however, research has found that this has not occurred. For example, the Centre for Public Services (2002) concludes that

The claim that PFI brings additional innovation to that which can be achieved by the public sector remains unsubstantiated, in particular, there is little evidence of innovation in the design of PFI buildings.

The National Audit Office's report of the first four DBFO (design, build, finance and operate) roads (1998a) has found that there was little innovation because most of the schemes had already passed the planning stage. Likewise, the practice of designing a hospital under the PFI process is similar to that of traditional procurement, in that professional medical staff discuss with externally appointed architects, surveyors and engineers how much of what size and type of facility to put where (Sussex 2003). Ball et al. (2003b) consider that much of the design innovation in their Scottish case came from the original project brief provided by the local authority, rather than from the private sector.

Ball et al. (2003b) report, however, that although there was considerable innovation in the financial package,

this may have benefited the contractor but added risk to the public sector. The preferred bidder for the High School project used a funding package that included only 1% equity funding, which reduced the annual unitary charge to the PFI Consortium by approximately £50,000. This option involved additional risk for the Council, which had to ensure that the senior lender was fully compensated under all situations. This liability would normally be fully covered in the form of a guarantee from the parent company (ie the construction company) and provision of latent defect insurance bonds. Nevertheless, in exceptional circumstances, particularly if a construction fault with a high cost of rectification occurred and the contractor's guarantee was inadequate, the cost could fall on the Council. Consequently, the low equity contribution from the sponsor reduced the risk transferred.

Grimshaw et al. (2002) suggest that, in fact, the private sector provider may be reluctant to innovate to meet certain objectives, for example that of 'joined up government thinking'. Innovations that reduce the size or complexity of tasks were unlikely to be seen as attractive by the service provider since this might allow the purchaser to bargain down the projected costs of the contract. Taken together, therefore, the evidence as it relates to innovation as a potential source of VFM is limited.

TRANSACTIONS COSTS

A number of authors have drawn attention to the transactions costs associated with the tendering processes of PFI, which are likely to be greater for both parties than for conventional procurements (Spackman 2002), and may be as high as £0.5 m per project (Travers 1996). According to Hewitt (1997) PFI provides new tasks for lawyers, such as the preparation of scored risk analysis, which add cost. In the NHS project Grimshaw et al. (2002) suggest that there had been excessive transaction costs in the bidding stage because bidders were required to submit very detailed plans for the project, including detailed financial and legal arrangements, which led to the trust spending large sums of money on advisers to help them verify and compare competing bids.

Sussex (2001) confirms their findings, citing the Health Select Committee (2000) to show that an average of nearly £3 m was spent per project on external legal, financial and other professional advice during the procurement process by the NHS trusts involved in the first 18 large PFI hospital schemes to be signed off. He also notes that the high costs involved in the bidding process were only partly related to contract price and that concerns had been raised that these costs were not falling as experience increased.

Hood and McGarvey's 2002 study reinforce concerns about the public sector's additional costs for consultancy fees, particularly in relation to risk. They examined nine local authorities that were either proceeding with a PFI or in the process of deciding to proceed and found that they all used risk management consultants, since none of the respondents believed that the in-house team could adequately provide the necessary expertise. Despite the additional costs, the authors questioned whether the nature of the advice was appropriate. One authority used an insurance company, one authority used a management consultancy and seven used insurance brokers. In two thirds of cases, these consultants were used in addition to the in-house risk management function to provide predominantly insurance-related advice. There was no evidence that they were giving advice on the more complex elements of risk identification, evaluation and transfer.

This situation is not restricted to the UK, since Whorley (2001) reports that in Canada much reliance was placed on the private sector for advice in the Ontario Government's PFI deal to provide management for the welfare benefit system. The issues not only involved cash costs, but also responsibility and accountability. He has found that the reliance on private sector advice

meant that Ontario's Community and Social Services Department subsequently found itself poorly positioned to answer for the project.

Sussex (2003) reports that the time taken for selection, bidding and contract negotiation processes may be months, or even years, longer than for Exchequer-financed schemes, introducing delay and extra costs to the procurement process. The PAC has confirmed this, criticising the lengthy procurement process and the excessive procurement costs for both public and private sectors in the PRIME project (PAC 1999b).

Finally, Howard (2002) makes an important point: that the high costs incurred by private contractors in unsuccessful bids have to be recovered later from successful bids. Thus successful bids incorporate the costs of past failures. Grimshaw et al. (2002) develop this. They suggest that the private sector regards the work and huge costs involved in successful bids as constituting a barrier to entry, which means that in the long run new competitors will be unable to enter the market. If this is widespread (and recent press evidence suggests that this may indeed be the case, with some projects failing to attract more than a couple of bids) then this will serve to reduce the competitive pressures that are believed to constitute a major source of VFM and hence to increase the cost of PFI contracts. The clear implication is that the additional high transaction costs in both the public and the private sectors need to be balanced by additional savings elsewhere before there can be an increase in VFM.

RISK TRANSFER

Issues associated with risk and its transfer from the public to the private sector are critical to justifying VFM and therefore an understanding of the processes that surround risk transfer is essential for evaluating PFIs. Post-implementation it is important to determine whether or not risk transfer has been achieved in the ways that the contract intended in order to decide whether or not VFM has been achieved. According to Grimsey and Lewis (2002), there is little empirical evidence to support or refute assertions that 'risk allocation would seem to have been achieved'.

There is, however, evidence to show that the Government has not always succeeded in transferring risk to the private sector, thus incurring extra costs for the public sector when the private sector contractor has failed to deliver the services as specified in the contract. First, in the case of the passport delays of summer 1999, the PAC stated:

Although the Agency transferred the risk associated with design and delivery of the new computer system to their private sector partners, Siemens, the significant risk associated with ensuring continuity and quality of service remained with the Agency. As a result, the Agency incurred additional costs of £12.6 million in an effort to maintain services, and only some of that sum will be recouped through the extra-contractual payment of £2.45 million which Siemens have agreed to pay over a number of years. The Agency needed to be more aware of the risks they carried, and to have prepared better contingency plans to ensure that operating capacity was not impaired to the extent it was. Had that been done, this considerable extra expense could have been avoided. (PAC 2000d, Recommendation 2)

Several interrelated points should be noted here. The public sector bears responsibility for service delivery if the private contractor fails for whatever reason, as the NAO has insisted (NAO 1999d). This means that the public sector must previously have appropriate contingency plans in place. Such capacity may no longer exist, and indeed some contracts preclude the retention of such expertise, which in any event would be an additional expense. Furthermore, penalties may be insufficient to meet the additional costs.

In the case of the Passport Agency, the additional costs

of the project that stemmed from the failure of the private sector contractor to deliver the service on time fell on the public as individuals, since the Agency is required to recover its costs via the passport fee. Furthermore, in order to reduce waiting times, shortcuts were implemented, which reduced security checks and secretly transferred risk to the public. The fact that these shortcuts were rescinded once they became publicly known suggests that there was never any belief that the public was prepared to accept this risk. In both cases, the risks were transferred not from the public sector to the private sector but to the public as individuals, a travesty of risk transfer (Edwards and Shaoul 2003). Other well publicised cases of IT project failure have resulted in risk and thus costs being transferred to the users, the public at large, the purchasing agency and/or other public bodies.

The public sector's contingency plans have been inadequate. As well as the Passport Agency's well publicised failure, the PAC criticised the Benefits Agency for its lack of contingency plans to cover the risk of delay in delivery in the event that its NIRS2 project failed, despite early indications that it was behind schedule (PAC 1998b, Recommendations 2 and 12). As in the case of the Passport Agency, the costs were borne by the Agency, service users and other public sector agencies, illustrating that risk transfer did not operate as anticipated. The PAC also criticised the Benefits Card Payment project:

The various parties identified many of the risks at various stages, but did not always share this information. Risks were 'cleared' without justification, and 'cleared' risks were not well monitored and so re-emerged. (PAC 2001a, para. 24)

Other project failures have resulted in extra costs to the public sector, suggesting that risk transfer is not easy to accomplish. For example, the Royal Armouries PFI project transferred demand risk to the private sector operator but when visitor numbers were lower than anticipated, the Government was forced to step in and bail out the contractor (NAO 2001a). Such bail-outs of PFI/PPP (others include the Channel Tunnel Rail Link and the National Air Traffic Services PPPs), raise questions about who really bears the risk when essential projects fail, despite the introduction of procedures for managing risk (HM Treasury Minute in relation to PAC 2001a).

At least in part, these failures may be caused by the difficulty associated with assessing the impacts of risk transfer in practice. Akintoye et al. (1998) list the main techniques used for risk analysis and assessment in construction PFI projects as: risk premium, risk adjusted discount rate, subjective probability, decision tree analysis, Monte Carlo simulation and intuition. The public sector may, however, lack skills and knowledge not only of appraisal and evaluation techniques generally, but also of risk analysis techniques. For example, Hood and McGarvey (2002) have found that Scottish local authorities are ill prepared to manage the risk process inherent in PFI for a number of reasons, including the limited involvement of risk managers in the early stages of the PFI contracting process, although their involvement did increase after the initial approval of projects. They have therefore lacked the coordinated approach to risk assessment and the more holistic, corporate approach to risk management that might be expected to be found in the private sector.

In this context, it is interesting to note the finding of Akintoye et al. (1998), who have explored perceptions of risk burdens and risk analysis and management of PFI projects by clients (government departments), construction contractors and lending/financial institutions. They found that the different parties adopted different methods and techniques in dealing with risk assessment of PFI schemes. Hood and McGarvey (2002) believe that the low involvement of the risk manager/risk management function at the decision-making stage reflect a lack of expertise, and/or the fact that in many local authorities risk management

has been narrowly focused and interpreted as insurance management. Therefore, given that commercial operators have a substantial advantage over Scottish local government in the negotiation of risk transfer, risk transfer is likely to be poorly estimated, thereby rendering the VFM comparisons invalid. Recently, however, Sussex (2003) has commented that PFI has arguably made NHS managers more aware of risk management and better at it than previously.

There is a further point that is relevant to the control and transfer of risk. The NAO has made clear that the public sector must carry the ultimate responsibility for service provision and that this is not a risk that can be transferred. A number of authors have provided specific instances of cases where the public has blamed the public sector, not the contractor, for poor performance. For example, Edwards and Shaoul (2003) show that in the case of the Passport Agency the private sector escaped criticism and Grimshaw et al. (2002) comments that patients are likely to blame the trust not the private sector provider for poor performance. The Highways Agency recognised that there are risks arising from public-private sector working, including risks of damage to the Agency's reputation from joint working. This was highlighted in the failure of one of its contractors to grit the roads, leading to a traffic snarl up that left some motorists stranded in their cars for up to 20 hours (Transport Select Committee 2003).

Since these kinds of failure have led to increased costs for the public sector, the NAO has recommended that public and private sector partners should consider other actions which preserve the original allocation of risk, but which still help the private sector partner to improve a loss-making position (NAO 2003e). However, the kinds of actions that would ensure such an admirable outcome are not specified. The NAO stressed that any additional work provided by the public sector to the private sector should be properly benchmarked and decisions made fully auditable, and that public sector partners should have in place contingency plans in case of private sector default. The PAC made it clear in its report *Managing the Relationship to Secure a Successful Partnership in PFI Projects* that contractors should expect to lose their investment in PFI projects when things go wrong:

If contractors successfully manage the risks that have been allocated to them and deliver the required services then they will expect to earn rewards commensurate with the level of risk they have borne. But if they fail to manage the risks they have taken on then they should expect that part or all of their equity investment in the project may be lost. It will undermine an essential commercial discipline if contractors generally are given the impression that the Government will always bail them out, as has occurred in some individual cases, such as the Royal Armouries Museum or the Channel Tunnel Rail Link. (PAC 2002a, Recommendation 3).

Although the above examples of project failure illustrate how risk transfer is effected in practice, even some apparently successful projects may demonstrate how risk transfer may be changed as a result of extra-contractual processes. The refinancing of Fazakerley prison after the completion of the construction phase, which most believe to be the most risky part of the project, provides an illustration of this (PAC 2001b). In this case, the private sector did share some of the benefits of refinancing its debt with the Prison Service, although the PAC noted that these could have been shared more equitably. More importantly from the perspective of risk transfer, the private sector's debt repayment profile was restructured, leaving the public sector exposed to additional termination liabilities, should the contract be terminated for any reason. This increased exposure would occur when the private sector had received most of the benefits and would be facing additional costs associated with long-term maintenance, thereby tempting the private sector in adverse circumstances to 'cut and run'. In other words, the refinancing served to increase public sector risk and

by implication lessen that of the private sector. This is important because refinancing of the SPV's debt after construction completion has now become commonplace. The NAO (2002e) has noted that, following extensive work by the OGC, refinancing gains arising from both early and new PFI contracts will be shared in a more equitable manner in future, so that the private sector does not receive rewards that are not commensurate with the level of risk borne.

CONCLUSION

Potentially there are a number of sources of VFM, but the evidence outlined above about their ability to deliver actual improvements in VFM is mixed. In particular a number of problems may be identified.

- Competition may not be an effective source of VFM because procurers become locked in to projects.

- The partnership between the public and private sectors may not deliver good contract management.

- Innovation in the design of buildings has been limited.

- PFI generates transactions costs that need to be covered before PFI can hope to deliver improved VFM.

- The public sector ultimately carries responsibility for service delivery and so risk transfer may not always occur in the ways in which the contract intended.

The literature indicates that PFIs may bring both costs and benefits compared with publicly financed alternatives but the evidence is finely balanced (Sussex 2003) or often unclear (Spackman 2002). The PAC drew the following main conclusions from its summary analysis of PFI projects *Delivering better Value for Money from the PFI* (PAC 2003e).

- There are potential advantages as well as potential drawbacks to using PFI.

- Although there are examples of good practice, many departments need to get better at procuring and managing contracts.

- Although PFI is an addition, not an alternative, to the public sector capital programme, too often it is seen as the only option.

- Departments are too willing to bail out PFI contractors who get into trouble.

Taken together, these findings show that the measurement and actual achievement of VFM has proved more difficult than PFI's proponents expected. It is not clear that there is a useful way of measuring a concept as ambiguous as VFM, and the Government's methodologies are likely to have only limited value. It appears that additional evidence should be sought about projects' outcomes.

Examining the potential determinants of VFM

Such evidence as exists, shows that private finance is not unproblematic in areas that are of interest to this study: cost, accountability and transparency.

DBFO and roads

This chapter presents an analysis of the use of the Private Finance Initiative in roads, where it is known as DBFO. It has several sections. The first explains the origins, development, nature and scale of DBFO. The second considers the objectives of the policy. A third section reviews the official reports on DBFO in roads, the research literature and other commentaries as they relate to such projects and the Highways Agency's response. The fourth section presents an analysis of DBFO. Although DBFO contracts may take various forms, the first tranche of projects signed by the Highways Agency are all roads projects and these first eight are the subject of our investigation. We present a financial analysis of how DBFO operates in roads, its costs, VFM, risk transfer and accountability. It is based upon the Highways Agency's financial statements, with some additional input from the Agency, and the private sector's annual reports and accounts.

HISTORY AND DEVELOPMENT

The use of private finance in public infrastructure in Britain since the 1980s has to be seen in the context of the then Conservative Government's wider policy of reconstituting government as the procurer and regulator rather than the provider of services. In the field of transport, numerous measures were taken to liberalise transport, reduce regulation, remove the barriers that prevented the private sector from entering public transport, including air, sea ferries, coach, bus and rail, and to create a market for transport.

The use of private finance, which began in the 1970s and 1980s in the international arena, had by the 1990s gained some momentum in the transport, power and water sectors. The UK was one of the first countries to turn to private finance, with the DoT being the first department to use it to any significant degree. By 1994, the UK had made more use of private finance in transport, by far the largest sector, than any other country apart from China (Levy 1996). Early transport projects included: the Channel Tunnel (signed

in 1985 and opened in 1993), the Queen Elizabeth II toll bridge over the Thames at Dartford (signed in 1987 and opened in 1991), the second Severn Bridge (signed in 1990 and opened in 1996), the Skye Bridge (signed in 1991 and opened in 1995), the Birmingham North Relief Road, Britain's first ever privately owned inland toll motorway (signed in 1992 and opened in 2003), the Channel Tunnel Rail Link (signed in 1996) and the Croydon Tramlink (signed in 1996 and opened in 2000). All these were to be new builds, usually privately owned, and were to be privately managed with user charges. Other recent projects included several light rail systems, usually municipally owned. The 1990 New Roads and Street Works Act had given the Secretary of State for Transport, ie central rather than local government, the power to initiate new roads and bridges and to charge users directly for new, but not existing, roads and bridges. This represented a significant change at the time because although a handful of bridges and tunnels owned by local authorities were tolled, those run by central government were free.

However, the Labour Government has taken these developments a step further. It has introduced legislation that allows local authorities to charge road users directly for existing roads through the use of a congestion charge. It has signed large-scale projects that include the National Air Traffic Services and London Underground PPPs, both of which organisations already charged for their services, and rescued the privately financed Channel Tunnel Rail Link with a loan guarantee. By early 2003, the capital value of signed contracts in the UK transport sector, including both central and local government, was £30 billion, far exceeding any other functional area (PPP Forum 2003c).

In the context of roads, prior to the early 1980s when public investment had fallen to about £4 billion from its peak in 1975 of about £6.5 billion (in 1995 prices) following the 1976 cuts (DoT 2003), the DoT carried out much but not all infrastructure design, commissioning the construction or enhancements from the private sector. Trunk roads and motorways were operated and maintained by the local authorities as the Department's agents, which in turn used their own Direct Labour Organisations (DLOs) to carry out such work. From the early 1980s, the design work increasingly went to private consultant engineers. Under the 1981 Direct Labour Organisations Act, local authorities were required to subject their operations and maintenance to compulsory competitive tendering (CCT) and outsource the work to private contractors when their prices were lower than the DLO's, in line with the Government's wider policy of 'rolling back the state'. Thus, by the mid-1990s, the design, construction, operation and maintenance, but not the management or financing of the main network, were carried out by the private sector. In 1997, the number of agency areas was reduced to 24 and management too was outsourced. Local authorities ceased to act as the Highways Agency's agents and the management of road operation and maintenance in the 24 areas was put out to private contractors on seven-year contracts with incentive schemes. Since then the number of maintenance areas has been reduced to 20 and was expected to be reduced to 14 once an operational review was put into effect (Rowsell 2001).

Although the early private finance transport projects were for new builds, the Conservative Government wanted to extend this to improving and maintaining existing roads. It outlined its proposals to use a form of PFI in its Green Paper 'Paying for Better Motorways' (DoT 1993) and 'Design, Build, Finance and Operate Concessions for Trunk Roads and Motorways' (DoT 1994). Under such DBFO concessions, the private sector would be invited to extend or enhance a road to the Department's requirements, operate and maintain it and a further stretch of road for a 30-year period. The 30-year period was chosen because the payment mechanism had to enable the debt finance, which typically has a repayment period of 20 years, to be

repaid and ensure a return to the equity investors. Road users would not pay directly for the use of the roads. Instead, the Government would pay the contractor on the basis of a shadow toll. The system of shadow tolls was designed by the Government's advisers, Price Waterhouse, to allay the private sector's fears that direct tolls would arouse political opposition, making DBFO unviable. Payments would be based on the number of vehicle kilometres travelled by short vehicles (cars) and long vehicles (heavy goods vehicles), in a series of bands, which would be capped at a certain level. The Government saw the system of shadow tolls as a precursor for tolling the motorways as set out in its 1993 Green Paper. Indeed the contracts have significant provisions in them related to the transition to user paid tolls (Abadie and Larocca 2003).

The DBFO roads projects were selected from a list of completed design projects that had already obtained planning permission and had been languishing on the shelf because of lack of public funding. They were chosen as a way of exploring different approaches to DBFO road concessions, and were not necessarily the most appropriate for private finance. Of the ten proposed DBFOs announced in 1994, eight went ahead, albeit some in a slightly different form than originally announced. Another 11 road DBFOs planned for 1995 and 1996 were held over. According to Levy (1996), one of the main accounting firms accused the Government of trying to offload too much risk onto the private sector thereby reducing enthusiasm for many of these projects, although the NAO (1998a) reported considerable enthusiasm on the part of the larger consortia despite misgivings about the cost of bidding. The procurement process for the first eight DBFOs took place over a protracted period between 1993 and 1996, with a further one in Scotland, making a total of nine DBFO projects signed by the Conservative Government.

In the meantime, in 1994 the DoT established the Highways Agency, which would manage the 6,500 miles of motorway and trunk network, including the

DBFO concessions for trunk roads, as part of the DoT's policy of establishing executive agencies responsible for the implementation of Government policy. The Scottish, Welsh and Northern Ireland Offices would manage any concessions in their regions. The Secretary of State for Transport retained responsibility for deciding which large schemes would go ahead, the policy on road user charging and the development of the use of private finance for roads, and the methodology to be used in the appraisal of road improvement schemes (Highways Agency 1999a, 1999b).

As Table 5.1 (see page 76) shows, although DBFO largely came to a halt after the Labour Government came to power in 1997, pending a wider-ranging review of transport policy, a further five projects have reached financial close, including three now managed by local authorities and the Welsh Office. Table 5.2 (see page 77) shows the value of all maintenance and construction projects (DBFO and non-DBFO) signed by the Highways Agency between 1992 and 2001 (ie for trunk roads in England only, excluding local authorities and the regions). The construction value of the eight DBFO projects signed by the Agency in 1996 accounted for about 35% of all new construction projects between 1996 and 2001. Thus DBFO was by no means the only form of finance for construction projects. The Government's national 10-year transport plan, *Transport 2010* (DETR 2000) has allocated £21 billion to the strategic highway network, 25% of which will involve private finance. According to Highways Agency personnel, this investment is likely to focus on motorway widening contracts rather than further road construction or maintenance, with three important motorway expansion schemes, each worth about £1.5 billion, under consideration for DBFO or some other form of private finance. Taken together, although successive governments have been keen to expand DBFO in roads, a policy that has attracted little political opposition or even attention, it is significant that there has not been such marked continual expansion in other areas such as health.

OBJECTIVES

The Highways Agency identified the five most important objectives for the DBFO projects (NAO 1998a):

- to maximise value for money by allocating risks appropriately between the public and private sectors

- to ensure that the new roads would be constructed, operated and maintained with minimal adverse impact on the environment, maximum benefit to road users and minimal financial contribution from the public sector

- to promote innovation in technical, operational, financial and commercial arrangements

- to test the enthusiasm of the market for DBFO roads contracts across a range of different roads projects

- to develop a private sector road operating industry.

Thus the Government conceived DBFO contracts, together with its proposals on motorways, as part of a wider policy of introducing road pricing and creating a market for roads and a private road operating industry. These were objectives that had the potential, at least, to conflict with the desire to achieve better VFM than under conventional procurement.

Given that there is a direct relationship between the way a road is designed and constructed and its whole-life operational costs, the Government expected that the private sector would consider its obligations over the 30-year life of the contract, together with the contractual requirement to return the road to the public sector with a specified life expectancy at the end of that period. Compared with the previous system of letting contracts for the separate tasks that are needed to create, operate and maintain a road, it was expected that this integrated approach would result in lower

Table 5.1: DBFO schemes

Scheme	Contract award	DBFO company	Capital cost (£m)	Length (km) and summary description
Highway Agency schemes				
Tranche 1				
A69 Newcastle–Carlisle	01/96	Road Link Ltd	9	84km Construct 3.5km by-pass
A1(M) Alconbury–Peterborough	02/96	Road Management Services (Peterborough) Ltd	128	21km Motorway widening
A417/A419 Swindon–Gloucester	02/96	Road Management Services (Gloucester) Ltd	49	52km Three new sections of road
M1–A1 Motorway Link	03/96	Yorkshire Link Ltd	214	30km New motorway, motorway widening and new interchange
Tranche 1A				
A50/A564 Stoke–Derby Link	05/96	Connect (A50) Ltd	21	57km Construct 5.2km by-pass
A30/A35 Exeter–Bere Regis	07/96	Connect Ltd	75	102km Construct two new sections and 9km by-pass
M40 Denham–Warwick	10/96	UK Highways (M40) Ltd	65	122km Motorway widening
A168/19 Dishforth–Tyne Tunnel	10/96	Autolink Concessionaires (A19) Ltd	29	118km Online widening
Tranche 2				
A13 Thames Gateway*	04/00	Road Management Services (A13) Ltd	146	24km Online upgrade and improvement schemes
A1 Darrington–Dishforth	09/02	Road Management Services (Darrington) Ltd	210	22km Construct two new sections of motorway and communications
Scottish Office schemes				
M6/A74	12/96	Autolink Concessionaires (M6) Ltd	96	90km Construct new sections of motorway and trunk road
Welsh Office schemes				
A55 Llandegai–Holyhead	12/98	UK Highways (A55) Ltd	120	50km Construct section of trunk road
Local Authority schemes				
A130 (A12–A127)	10/99	County Route	75	15km Construct section of trunk road
Newport Southern Distributor Road	06/02	Morgan Vinci Ltd	50	9.3km New river crossing
Total			**1,300**	**796.3km**

Source: Department of Trade and Industry (2002).

* in July 2000, project responsibility passed from the Highways Agency to Transport for London.

Table 5.2: Highways Agency's PFI and non-PFI maintenance and new construction projects (England only)

(£m)	Maintenance contracts	Non-PFI new construction	PFI new construction
1992	196	270	
1993	319	553	
1994	209	442	
1995	183	545	
1996	273	312	590
1997	71	0	
1998	326	60	
1999	208	154	
2000	297	186	
2001	154	378	

Source: Department of Trade and Industry (2002).

costs because previously there was insufficient incentive for the various parties to collaborate to maximise VFM, especially in relation to whole-life costs and quality. Under the previous regime claims could be made to the Agency for additional costs to cover, for example, unforeseen ground conditions, and an NAO survey (NAO 1988) suggested that such costs might represent a 28% increase from tender to outcome price. An important objective of DBFO was to:

Minimise claims by transferring certain risks and responsibilities to the private sector in order to achieve better value for money. As a consequence there are very few circumstances in which the Agency's liabilities under the DBFO contract, agreed at the outset, can be increased. (Highways Agency 1997)

The Government sought to transfer all or part of the following risks: design and construction, latent/inherent defects, downside volume, operation and maintenance, protestor action, insurance and indemnity risks, and legislative risks unless they were discriminatory against the DBFO roads.

Seventeen consortia, from some 70 companies, submitted pre-qualification bids for the first four contracts (NAO 1998a), four of which were short-listed for each contract. The Highways Agency assessed the costs of a hypothetical public sector comparator (PSC), including the cost of risk transfer, against the costs of DBFO over the life of the project. DBFO contracts would normally be awarded only if the net present cost (NPC) of the final bid was lower than conventional procurement.

The Highways Agency used a team of private legal, financial and engineering consultants to evaluate the bids against the Agency's own traffic forecasts and different scenarios and to compare the value for money of the public and private procurement routes. The use of private sector advisers, in a new market likely to expand if these bids are successful, creates the potential for a conflict of interest as the NAO implicitly recognised in the case of National Air Traffic Services PPP (NAO 2002d). It cannot therefore be assumed that the advisers act in the taxpayers' best interest, particularly under conditions where the Government is known to be committed to the policy.

DBFOs in roads have generally had a low public visibility and have been accompanied by little public discussion. Unlike the full business cases for hospitals and schools, those for DBFOs that establish the VFM case and show whether the schemes are economically sound and affordable are not in the public domain, even after financial close. Neither are the terms of the contract, including the incentives and penalties for failing to operate and maintain the network. According to the NAO (1998a), it was the Government that required the private sector to refrain from publishing the financial details, which raises questions about public accountability and scrutiny. It is therefore impossible to make an independent assessment of the expected VFM case and reliance must be placed upon the NAO's studies, generic research on the financing of transport projects and any case studies made with access to detailed information.

THE EVALUATION LITERATURE

The literature relating to DBFOs and their evaluation derives from several sources: academic research papers, official reports and commercial reports produced for investors. We consider each in turn, including the Highways Agency's response to some of the issues highlighted by the official reports, which provides indirect evidence of the VFM implications of the early projects.

Research papers

Although there are books, papers and articles about private financing of infrastructure in general and roads in particular, most of these simply describe the policy, its objectives, the procurement process and particular projects, often in very glowing terms, and sometimes point out actual or potential problems (see for example, Miquel and Condron 1991, World Bank 1994, Levy 1996, Ridley 1997, Glaister 1999, Debande 2002, Grimsey and Lewis 2002). A few of these were commissioned or published by institutions that have played an active role in promoting these policies, such

as the World Bank and OECD, and their view is that private finance can play a very positive role in infrastructure provision. There are few studies, however, that provide a soundly based theoretical justification or sufficient detailed financial evidence to make a judgement about the value of private funding of transport infrastructure or DBFOs to the procurer, either before or after implementation. Indeed, the literature is characterised by little evidence about either the financial plans and outcomes or the performance of the contracts.

In part, at least, this is because of the lack of information in the public domain, owing to Government restrictions and commercial sensitivity. But Mackie and Preston (1998) argue that appraisal of transport projects in general is far from straightforward and caution that critical judgement is required at all stages. They identified twenty-one sources of error and bias with evidence from the UK experience of cost–benefit appraisal of transport projects for implementation. Some of the most important were the prior commitment of the politicians and/or scheme promoters and the tendency to overestimate the benefits and underestimate the costs.

The empirical studies which do exist do not provide conclusive evidence of the superiority of private finance. In their international survey of large-scale transport projects, Flyvbjerg et al. (2003) found that cost and time overruns were by no means confined to the publicly funded projects. The projects' promoters underestimated the costs and overestimated revenues, they underestimated the environmental impacts and overestimated the wider economic and social benefits. The authors deduce that these were not mistakes but deliberate attempts to get the projects off the ground, and that all the interested parties colluded in the process: the sponsors, their commercial consultants, the financiers, the public sector bodies and governments. In so doing, the promoters spawned projects that were enormously risky and whose risks and costs were concealed from those who ultimately bore the cost, either directly or indirectly. If the outcomes had been known, the projects would not have been undertaken, or would have been done differently, or other projects would have been carried out in their place. The authors point to the lack of accountability throughout the project life cycle, not the lack of technical skills or sound data, important though these were, as the cause of the problem.

Mills (1991) makes a critical appraisal of the practical implementation of two Australian cases, the Sydney Harbour Tunnel and the new facilities at two corporatised airports, Darwin and Alice Springs. Mills' description of the Sydney Harbour Tunnel, built and managed by a private company, although not strictly a PFI/PPP arrived at by competition between bidders, is of interest. In essence, the company acted as an agent for the New South Wales Government, which bore most of the risks and in the end paid all the costs. The commercial arrangements failed to improve the standards of economic appraisal, making it easier to go ahead with projects irrespective of whether they were economically viable since they were paid for via a stream of annual payments rather than up-front and financed by government debt. These limitations were exacerbated by the lack of public scrutiny, fostered by the Government's presentation of the project as a *fait accompli* and complex, not to say abstruse, documentation. Mills concluded that although there are difficulties in ensuring adequate arrangements for private ownership and control of such projects, there was a stronger case for the private *management* of construction.

Silva (2000), reporting for the World Bank, which has vigorously promoted the turn to the private sector for construction, management and maintenance of toll roads, was very supportive of the approach. She notes that although shadow tolling had been used in some industrial countries such as Greece, Portugal and the UK, it had not been tried in developing countries. Her

report analyses the main trends in private participation in toll roads in developing countries. She notes, without citing sources or providing details, that the majority of projects have been successful and that only a minority of projects have had problems. Of the 279 projects awarded during the 1990s, 21 projects in Hungary, Mexico, Indonesia and Thailand – accounting for $9.5 billion, approximately 10% by value – had to be taken over by the government. In other (unspecified) cases, performance had been poor and contracts had had to be renegotiated. Factors contributing to the lack of success included: overestimation of traffic, inflexible contracts that constrained the private sector's ability to manage market and construction risks, inadequate strategic network planning, the private sector's preference for construction rather than operation, and voters' dislike of toll charges. In other words, the contracts had failed because they were, for various reasons, simply not profitable enough for the private sector and/or the public, which was opposed to them, and the government was forced to close them down. Despite this, she concludes that governments need to address why these projects have failed and to ensure that the projects are made more attractive to the private sector and the electorate. In effect, governments have somehow to overcome the financial constraints of the sector that have meant that roads have never, in the modern era, been run for private profit.

Estache, Romero and Strong (2000) have written extensively for the World Bank, outlining the benefits of private finance in roads and the regulatory, economic and financial conditions that enable private finance to work well, implicitly acknowledging that not all projects have been successful. Freeman (2004) reports that the World Bank has not undertaken formally a complete evaluation of the road sector, although there have been individual highway evaluations and specific Bank studies of tolls roads. It has evaluated 75 roads and highways projects and of these 64, or 83%, were rated satisfactory, although no evidence or sources are cited.

In contrast to much of the literature, some of which is written, commissioned or published by interested parties and is supportive of the use of private finance but provides little systematic evidence, the Australian academic accountants, Walker and Con Walker (2000), have compiled evidence from a range of secondary sources on the use of private finance in infrastructure projects. They are not persuaded that the huge cost of 'take or pay' contracts or Build, Own, Operate, Transfer (BOOT) schemes outweighed the benefits. Under a 'take or pay' scheme, the government paid a minimum payment to the private sector for constructing the infrastructure asset irrespective of usage, in effect guaranteeing the cash flow to service the debt. Under a BOOT scheme, the private sector builds, owns and operates the asset in return for all or part of the associated revenue stream for a defined period, after which it transfers the asset back to the public sector. Walker and Con Walker observe that since these schemes involved off budget financing, their arrangements were not only very popular with the private sector but also served to conceal the full scope and scale of the government's financial dealings with the private sector from both the taxpayers and financial markets.

They note that evidence of the private sector's profits from such schemes – and hence some indication of the financing costs to government of 'privatising' operational responsibility for infrastructure development – was hard to come by. Such evidence as existed was typically 'snippets' in the financial press, which included:

- 1998 Australian press reports that the private sector acknowledged a net return of 11–13% on BOOT projects, which the authors think could be conservative

- the Melbourne City Link project's prospectus, which anticipated that initial investors would get a real post-tax return over the life of the project of 17.5%

- according to NSW's Auditor-General, investors in Sydney's M2 motorway would get a pre-tax return of 24.4% per annum if traffic forecasts were valid.

They cite an analysis by one of the authors of the feasibility study for Sydney Airport Link, which suggested a 'real' internal rate of return of 21% per annum over the 30-year project life. Although the subsequent deal was negotiated several points below first estimates of 21%, this was nevertheless a very high cost of finance for the state government. The authors also raise the point that the consortium made additional profits through its acquisition of land for development near the sites of the new rail stations – the classic way that railways have generated profits. Walker and Con Walker report that the period of BOOT schemes has been getting longer, with standard clauses to extend the contract if the operator have not enjoyed a cumulative minimum rate of return.

As well as collating information about the financial returns to the private sector, Walker and Con Walker also report that the NSW Auditor-General has raised concerns about the lack of 'auditable controls and guidelines' for these schemes. This could lead to a rapid over-investment in toll roads simply because they produced a stream of cash flows – little different in essence from the securitisation of receivables – at the expense of other potentially more socially useful schemes that could not generate such cash flows. Such a deal-driven process could, they argue, distort the planning process.

They are also concerned that it is difficult to find out the extent of such off-budget deals, in part at least because it is difficult to measure what governments do not wish to disclose. In the absence of reporting by government, reliance must be placed on a wide range of sources, including reports by the central bank, state auditor generals and other public agencies. Walker and Con Walker are particularly concerned about the lack of transparency and accountability as off budget financing means that the scale of public liabilities – 20% of NSW's gross liabilities in 1993 – is hidden from public view. The private sector has resisted publication of the contractual arrangements, arguing that the arrangements were commercially sensitive and/or contained significant intellectual property, despite the fact that such schemes used public assets and may have had a government-controlled natural monopoly. Such projects have typically by-passed traditional public scrutiny because they did not involve budgeted expenditure and governments had colluded in this in order to prevent the public from realising just how profitable these schemes were. In Victoria, for example, the Freedom of Information Act was explicitly amended to exclude one such deal. In the absence of public scrutiny, these projects may burden governments with hidden subsidies, diversion of revenue streams and loan guarantees whose impact on public finance may not become apparent for many years.

In short, although there are numerous studies supportive of the use of private finance in roads, there is very little in the way of detailed evidence about either its *ex ante* financial appraisal or *ex post* financial evaluation in the literature or about the operation of the post-implementation phase of road tolls. Such evidence as exists shows that it is not unproblematic in areas that are of interest to this study: cost, accountability and transparency.

Official reports

The first publicly available evaluation in the UK emanates from the NAO (1998a) which carried out a review of the first four DBFOs shortly after financial close, describing the pre-tendering process, the level of competition, method of ranking and selecting the bidders, the bidding process and the bids themselves. It noted that the short-listed bids were not necessarily the cheapest but the ones that were most likely to be financially sound and thus likely to be deliverable and that, compared with traditional procurement, the process was time consuming and very costly. The DoT

and Highways Agency spent £8.2 m on legal and financial fees that would not normally have been incurred, although the successful bidders spent typically more than £3 m per contract, with the 12 short-listed bidders spending up to £2 m. This and the high cost of private finance, which the NAO did not detail, meant that the VFM case rested upon risk transfer, innovation and efficiency gains. The nature of the projects chosen and the fact that they had already received planning permission meant, however, that the projects were less risky than might otherwise have been the case and there was little possibility for innovation.

Although the NAO considered that most of the risks were allocated to the party best able to manage them, it criticised the payment mechanism, shadow tolls. This transfers the risk of falling demand (lower traffic volume) to the private sector, which has no means of influencing the volume of traffic using the roads, although their revenues and costs depend upon it. Conversely, if volumes rose more than anticipated, the government could face higher than expected charges This is important because traffic flow forecasting is not an exact science, making it difficult to forecast revenues over the life of the contract. Thus it is the government that bears the upside demand risk in the context of rising traffic. The NAO reports that the DoT has not been very successful in its predictions of traffic flows for road construction projects. The DoT is 'reasonably satisfied' if the original traffic flow forecast for the first year of operation is within 20% of the actual flow for that year (NAO 1988, p. 2). Out of 41 road schemes analysed, 22 were within this limit. The 19 schemes for which there was a much wider variation contained examples where differences between forecast and actual flows ranged from –50 to +105%. Where traffic volumes have been significantly lower than expected, these are often because they are new road schemes that are inherently harder to predict and/or depend upon other developments. For example, in the case of the Humber Bridge – a new road scheme

– where traffic flows were only 25% of those forecast in the opening year, this was the result of a change in the regional economy and feeder roads that were never built. Flyvbjerg et al.'s study (2003) shows that actual traffic forecasts were on average 9% higher than forecast, in the context of rising traffic.

In Britain, traffic on motorways and main trunk roads rose by 36% and 24% respectively between 1992 and 2002, with some regional variation (Department of Transport 2003). Thus since the DBFO schemes were to widen or improve existing important trunk roads and motorways, or connect a main road and motorway, the private operators faced little downside risk. Conversely, it means that a contract whose payments are based on the Highways Agency's estimates of traffic flows could turn out to be very costly for the Agency, both because of poor estimation and rising traffic volumes. This suggests that transferring demand risk is inappropriate since volume is determined by external factors over which the private operators have no control. Thus, as the NAO explained, shadow tolls introduce a new risk that increases costs, offsetting other possible gains. Low volumes, resulting from, say, high petrol prices or policies aimed at encouraging public transport, would undermine the financial viability of the project, lead to financial collapse and the need to bail out the concessionaire and/or its bankers, and conversely, high volumes could create affordability problems for the Highways Agency. Furthermore, although the private operators have a commercial interest in volumes rising, this may conflict with wider transport and environmental policies.

The NAO found that the Highways Agency had overstated the benefits of using DBFO since it had used an 8% discount rate to compare the bids, the rate traditionally used in the DoT for comparing transport projects for road versus rail decisions. Since the decision was whether to use public or private finance, the 6% discount rate should have been used to compare the cost of the public and privately financed

options as required by the Green Book (HM Treasury 1991). Since discounting in general favours a stream of payments spread over 30 years rather than large up-front expenditure with subsequent small payments for operations and maintenance, the higher the discount rate, the greater the advantage to the scheme, with payments spread evenly throughout the lifespan of the project. The higher discount rate therefore increases the apparent advantage of the privately financed option relative to the public alternative.

Table 5.3 presents the NAO's data comparing the DBFO contracts with the PSCs. A comparison of lines 9 and 12 of Table 5.3 shows that at the 6% rate recommended in the Green Book for investment appraisal (HM Treasury 1991), only two met the VFM criteria, the M1–A1 and the A1(M), while the A419/A417 and A69 projects did not. In other words, under the Government's own financial criteria, if not the DoT's, which was changed in 1997 to 6%, only two of the projects should have been allowed to proceed.

When the composition of costs is examined more closely (line 15 of Table 5.3), it is clear that two projects, the A419/A417 and the A69 have low capital costs in both absolute terms and relative to total project costs. A comparison of lines 9 and 10 shows that conventional procurement was cheaper than DBFO for each project. It was only after risk transfer (line 11) was factored into the PSC (line 12), that two of the four projects had a lower NPC than conventional procurement. Line 13 shows that risk transfer was the balancing factor, accounting for 31% of the largest project's PSC (the M1–A1) and 12% of the smallest (the A69). Even after factoring in risk transfer, however, two of the projects were still more expensive than conventional procurement. Only the two largest projects, the M1–A1 and A1(M), the costs of which were predominantly construction costs (76% and 67% respectively), were VFM (see line 15). This could be expected since the discounting methodology favours projects where costs arise later rather than sooner. In

Table 5.3: Value for money and risk transfer for the first four DBFOs

Line	(£m)	M1–A1	A1(M)	A419/A417	A69	Total
	Using 8% discount rate					
1	NPC of shadow toll (DBFO)	232	154	112	62	560
2	NPC of traditional procurement	238	167	96	50	551
3	NPC of PSC risk transfer	106	37	27	7	177
4	NPC of total PSC	344	204	123	57	728
5	NPC risk as % PSC	31%	18%	28%	22%	24%
6	Capital cost (cash)	214	128	49	9	400
7	Capital cost as % DBFO	92%	83%	43%	15%	71%
8	NPC risk as % of capital cost	50%	29%	55%	74%	44%
	Using 6% discount rate					
9	NPC of shadow toll (DBFO)	282	192	140	78	692
10	NPC of PSC without risk transfer	257	182	106	58	603
11	NPC of PSC risk transfer	115	40	31	8	194
12	NPC of total PSC	372	222	137	66	797
13	NPC risk as % PSC	31%	18%	23%	12%	24%
14	Capital cost (cash)	214	128	49	9	400
15	Capital cost as % DBFO	76%	67%	33%	12%	64%
16	NPC risk as % of capital cost	54%	31%	63%	85%	49%

Source: National Audit Office (1998a).

other words, under DBFO, the high capital costs are spread over 30 years, compared with the need to pay them upfront with conventional financing.

The NAO did not explain either the basis of the risk assessment methodology or the relative weighting of different elements of the risk assessment. It did note that the majority of risk transfer relates to the construction phase of the projects, without apportioning the risk between the construction and operational phases. This is contradicted, however, by line 16 of Table 5.3, which shows that the discounted value of the risk transfer (at 6%) as a percentage of the DBFO's construction costs varied from 85% to 31% of construction costs. The A69 project, the one with the lowest proportion of new build, had the highest amount of risk relative to its capital cost (85%), something that

the NAO did not explain. Neither did the NAO explain why the projects with the largest absolute risk transfer (line 11) were better VFM, rather than simply more costly. The somewhat subjective nature of risk transfer methodology may be inferred from the fact that the NAO noted that if the Highways Agency had informed the bidders that a 6% discount rate was to be used, the bids might have been constructed differently. Nonetheless, if the main risk is indeed construction risk, then this means that the Highways Agency is paying a significant premium over and above the construction cost to ensure that the project is built to time and budget.

Finally, the NAO concluded that there were such large uncertainties inherent in quantifying the costs of the public sector comparator that it was very difficult to rely on it. The implication is that most of the 'large uncertainties' lie with forecasting the cost of risk transfer rather than with construction, operational and maintenance costs. Although the report focused on the expected costs, such reservations do raise questions as to whether the DBFO projects were more economical than public procurement and would in practice be cheaper over the life of the project.

The NAO reported that the construction phases of the projects were complete and that they had been built to time and budget in contrast to conventional procurement, which had a history of cost and time overruns, although these were not quantified or evidenced. It then examined the arrangements for monitoring the contracts and noted that the Highways Agency was dependent upon the contractors' own quality assurance systems and had not, at the time of financial close, developed its own plans for auditing them. It noted that the accuracy of the shadow payments depended not only on the estimates of traffic volumes that would need verifying but also on the reconciliation with the estimates paid in the previous year, which would need indexing. Thus, there was a need for careful audit of the payment mechanism.

The NAO reported on a number of features of the contract relating to the allocation of risks between the Highways Agency and other parties to the contract. First, there were specific clauses built into each contract to prevent roads being handed back in a poor condition and to ensure that the NPV of net cash flow remained unaltered should changes be required that would lead to adjustment of toll levels. Secondly, there was a system of penalty points so that, if contract performance fell below that specified, an accumulation of such penalty points could lead to the banks stepping in and replacing the contractor, subject to the approval of the Highways Agency. Failure to appoint a satisfactory replacement could lead to the Highways Agency terminating the contract. Thirdly, should the private sector default on its loans for whatever reason,

the banks would have to take operational control and appoint a replacement contractor, subject to the approval of the Highways Agency. It is unclear, however, how this and any subsequent renegotiation of the contractual terms would affect the Agency's costs and risk allocation.

In the case of the East Lothian schools contract where the SPV's parent construction company became insolvent during the construction phase of the project, it was claimed that: ' . . . the contract structure together with the commitment of the interested parties to the project ensured that the public sector was insulated from the resultant cost increases and this stands favourable comparison with traditionally procured projects faced with the same scenario' (Methven 2004, p. 45). However, a close examination of the changes in the risk allocation contradicts this assertion and the education authority's insistence that no increases in cost or changes in risk allocation would be allowed (Methven 2004). Although costs rose, it is unclear who bore them.

Lastly, the Government guarantees the Highways Agency's payments to the DBFO companies, in effect underwriting their debt and reducing their risks. This raises questions about who is really bearing the risk of default.

In short, the NAO report provides very limited financial information about the schemes. In general it describes, rather than analysing or criticising, the evidence it does present and then fails to bring out the significance of its findings, particularly in relation to the payment guarantees and demand and default risk. Although the NAO believed that it was difficult to compare the costs of the alternatives methods of financing the schemes, given all the measurement uncertainties, it did not explicitly reject the methodology. Although it noted that two of the projects were not VFM at the 6% rate, it seemed to excuse the absence of VFM on the basis that the Highways Agency was charged with developing the private sector's ability to provide these services. Arguably, this comes very close to using PFI/DBFO as an explicit subsidy to the private sector. Finally, although the NAO believed that shadow tolls and private finance introduce extra costs, risk and therefore costs that offset other risks, it did not draw the conclusion that therefore all these schemes were not, in terms of the Government's own methodology, VFM. In other words, it stopped short at the very point at which it could most usefully fulfil its remit to evaluate value for money.

The Public Accounts Committee (PAC), in reviewing the NAO report, was more explicit:

By failing to select the best qualified bidders to tender for two of the four projects, the Agency was on dangerous ground. They risked giving the message that they were more interested in spreading the contracts around than encouraging the innovative and keenly priced bids which are necessary if PFI is to deliver good value for money. (PAC 1998d, Recommendation 1)

However, it failed to follow through the implications of both this and other limitations identified by the NAO.

In its report on the contract on the A74(M)/M74 Motorway in Scotland DBFO, now known as the M6 extension, the NAO reiterated many of the same points (NAO 1999a). The report presented very little useful financial information and showed how the present value of the DBFO option changed through the bidding process and after, given that the private partner completed construction ahead of schedule, thereby adding to the shadow tolls. The use of numerous DBFO values makes it difficult to present a consistent analysis of the relative costs of the two options.

The present value of the DBFO option at the DoT's final assessment was £193 m compared with a PSC of £210 m (at the 6% discount rate). Financing charges accounted for 16% of the total discounted cost and were higher than under conventional procurement. The NAO's view was that, provided the finance was raised competitively, this extra cost should reflect the risk transfer. On the key issue of risk transfer, whose costs were not presented, the NAO was concerned that the use of shadow tolls created a risk that the private sector could not manage and which therefore could be expected to increase the cost of the contract to the Department. Furthermore, since the contract provided an incentive for the contractor, Autolink, to complete the construction phase as soon as possible, this increased the cost of the road by £10 m because of extra shadow tolls as a result of early opening, thereby reducing the margin between the expected price and the PSC. This, and the possibility that the Department had overstated the cost of the public sector comparator by £10 m, eliminated the DBFO's margin of superiority. Despite this and its belief that it was 'not realistic to expect a very high degree of precision and accuracy in such forecasts', the NAO's contradictory conclusion was that, while not clearly demonstrating VFM, it was likely to remain VFM. In other words, it drew conclusions that were not justified by the evidence.

The NAO's evidence from these two reports, if not its conclusions, is important because it shows that the Highways Agency was unable to demonstrate (even using the Government's methodology, which favours private finance over public finance) that these DBFO schemes had lower whole-life costs than conventional procurement. Since the discounting methodology serves to reduce the apparent cost of the DBFO option, this means that the cash cost of DBFO must be very much more than a publicly funded option and that DBFO is a very expensive way of constructing, operating and maintaining roads. This in turn means that DBFO comes at the expense of other roads and/or other public services.

There is little information about how these DBFO contracts are working in practice. A recent report, however, by the Transport Select Committee (2003) lends an interesting perspective to the Highways Agency's management of its maintenance contracts, which is not dissimilar to the operational phase of DBFO contracts. The failure of one of the Agency's contractors, Carillion URS, to grit the roads before an expected snowfall in January 2003 led to the M11 and surrounding roads in Essex and Cambridgeshire being blocked. Hundreds of thousands of commuters were stranded overnight in freezing conditions for up to 20 hours in their cars, unable to move. Police described the M11 as 'effectively a car park', which in turn affected traffic flow in the surrounding area. The resulting gridlock made for good aerial shots, ensuring that it got maximum television time and column inches.

Although the contractors are responsible for all the decisions relating to winter maintenance, the Transport Select Committee blamed the Highways Agency for failing to coordinate the maintenance activities, saying that their 'arrangements manifestly did not work'. Carillion's radio communications had not been working for four days. Neither did its mobile telephone network function. Although repairs had been requested, Carillion had taken no action and even more importantly, the Highways Agency was not informed. The Committee found it 'utterly astounding' that repair procedures were so slack and was 'dismayed that the Highways Agency should have been unaware of this'. It expected the Agency to be aware of such problems.

The Committee attached even more importance to the fact that the Highways Agency could take no financial action against the contractor: according to the contract, penalty points were not awarded for poor performance alone but only for failure to respond to problems. Furthermore, no penalties were awarded because the Highways Agency believed that the contractor had acted promptly to address the problems raised by the review of the incident. The Committee said:

It is intolerable that the Highways Agency has no immediate financial sanction available where a contractor fails to keep the motorway and trunk roads system free of ice and open. The Agency's stated desire to work in positive partnership with its contractors is admirable. This cannot substitute however for appropriate contractual sanctions to enforce high maintenance standards. While these standards are not upheld, as happened on 30 and 31 January, it is the travelling public who pay an unacceptably heavy price. The Agency must review its contractual arrangements with maintenance agents urgently. (Transport Select Committee 2003)

Furthermore, the Highways Agency was unable to provide the Committee with information about its contracts at the hearing. The Committee complained that the Agency took an unprecedented 11 weeks to provide the required information, which was not complex. The Committee's report of contract failure is important because it provides crucial information about the nature of the Highways Agency's contracts, its monitoring and penalty system, and attitude to contract enforcement, which is not otherwise publicly available. There is no reason to believe that the DBFO contracts are substantially different.

Despite the problems raised by the NAO, the Highways Agency publicly proclaims that the DBFO contracts have been successful, stating:

The DBFO roads programme is a success story that needs to be told. One of the principal messages is that the use of PFI for road procurement has delivered contracts representing real value for money. This means that the public will receive a high standard of service on DBFO roads at lower cost. (Highways Agency 2003)

This is based on the Highways Agency's own review, *Value in Roads* (Highways Agency 1997), which relates to the expected VFM case and subsequently formed the basis of a paper by Highways Agency personnel, including the chief executive, in an academic journal (Haynes and Roden 1999). Their work concluded that:

These projects were delivering new and improved road construction and maintenance, providing better services to users of the country's strategic road network and achieving significant value for money savings for taxpayers. (Haynes and Roden 1999, p. 1)

Since the paper is largely descriptive, however, and provides little additional financial information or evidence to substantiate its claims over and above that contained in the NAO reports reviewed above, it is difficult to give much credence to the claims. The Highways Agency itself links value for money in DBFO closely with the transfer of risk from the public to the private sector, as demonstrated by the following statement.

Under each DBFO contract the private sector assumes substantial risks, including those relating to designing, building and operating the road. The private sector is reasonably expected to be able to manage these risks better than the public sector under traditional methods of procurement. The placing of risk appropriately in this way is likely to provide better value for money than placing risks with those not well able to manage them. The fact that the procurement process for each scheme was highly competitive gives assurance that the terms obtained were the best obtainable from the market for deals of this type at this time. (Highways Agency 2003)

But Haynes and Roden argue, without referring to the problems and issues cited above, that VFM (as reflected in the difference between the public sector comparators and the shadow tolls) had been delivered. Using the 8% discount rate, the first four projects had saved a total of £168 m and the first eight a total of £314 m, equal to an average saving of 22%. Using HM Treasury's 6% discount rate, the savings on the

eight DBFOs were estimated at about £230 million or 13%, ie in aggregate VFM was delivered.

Haynes and Roden have also produced disaggregated data (see Table 5.4 on page 88) that present a rather different story. Table 5.4 shows that two of the eight projects were either almost identical to or more expensive than the PSC at the 8% discount rate: the A69 project previously identified by the NAO as more costly than the PSC, and the A30/A35 project from the second tranche of the eight DBFOs that the NAO did not examine. Although they do not show comparative data at the 6% discount rate, this must mean that at the 6% rate at least three of the eight failed to demonstrate VFM, since the NAO report had shown that two of the first four schemes were not VFM at the 6% rate and Haynes and Roden's work suggests that the A30/A35 was not VFM. Thus the schemes were only VFM in the aggregate, not in each case. Haynes and Roden do not comment on this, or on the fact that at the 8% rate the A30/A35 was only marginal, nor do they explain why the VFM rule had been breached at the 8% rate in the case of the A69 project.

The three schemes (the A69, A419/A417 and the A30/A35) that were either marginal or not VFM were small schemes and had a small construction element relative to operations and maintenance. One interpretation of this is that DBFO is appropriate only for relatively large projects with a significant construction element. Another, and related explanation, is that the large schemes appear to offer VFM because the discounting methodology favours large, privately financed construction schemes that are paid for through a stream of broadly equal payments for 30 years, rather than a large initial outlay with limited future costs.

The Highways Agency (1997) also claims success in relation to innovation, the transfer of risk in relation to protestor action and latent defects, and the development of a road operating industry, without presenting any evidence. In fact it is too early to assess

Table 5.4: VFM comparison for first eight DBFOs at 8% discount rate

Project	Public sector comparator (£m)	Winning DBFO (£m)	Saving (£m)	Percentage saving
M1–A1	344	232	112	32.6%
A1(M)	204	154	50	24.5%
A419/A417	123	112	11	8.9%
A69	57	62	−5	−8.7%
M40	276	182	94	34.1%
A19	177	136	41	23.2%
A50	77	67	10	13.0%
A30/A35	149	148	1	0.7%
Total	1,407	1,093	314	22.3%

Source: Haynes and Roden (1999).
Note that similar data were not provided at the 6% rate.

whether the innovation has proved successful. The Highways Agency (1997) notes the importance of disseminating accumulated knowledge and training staff in negotiation to improve the quality of DBFO projects and indicates the need for future projects to transfer some planning risk to the private sector. It is noteworthy, however, that the assessment under the heading 'Key messages' does not make any mention of the Highways Agency's first objective. In other words, there is no assessment of whether the projects have been designed, maintained and operated in such a way as to minimise any adverse impact on the environment or to maximise the benefit to road users.

The Highways Agency's response to the official reports

Despite the upbeat nature of its own review, the Highways Agency has proposed and/or initiated a number of changes (Highways Agency 1997, 2002, 2003). First, the criterion on safety payments is to be changed so that if the DBFO project has a higher

accident rate than the national average a deduction will be made. Second, contractors will be required to produce a five-year rolling plan with proposals on issues such as safety, facilities for pedestrians and environmental protection. The proposed control mechanism in relation to these plans is worthy of note: there is to be no performance payment attached to these plans but:

The Agency will reserve the right to publish them so that the road user will be able to monitor performance against expectations. (Highways Agency 1997)

Recent publications from the Highways Agency, such as Improving DBFOs – A Consultation Document (Highways Agency 2002), show how the Agency intends to speed up delivery, reduce transactions costs and improve flexibility of contracts and integrated team working. In particular, the Agency is seeking to develop new forms of contracts and is also investigating the adoption of performance specifications as a driver to innovate more cost-effective methods of work, reduce administration costs and increase efficiency (Highways Agency 2003).

As a result of criticisms of the use of shadow tolls in roads, including the criticism that it can incur higher charges for the public sector (NAO 1999a, PAC 1998d), and the use of tolls for the Skye Bridge paid by users (PAC 1998a), the Agency has sought alternatives (2003). The Highways Agency, as purchaser for the urban A13 Thames Gateway DBFO Project, has used a new mechanism, called the Availability Payment Mechanism, which incorporates refinements on availability, HGV/Bus shadow tolls and bus journey reliability times, in addition to safety. The A1 Darrington to Dishforth and A429 Stockbury to Sheerness projects will use another new payment mechanism, the Active Management Payment Mechanism, whereby congestion management together with a safety performance adjustment form the basis of the payment (Highways Agency 2003).

The Government chose a 30-year contract period because the payment mechanism had to allow for a reduced payment stream in the initial construction phase and a buffer period after repayment of the debt – assumed to be 20 years – in case cash flows were less than, or occurred later than, expected. The Government also believed that this was long enough to encourage the DBFO company to consider the whole-life costs of the project. With a more mature PFI debt market, however, debt may be repaid over a longer period than originally anticipated and the Government therefore believes that a longer contract may encourage further cost savings. The Agency therefore plans to allow bidders for future contracts to provide variant bids based on their preferred contract period.

Commercial reports to investors

Although the Department of Transport and the Highways Agency make little information available to the public either as taxpayers or end users, stock

exchange regulations and investor demand mean that some financial information must be made available to the capital markets. Although, in principle, the offer documents (IPOs) accompanying bond issues could provide a useful source of information, since most PFI bonds are insurance wrapped, they contain little useful financial information when viewed from the perspective of this study.

The credit ratings agencies, Fitch Ratings and Standard and Poor's, nonetheless provide an important source of information about PFI in general and the DBFO road projects in particular and lend an interesting perspective to the evaluation of DBFO in roads (Fitch Ratings 2003, Standard and Poor's 2002, 2003). Standard and Poor's makes the point that while experience as yet is limited, the private sector is being required to assume more risk in the most recent PFI projects than in the earlier projects. The clear implication is that the early projects were a safe investment for bondholders. Fitch Ratings is more explicit. It notes that there have been few significant problems in more than 200 projects even in the construction phase and although the Government wants to transfer more risk to the private sector, there has been 'significant government support' to offset the additional risk. This implies that the Government has been willing to pay for this additional cost in one way or another. Fitch Ratings cites the example of insurance risk: whereas the early projects required the private sector to shoulder the full cost, now the Government shares the risk by taking the 'insurer of last resort' role. Fitch Ratings concludes its report (2003) by saying that it expects the PPP sector to remain as investment grade and to 'continue to offer a comparatively safe haven in times of economic downturn'.

Standard and Poor's notes that the DBFO road projects have a number of strong credit features, including a contract signed and payments guaranteed by the department head, contractually stable income stream, little or no volume risk to debt holders and relatively low operational risk. Its report points out that the construction phase represents the largest single risk to a PFI project, although this is less in shadow toll projects. In some cases the construction risk has been structurally removed. Once the building phase has been completed, it has been possible for the consortium to take advantage of lower interest rates and a reduction in project risk to refinance its debt, as in the case of Autolink Concessionaires (M6)'s contract for the M6–A74(M)/M74 link. In general, Standard and Poor's believe that PFI construction risk is low compared with other infrastructure projects, being low tech, using tried and tested building techniques, design and materials, and employing experienced contractors. This statement to the capital markets, combined with that of the NAO's cited earlier, provides an interesting contrast to the Government's rhetoric that private sector innovation in PFI contracts provides one of the three main sources of VFM. Standard and Poor's note that the consortia had sought to reduce their risk by turnkey, date and price-specific contracts that pass risks down to the subcontractors.

Although most PFI projects have little volume and demand risk, DBFOs, based on shadow tolls, do. In practice this has not been a problem owing to ever-rising traffic volumes. A significant downturn in the economy and a fuel shortage could affect traffic levels. Standard and Poor's report notes that the payment streams are subject to performance regimes that are complex – in some cases too complex to be applied effectively, an issue we will develop later – and subjective, which could lead to disputes. It notes, nonetheless, that there have been few payment reductions in practice.

Standard and Poor's report includes a summary of the risks of several individual projects.

The M6–A74 link contract was awarded to Autolink Concessionaires (M6) in 1996. The report notes that the successful completion of the construction phase

had removed a major risk and enabled a refinancing of the debt. Autolink had operated and maintained the road without incurring any penalty points. Although the company was exposed to traffic risk if traffic volumes declined, and indeed traffic growth had been less than expected, this had not been a problem since vehicle use had exceeded the base case traffic forecast by 7.9%. It identifies the following strengths: relatively stable revenue flows; less than budgeted expenditure on maintenance and operations, in part owing to less-than-expected traffic growth; the nature of the contract, which would make it difficult for the Government to terminate without compensation; and comfortable financial margins ensuring adequate senior debt coverage even without traffic growth.

The A1(M) Peterborough to Alconbury and A417/A419 Swindon–Gloucester contracts were awarded to Road Management Services Ltd in 1996 and financed by a single bond. Again, the construction phase has been successfully completed and the company have incurred no penalty points on the operational phase. Although car volumes have been lower than expected on the A1(M), this has been partially offset by higher than expected car volumes on the A417/A419. As with the M6 project, expenditure on operations and maintenance have turned out to be lower than expected. The report notes that senior debt repayment is assured 'even in downside stress scenarios', owing to profit margins that have held up well despite lower-than-expected traffic volumes.

The A1 Darrington–Dishforth contract was awarded in 2002 to Road Management Services Ltd, the largest DBFO contract to date. The risks are offset by the Government's commitment to DBFO, a tried and tested contract structure, 'limited scope for payment deductions despite onerous traffic operations and maintenance stresses', contractors' experience, the financing structure, robust revenues and ample headroom in the project for the different phases of the contract. Although it was concerned that the new payment mechanism – the gross congestion management payment – exposed lenders to the risk of congestion occurring outside set parameters, it believed this was 'partly mitigated by the Highways Agency's commitment to making this new arrangement work effectively'. In other words, the Agency would not interpret the agreement rigidly.

Taken together, the credit ratings reports show that the combination of secure revenue streams, performance regimes that are not particularly onerous and lower than expected costs (by the SPV) means that DBFOs are highly profitable both for their investors and bondholders. This raises questions about the value of the PSCs used to evaluate DBFO deals and their actual VFM, including risk transfer, since profits held up well despite lower than expected traffic growth. More fundamentally, it refutes the Government's justification for refusing to disclose information about the DBFO projects on the grounds of commercial confidentiality, since the capital markets themselves require this information to be available to potential investors. In so far as some of the information is in the public domain, albeit unknown to a wider audience, this suggests that the Government and the private sector are only reluctant to disclose the information to the public at large.

There are several implications of this literature review for the present study.

- Although numerous studies have supported the use of private finance in roads, few provide much in the way of supporting evidence either for the *ex ante* appraisal or the *ex post facto* evaluation.

- The international evidence shows that although most of the projects have been successful, not all have been trouble free and some have had to be taken into public ownership or renegotiated.

- Some academic research has raised concerns about the cost, accountability and transparency of such deals.

- The UK Government has not published the projects' full business cases that were used to support its decision to use private finance in roads.

- The NAO's reports show that risk transfer has been crucial to the VFM case and criticise the use of shadow tolls that have created additional risks for the public sector that were not reflected in the appraisal methodology. The high cost of using private finance, the – at best – weak VFM case and the affordability problems raise questions as to whether and how VFM will be achieved in practice.

- Most of the risk transfer relates to the construction phase, which has generally been successful in delivering the new roads on time and to budget. Although the system of incentives has worked, it has come at a cost and it is unclear why similar objectives could not be achieved by appropriately designed construction contracts.

- Given the early stage of the policy, little is known about whether the system of incentives and penalties can and will deliver what is required in the operations and maintenance phase.

FINANCIAL ANALYSIS OF DBFOs IN ROADS

The subject of our analysis here is the first eight DBFO contracts in England managed by the Highways Agency. We chose these because they constitute the majority of the 14 projects (see Table 5.1 on page 76), and they have been going the longest, and most of the Government's publicly available data relate to these projects. We examine the Highways Agency's expenditure on DBFOs and how this is reported, the structure of the deals, the DBFO companies' income, costs, including the cost of capital, and returns to the parent companies, to provide evidence about the actual VFM, risk transfer and how PFI projects are reported and accounted for.

Highways Agency's expenditure on DBFOs

It is believed that the capital costs of the eight projects listed in Table 5.1 (see page 76) totalled £590 m and the total discounted cost over the life of the contracts was £1,093 m (Haynes and Roden 1999). It is impossible to get consistent information about either the capital or the total costs of all the projects as various official sources cite different figures. Although in part this may be due to definitional reasons – eg capital value as opposed to construction costs that may or may not exclude financing costs, cash versus discounted values and/or changes in the discount rate – it does not make for clarity, transparency or accountability. Neither the Department of Transport nor the Agency has published information setting out the expected annual cash payments to the DBFO companies for these projects, despite the fact that the Government guarantees the Highways Agency's payments on the contracts.

The Highways Agency, as an executive agency, publishes an annual report and accounts, produced as hard copy and also posted on the Agency's website, which could be expected to provide information about the annual payments. It applies the regulations laid down by the Treasury Taskforce (1999a) in its

amended Technical Note No. 1, which, following disagreement with the Accounting Standards Board (ASB), gave the Government's interpretation of the guidance given by the ASB (1998).

The accounts for 1999/2000 state that contract risk has been independently analysed according to the guidance laid down. For 1999/2000 it was considered that sufficient risk had been transferred to the operator and so seven out of the eight contracts were not shown on the Highways Agency's balance sheet, although intangible assets representing the reversionary interests were recognised. One unnamed contract was shown on balance sheet. In 2000/1 the accounting treatment changed, however, to show all eight contracts as on balance sheet assets. No information regarding this change in accounting policy is given, but we presume that this followed a reassessment of risk by its auditors, the National Audit Office. Maintenance expenditure was recognised in the operating cost statement while construction costs associated with the DBFO contracts came on balance sheet, together with the associated long-term and short-term creditors.

Table 5.5 (line 4) (see page 96) shows the annual payments made by the Highways Agency in respect of these DBFO contracts in England, currently running at about £210 m per annum. The first point to note is that these payments are shown only as a note in the accounts, not as an explicit programme cost, and are far from clear. The Agency does not explicitly state to which contracts the payments relate nor does it break the payments down by contract. Thus it is impossible to track individual project costs. Since the Agency's ninth contract was not signed until 2002, the payments relate only to the first eight contracts. Secondly, since the Agency did not, prior to the year ending March 2000, produce accrual or cash accounts that showed the payments to the DBFO consortia, there is no publicly available record of any payments to the DBFO consortia in the years ending March 1997, 1998 and 1999. Although this is surprising from an accountability perspective, it is by no means unique. In their study of NHS PFI contracts, Hodges and Mellett (1999) show that information about costs was not disclosed without a specific regulation requiring it. Thirdly, despite the designation of the payment mechanism as 'shadow tolls', payments are recorded in three forms:

- as interest on the DBFO finance lease for the capital element of the projects

- as shadow tolls for the operating element of the contracts and

- as finance leases.

Although the interest is declining on a year-on-year basis as the lease obligation reduces, the finance lease capital payment will increase. The shadow tolls vary from year to year. These payments are estimated in advance and in the following year an adjustment is made based on actual traffic flows. Recording payments in this form provides further evidence that

these DBFOs are non-separable service contracts and are therefore to be accounted for as finance leases on the Highways Agency's balance sheet, together with an accompanying service charge report in the profit and loss account.

These three payments are not the full cost to the Highways Agency of the roads under DBFO contracts. Since the roads remain the Agency's property, they appear on its balance sheet. As such, they are subject, as are all the Agency's assets, to a 6% capital charge, soon to be reduced to 3.5%, assumed to be the cost of past capital and payable in the form of a dividend on the Government's Public Dividend Capital – the equivalent of the Government's equity stake – to the Government as owner. Table 5.5 (see page 96) shows that after including capital charges on the assets, assumed to be worth the value recorded in the DBFOs' accounts, since the Highways Agency does not identify them separately, the eight roads accounted for 5–6% of total programme costs. However, this underestimates the total cost because the depreciation charge, which could not be identified, has not been included.

Figure 5.1: Payment profile diagram

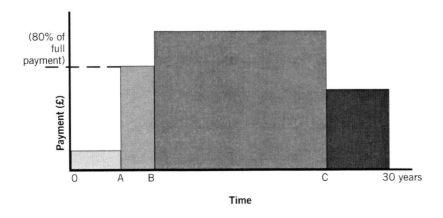

Figure 5.2: Relationships between the Highways Agency, the SPV, the parent companies and subcontractors

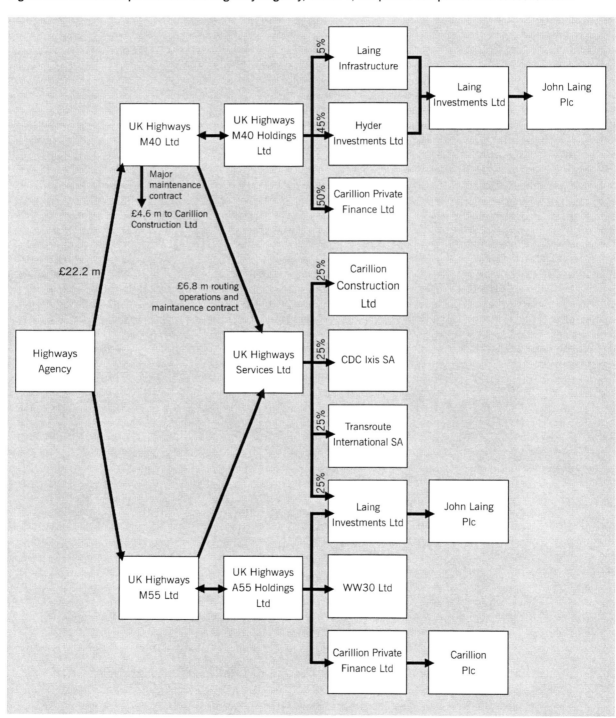

Source: Annual report and accounts of UK Highways M40 Ltd.

Note: Payments (in millions) relate to the year end 31 December 2002.

It is impossible to comment on how this compares with the expected payments since such information is not in the public domain. Although it is known in general that traffic volumes have risen and in a number of cases risen more than the companies expected, thereby increasing the payments to the private sector, it is unknown how these compare with the Agency's own estimates of expected traffic flows, since these too were never released.

Although the accounts also show the discounted value of the payments due over the remaining period of the contract, they do not show the expected annual cash payments. This is important as the Highways Agency's *Value in Roads – a DBFO Case Study* (1997) shows that there are step increases in the annual payments at two points, which appear to be around years four and seven, points A and B respectively in Figure 5.1 (see page 93), which is reproduced from the Agency's website. However, although the graph does not identify the scale of the axes and there is no other publicly available information on this, it does show that up to year B, payments are only 80% of the full payments. The significance of this is that the payments can be expected to rise by about 25% since the year ending March 2002 is only the sixth year of the contracts. However, the Agency was not able to clarify the point for our study.

Thus, in just three years (1999/2000 to 2001/2) for which financial information is available, the Highways Agency has recorded payments of £618 m. Given that payments are known to have started in 1997, this means that in just six years the Agency has paid very much more than the initial capital costs of £590 m. At the very least, it refutes one of the justifications for using private finance – that the Government does not have the money to finance infrastructure investment – and raises questions about its actual VFM.

Assuming £200 m costs per year over 30 years (although as we have shown this is higher and set to rise), then the total cash cost of the contracts is approximately £6 billion. This means that the remaining £4.8 billion due over the life of the contracts (since we assume that £600 m was paid in the years 1997–2000 as well as the £600 m paid in 2000–2) represents the premium paid for risk transfer and the cost of operatiing and maintaining the roads. The £6 billion whole-life costs imply a present value of about £2.2 to £2.5 billion, depending upon whether the 8% or 6% discount rate is used. Although clearly these assumptions can be varied even more conservatively, it is difficult to reduce this below £2 billion, a figure almost twice the net present cost of £1.093 billion cited by Haynes and Roden (1999). The reasons for this are unclear. One interpretation is that payments have been higher than expected.

Several further points follow from this. First, it seems that the contracts have turned out to be very much more expensive than implied by the NPC provided by the Highways Agency's most senior personnel (Haynes and Roden 1999). This, plus the fact that evidently less risk was transferred than expected since the schemes are on balance sheet, makes it unlikely that the contracts can or will deliver the anticipated VFM. Secondly, the estimated capital and interest payments of about £1.723 billion[2] mean that the finance element of DBFO is about three times the initial construction costs and nearly one third of the total cash costs of the project. Thirdly, most commentators argue that most of the estimated risk transfer relates to construction risk (NAO 1998a, Standard and Poor's 2003) and the NPC of risk transfer for the first four projects was £177 m at the 8% discount rate (the sum of line 3 in Table 5.3 on page 83). Then a conservative guess is that up to £100 m of this £177 m risk (56%) is attributable to construction risk. This means that the Agency was paying a £100 m premium on £400 m of construction

---

[2] Schedule of payments provided by the Highways Agency to the research team.

costs (the sum of the four schemes shown in line 6 of Table 5.3 on page 83) equivalent to 25% of construction costs to get the roads built to time and budget. Again, although this 'guestimate' can be varied, it does suggest that risk transfer does not come cheap. Fourthly, since these annual payments must be met out of a limited budget, this is likely to give rise to affordability problems: in other words the cost of these eight schemes can be met only at the expense of other capital and maintenance projects.

Although, in 2001/2, the HA overspent its net resources budget by £456 m, this was because expenditure budgeted as capital in the Agency's business plan had to be accounted for as resource expenditure following the introduction of Resource Accounting, and because the Agency under-budgeted for non-cash costs, eg depreciation, presumably including the depreciation for the DBFO assets now on balance sheet. Although DBFO accounts for about 5–6% of total programme costs without the depreciation charge for the assets that had been brought back on balance sheet it is, however, unclear how DBFO affects the Agency's budget, owing to its being subsumed within a larger resource envelope and thus the degree to which it contributed to the deficit.

The DBFO companies' financial performance

The Highways Agency makes payments to its DBFO partner or concessionaire, which is typically a consortium or Special Purpose Vehicle (SPV) with a number of related companies, some of which have similar names. We used the FAME (Financial Analysis Made Easy) companies' accounts database to identify

Table 5.5: DBFO payments made by the Highways Agency

(£m)	March 2000	March 2001	March 2002
Interest on DBFO finance lease	59	58	57
DBFO shadow tolls	119	142	130
Finance leases (due within 1 year) estimated	17	18	19
Total DBFO payments	**195**	**218**	**205**
Capital charges (6%) payable on DBFO assets	53	53	58
Total DBFO costs (DBFO payments + share of capital charges)	248	271	244
Total DBFO costs as % Highways Agency's total programme costs	**6%**	**6%**	**5%**
Amount payable under DBFO contract within next year	18	19	20
Amount payable under DBFO contract after one year (capitalised value of road improvements)	965	947	911
Commitment to shadow tolls under DBFO next year	184	210	209

Sources: Highways Agency accounts (several years) and information provided by the Highways Agency.
Notes
1. Although the Highways Agency did not produce accruals accounts for 2000, the 2000/01 accounts showed the information for the previous year.
2. 2000 figures have been restated to be consistent with accounting policies of later years, using information provided by the Highways Agency.

the company, its parent and related companies, and then obtained the concessionaires' accounts, since their inception, from Companies House. However, we were unable to obtain a full set of accounts for 2002 for one of the companies, Autolink Concessionaires (A19) Ltd, as its parent company, Amey Plc, was involved in considerable restructuring, including the disposal of substantial equity stakes in its PFI projects during this period. This makes our financial data for 2001/02 incomplete.

The consortium is made up of a bank or finance house and a construction company that typically invests 3–7% of the capital required from its own funds as equity in the new company. The consortium has no recourse to its parent companies but raises the rest of its finance as debt from the banks, its parent finance house or more typically the bond market. Although a high level of gearing generally yields little in the way of return for shareholders, in practice, as we have shown, under conditions where there is little downside risk the cash flows that remain after debt service potentially provide a high rate of return to the parent companies on their small equity stakes.

It was clear from their accounts that in nearly every case, the SPV is a shell company whose only activities and income relate to its DBFO contract. It has no employees but serves as a conduit to channel the payments received from the Highways Agency to its subcontractors, which are typically subsidiaries of the SPV's parent companies. This arrangement creates the possibility for transfer pricing, with profit being recorded in related parties rather than the SPV. This means that the parent companies may profit from the DBFO in several ways: their equity stake in both the SPV and the subsidiaries that carry out work for the SPV, and interest on any loans to the SPV.

Since the SPVs operate as close companies,[3] they are not required to disclose the size of the payments made to related parties. Only one of the 10 consortia's

accounts that we examined disclosed this: UK Highways M40 Ltd. Figure 5.2 (see page 94) shows the structure of this consortium, which is typical of the other SPVs, and the financial flows of this corporate group. This complex structure and elongated chain of command could, however, lead to communications problems, extra monitoring costs and disputes as evidenced by the experience of the privatised rail infrastructure company (Shaoul 2004a). Furthermore, should the contract with the SPV be terminated for whatever reason, the Highways Agency would not only have to honour its debts, but could also find itself locked into long-term contracts with the subsidiaries of the SPV's parent companies. La Trobe Regional Hospital in Victoria Australia, for example, found itself locked into long-term contracts when it was forced to take back the privately financed and operated hospital into public ownership.[4]

Before presenting the SPVs' income from their DBFO contracts, it is useful to outline the accounting treatment. The shadow toll payment from the Agency is split into two parts. Current income is shown in the profit and loss statement, although for some companies any amount in excess of operating costs is shown as deferred income in the balance sheet until completion of road

---

[3] A close company, subject to certain exceptions, is broadly a company:
- which is under the control of
  - five or fewer participators, or
  - any number of participators if those participators are directors,

  or
- more than half the assets of which would be distributed to five or fewer participators, or to participators who are directors, in the event of the winding up of the company.

(Inland Revenue 2004)

[4] Interview with the finance director of La Trobe Regional Hospital.

improvements, when it will be amortised over the life of the concession. This means that in the early years, turnover may not reflect total income received and the companies varied in their revenue recognition policy.

All the SPVs concerned show the contract asset as a depreciating tangible fixed asset on their balance sheet. Taken together with the income treatment, this means that the SPVs consider sufficient risk, especially the demand risk, to have passed from the Agency to the private sector. The fact that the Agency now also shows all eight contracts on balance sheet in its own financial statements shows that such a determination of risk transfer is not straightforward. Clearly the Agency's auditors consider that the public sector still retains a large element of risk in relation to the contract, requiring the full assets to be kept on balance sheet together with the related financial obligations. As there is no requirement in the accounting standards or

Treasury guidance for the public or private sector to disclose details of their risk assessment it is not possible to follow how such conclusions on accounting treatment have been reached by either party to the contract. This means that the substantive question – the judgement as to how the risk is being allocated – must be finely balanced for the different parties to arrive at asymmetric accounting treatments.

Table 5.6 shows the turnover recorded by each of the eight SPVs for the years 1997 to 2002. The first point to note is that, despite the absence of such information from their own accounts, the Highways Agency was making payments from 1997. Although the SPVs record an income of £241 m over the first three years, this underestimates the total received by about 10%, since some is shown as deferred income. Secondly, most of the projects appear to have become fully operational by 1999 when income stabilised. Thirdly,

Table 5.6: DBFO companies' income from the eight contracts

(£m)	1997	1998	1999	2000	2001	2002	Total
Autolink/A19	8	13	20	20	16	N/A	77
UK Highways/M40	16	17	21	21	22	22	119
Connect A30/A35	11	12	12	11	26	29	101
Connect A50	2	8	7	6	9	10	42
Yorkshire Link A1–M1	0	0	17	35	47	46	145
RMS Gloucester A417/419	2	13	15	16	16	17	79
RMS Peterborough A1	1	4	22	23	23	24	97
Roadlink A669	4	7	8	8	8	8	43
Total 8 Companies	**43**	**74**	**124**	**141**	**168**	**155**	**707**
Payments made by Highways Agency	N/A	N/A	N/A	195	218	205	N/A
Payments made by Highways Agency ex-VAT on shadow tolls	N/A	N/A	N/A	174	183	182	N/A

Sources: annual reports and accounts of DBFO companies (various years) and Highways Agency.
N/A = not available.

although the ranking of their income largely followed that of the capital cost of the contracts, in one case, the A1(M) Peterborough–Alconbury contract had an income considerably lower than the capital cost of the project would have suggested. This may be due to the fact that, as Standard and Poor's noted, traffic volumes were less than the SPV expected. Alternatively, it may be because the SPV recorded some of its income in 2000 and 2001 as deferred income. Fourthly, the eight SPVs' income has risen continuously from £43 m in 1997 to £168 m in 2001, the last year for which we have complete information, in part at least because traffic volumes have increased. By 2002, the SPVs had received from the Agency more than the £590 m capital cost of the projects.

One perhaps surprising point that emerges from Table 5.6 is that the SPVs' income does not match the Highways Agency's total DBFO payments shown in Table 5.5 (on page 96) and reproduced at the bottom of Table 5.6. It is about 30% lower than the Agency's payments. There are several possible reasons for this. First, the SPVs and the Agency have different year ends. Secondly, some of the SPVs changed their year end in 2000 and so Table 5.6 shows an estimated value for 2000 based on pro-rating the monthly averages. Thirdly, the 2002 accounts for one of the companies were not available. Fourthly, three of the SPVs record some of their income as deferred income, but this is small and in the early years of the contracts. Lastly, depending upon whether the Agency's activities are zero-rated or exempt from VAT, its payments include VAT, whereas the SPVs' turnover is reported net of VAT. However, even assuming that all the shadow toll payments include VAT, the SPVs' income from the contracts is still 15–20% less than the Agency's payments, which relate only to the eight contracts in this period. This is something we are not able to explain.

Table 5.7 (see page 100) shows the total profits before interest and tax, and the profit margins for the eight SPVs over the life of the contract. These were generally

rising and by 1999, when the projects became fully operational, profit margins averaged a very high 54% of income. By 2002, profits had risen to £106 m (from £6 m in 1997) and profit margins had risen from 13% to 68%. Since the SPVs had no employees, almost all their operating expenses, except depreciation and a management fee to their parent companies, must represent payments to their subcontractors. These were typically about £50 m a year. Since operating profits have risen more than turnover and payments to subcontractors, it seems likely that the SPVs arranged fixed price contracts with their subcontractors for operating the roads and have earned more from the Highways Agency than expected owing to higher traffic flows. Thus the SPVs benefited in the short term at least at the expense of their subcontractors who carried out the operational services. The high volumes must in turn lead to higher maintenance costs later.

Table 5.7 (see page 100) shows that the amount of corporation tax payable was very small, rising from zero in 1997 to £9 m on profits of £106 m (about 8%) in 2002. The total amount of tax payable by the companies over the period was £25 m. This constitutes an effective tax rate on operating profit of 7% on total operating profits of £384 m for the period, despite the fact that the current rate of corporation tax is 30%, largely because of tax relief on net interest paid. Even this is an over estimate of actual tax paid, however, since most of it is deferred tax. We would expect the tax payable to increase in the next few years. This finding is important because it challenges a crucial part of the VFM methodology set out in the revised Green Book (HM Treasury 2003a) and based on guidance provided by KPMG, a key player in the PFI market. The new methodology assumes that corporate tax receipts will increase under PFI and that therefore the PSC should be adjusted by 22% to reflect this. This is in contrast to the earlier versions of the Green Book (HM Treasury 1991, 1997a) that assumed a tax contribution of one per cent or less. Our evidence shows that this key assumption, which will distort the

Table 5.7: DBFO companies aggregate cost of capital

(£m)	1997	1998	1999	2000	2001	2002	Total
Turnover	43	74	124	141	168	155*	707*
Payments to subcontractors	37	49	53	59	70	50	323
Operating profit before interest and tax	6	25	69	82	98	106	384
Interest receivable	0	2	1	3	6	4	17
Interest payable	23	49	69	73	102	83	399
Tax	0	3	3	3	7	9	25
Profit after tax	−5	6	9	9	6	20	45
Dividends payable	1.50	0.00	0.01	0.00	2.75	8.75	11.52
Debt	557	810	850	851	951	884	
Shareholders' funds	18	52	49	51	51	68	
Total capital employed	575	862	899	902	1002	952	
Key ratios							
PBIT/turnover	13%	33%	55%	58%	58%	68%	54%
Effective tax rate	0%	12%	4%	4%	9%	8%	7%
Interest rate on debt	4%	6%	8%	9%	11%	9%	
Effective total cost of capital	3%	6%	9%	9%	11%	11%	
Gearing ratio	97%	94%	95%	94%	95%	93%	
Return on shareholders' funds							
(post-tax profit/shareholders' funds)	−25%	11%	18%	17%	11%	29%	

Source: annual report and accounts of DBFO companies (several years).

Notes

* One company's data still missing in 2002.

Payments to subcontractors = turnover less operating profits, management fee and depreciation.

Effective total cost of capital is operating profit before interest and tax/long-term debt and shareholders' funds.

Effective tax rate on operating profit = tax payable/profit before interest and tax.

Gearing ratio = debt/(debt + shareholders' funds).

Effective total cost of capital = (interest payable plus post-tax profit)/(long-term debt and shareholders' funds).

Profit after tax is affected by other income.

VFM analysis in favour of private finance, is inappropriate, certainly for the early years.

High operating profits are necessary to cover the cost of capital: interest payments on debt and returns on shareholders' funds to the parent companies. They therefore provide an estimate of the SPVs' total cost of capital and thus serve as a proxy for the Highways Agency's cost of using private finance.

First, Table 5.7 shows that debt had risen from £557 m in 1997 to £951 m in 2001, the last year for which complete information was available. This was considerably higher than the £590 m construction costs which, as the NAO reported, had resulted from the additional costs of private finance, the high transaction costs and risk transfer (NAO 1998a). Interest payments on debt had increased over the period from £23 m in 1997 to £83 m in 2002 and, by 2002, the seven SPVs were paying an effective interest rate of about 9%, considerably higher than the cost of Treasury stock, currently about 4.5%. Secondly, the table shows that shareholders' funds rose from £18 m in 1997 to £51 m in 2001 and £68 m in 2002, in part because of retained profits. The parent companies' post-tax profits rose from a loss of £5 m in 1997 to a profit of £6 m in 2001 and £20 m in 2002, equal to a rate of return on shareholders' funds of 11% in 2001 and 29% in 2002.

This means that in 2002 the SPVs' total effective cost of capital for seven of the eight contracts was about £103 m (interest payable plus post-tax profit) or 11%, several points above either the cost of Treasury gilts or the Government's 6% cost of capital implicit in its 6% capital charging regime and test discount rate. This additional cost must represent, as the NAO explained (1998a), the cost of risk transfer. This implies a risk premium of about six percentage points, equal to about £56 m. However, there is no yardstick against which to evaluate whether this cost constitutes VFM.

Considering next the SPVs' rate of return on shareholders' funds, we use, by way of a benchmark, the evidence given on 'normal' rates of return on PFI projects by the National Audit Office to the PAC, citing the Office of Government Commerce (PAC 2003d, Figure 2). The 'normal' rate of return (post-tax) on the construction companies' investments (not defined) in PFI companies was 8–15% for 2001. Thus our companies have exceeded the 'normal' rate of return. Our analysis is confirmed by the industry itself, which uses a variety of different and undefined measures of returns to shareholders, therefore making precise comparison difficult. According to a report in *The Guardian* (8 September 2003), the Major Contractors Group (MCG), which represents PFI contractors such as Carillion, Costain and Amec, said that they expected to make between three and ten times as much on their stakes in PFI as their traditional contracts with equity returns in the region of 10–20%. A segmental analysis of their main business areas as revealed in their annual report and accounts and carried out as part of the present study confirms that this is indeed the case. The chief executive of Mowlem, another MCG member, justified the higher returns on the basis of the substantial risks associated with PFI. In other words, it is more beneficial in terms of capital employed (although not necessarily in absolute terms) to have stakes in the SPV than actually to carry out the construction or even the service provision. Confirmation of MCG's viewpoint is shown by John Laing's sale of its construction company in order to buy up equity stakes in PFI contracts.

This analysis of the SPVs' total effective cost of capital as a proxy for the Highways Agency's cost of private finance tells only part of the story. First, as explained earlier, the SPVs typically subcontract some of the operations and maintenance work to subsidiaries of their parent companies (Figure 5.2 on page 94). In only one case, UK Highways M40 Ltd, did the SPV disclose sufficient information in its accounts to enable an analysis of the subsidiary's financial performance. In 2002, UK Highways M40 Ltd was paying about

Table 5.8: Financial performance of a DBFO's subcontractor (UK Highways Services Ltd)

(£m)	1997	1998	1999	2000	2001	2002	Total
Turnover	6.25	6.55	6.54	7.07	7.17	7.61	41.19
Operating expenditure	5.40	5.21	5.36	5.70	5.74	5.87	33.28
Operating profit before interest and tax (PBIT)	0.85	1.34	1.18	1.37	1.43	1.74	7.91
Interest receivable	0.02	0.05	0.03	0.04	0.04	0.03	0.21
Interest payable	0.02	0.07	0.06	0.06	0.05	0.04	0.30
Tax	0.27	0.43	0.34	0.41	0.43	0.52	2.40
Profit after tax	0.58	0.89	0.81	0.95	0.99	1.22	5.44
Dividends payable	0.30	0.79	0.81	0.76	1.03	1.06	4.75
Debt	0.67	0.62	0.56	0.50	0.43	0.34	
Shareholders' funds	0.77	0.18	0.05	0.24	0.21	0.37	
Total capital employed	1.44	0.80	0.61	0.74	0.64	0.71	
Key ratios							
PBIT/turnover	14%	20%	18%	19%	20%	23%	19%
Effective tax rate	31%	32%	29%	30%	30%	30%	30%
Interest rate on debt	3%	11%	11%	12%	12%	12%	
Effective total cost of capital	40%	114%	136%	130%	156%	172%	
Gearing ratio	45%	78%	92%	68%	67%	48%	
Return on shareholders' funds (Post tax profit/shareholders' funds)	**75%**	**494%**	**1620%**	**395%**	**471%**	**329%**	**299%**

Source: annual report and accounts of UK Highways M40 Services Ltd (several years).
Notes
Effective tax rate = Tax payable/Profit before interest and tax.
Gearing ratio = debt/(debt + shareholders' funds).
Effective total cost of capital = (operating profit before interest less tax)/(long-term debt and shareholders' funds).

£6.8 m or 34% of its income to its sister company, UK Highways Services Ltd. With operating profits accounting for a further 35% of its income, this means that UK Highways M40 Ltd paid 31% to other (unknown) subcontractors and suppliers.

Table 5.8 (see page 102) shows UK Highways Services Ltd's income from this and another DBFO contract, its profit margin and return on shareholders' funds. Turnover rose from £6.25 m in 1997 to £7.61 m in 2002, with nearly all its income (£6.8 m out of £7.61 m) in 2002 coming from the M40 contract. Profit margins rose from 14% in 1997 to 23% in 2002 and were typically 19% of income over the period. The effective rate of interest payable on debt rose from 3% in 1997 to 12% in 2002 on debt that fell from £670,000 to £340,000 over the same period. After paying about 12% interest on its debt in 2002 and corporation tax at 30% of operating profits most years, it generated a post-tax return on shareholders' funds of 75% in 1997, rising to 329% in 2002. This was considerably higher than that of the SPV. Therefore, if these results are typical, the total returns to the parent companies on DBFO contracts are much more than simply the SPVs' returns.

Secondly, as the PAC (2003d) supplementary memorandum explained, the total returns to the SPVs' parent companies also would need to include the interest paid to the parent companies' finance subsidiaries, the benefit of any refinancings during the contract period – and at least one of the SPVs, Autolink A19 Concessionaires, has refinanced its debt – realised gains on the disposal of any investments in the SPV and any unrealised gains from increases in the value of such investments.

Thirdly, the notes to the SPVs' accounts provide interesting examples of how the parent companies benefit in other ways. To cite but one example (and there are others), Yorkshire Link (Holdings) Ltd, the SPV's parent, has made two interest-free loans totalling

£36 m of unstated duration to its parents, Balfour Beatty Plc and Macquarie Infrastructure (UK) Ltd, which thereby improve the parents' cash flow position at no extra cost to them. The holding company was able to do this because the SPV took out a loan, which among other things financed the holding company's upstream loan. Not only does this provide benefits to the private sector, it also creates additional risk for the Highways Agency, since should the parents go under, for whatever reason, the SPV will no longer have the cash to carry out the expensive maintenance work required later on in the contract, for which the Highways Agency has already paid through the front loading of the payment mechanism. There appears to be no ring-fencing of the SPVs' finances.

Thus the 68% profit margin on income received from the Highways Agency in 2002 (Table 5.7 on page 100), adjusted to 63% when £9 m corporation tax payable is taken into account, is attributable to the SPVs' cost of capital, which we suggested could be used as a proxy for the Highways Agency's cost of capital, and considerably under-represents the total cost. For as well as including the SPVs' interest payments on debt and returns to shareholders, any estimate of the total cost should include the profits of the parent companies' construction subsidiaries and the interest and profits of their finance subsidiaries, the tax revenue lost through deferred tax, profits on refinancing, etc. Little of this information is available in a way that makes it possible to assess the total cost of using private finance.

All this means that considerably less than half the payments made by the Highways Agency are actually spent on the construction, operation and maintenance of the roads. This raises questions about the DBFOs' actual VFM. In principle it should at least be possible to assess the actual VFM by comparing the Highways Agency's costs and the SPVs' returns against the financial models submitted as part of the bidding process. However, the bidders' financial models are not in the public domain. The results of such a comparison have not been published, neither is it known whether the Agency has indeed carried out such an analysis.

More importantly, it also raises questions about affordability, the implications for the rest of the Highways Agency's expenditure, and the extent to which the use of private finance is a good use of the taxpayers' money. At the very least, the experience of DBFOs does not sit comfortably with the general aim of controlling public expenditure.

In conclusion, the literature has shown that:

- despite general support for DBFO, there has been little empirical *ex ante* or *ex post* financial research into the use of private finance in roads in general and DBFOs in particular; such financial evidence as exists consists of snippets from diverse sources

- there is almost no information in the public domain about either the business cases or the contracts

- there is little evidence as to how the operational phase is working

- more information appears to be made available to the capital markets than to the public at large, despite their interests as taxpayers and users

- such financial information as is available suggests that the risk transfer on construction costs and delays provides much of the financial justification for DBFOs

- given the high cost of risk transfer, this suggests that the Highways Agency paid a high premium to ensure that the roads were built to budget and on time

- the National Audit Office does not yet appear to have exercised its 'right to roam' through the books of the complex web of DBFO road companies.

The financial analysis in relation to the Highways Agency has shown that:

- the Agency's financial reporting of its DBFO contracts is limited and opaque

- despite an annual cost of about £210 m and the Government's payment guarantees of contracts worth £6 billion in total, there is little information available to the public as taxpayers and users.

- this cost appears to be more than expected at financial close since the NPC of such payments is about twice that of the NPC in the public domain

- in the three years for which figures are available, the Highways Agency has paid out more than the construction costs of the projects, refuting one of the justifications for DBFO

- since the full business cases are not in the public domain, there has been little external financial scrutiny of the deals and it is unclear post-implementation how the actual cost of DBFO compares with the expected costs; our evidence suggests that it has turned out to be more expensive than expected; how this affects the Highways Agency's ability to fund other maintenance projects is unclear

- given the high cost of risk transfer as reflected in the risk premium (approximately 7 percentage points), the Highways Agency seems to have paid a high price to get the roads built to time and budget

- the lack of information in the public domain makes it difficult to estimate the exact extent of the commitments incurred by the Highways Agency and the DoT and therefore provides little accountability to the public.

In relation to the private sector partners, the analysis has revealed a number of factors.

- The SPVs operate in a complex and opaque web of contracting that increases the costs and makes it impossible to assess their returns and thus the total cost of private finance to the public purse.

- Current regulation permits a lack of disclosure of related party transactions.

- The seven SPVs report an operating profit before interest and tax of 68% of their receipts from the Highways Agency, and this is after subcontracting to sister companies. This operating profit (less tax) is in effect the cost of capital.

- About 35% of the SPVs' income from the Highways Agency is paid to their operations and maintenance subcontractors, typically sister companies, including an unidentifiable profit element for the subcontractor. Given that this is still early in the contract, this is likely to be the cost of operations rather than maintenance.

- Subcontracting in this way means that it is difficult to isolate the costs of operations and maintenance in DBFO contracts since the subcontractor may have multiple contracts elsewhere.

- The absence of such information makes it difficult for the public sector when it comes to amending the contracts and negotiating new ones.

- Although the amount of tax payable by the seven SPVs over the whole period is only 7% of operating profits, even this overstates the actual tax paid since it includes an element of deferred tax.

- This low tax rate in the early years at least challenges an important part of the Treasury's new appraisal methodology for PFI, which assumes that tax payable will be about 22%, which in turn will distort the VFM analysis in favour of PFI.

- The seven SPVs' interest rate of 9% in 2002 and the high level of debt, which is greater than construction costs, mean that the DBFO contracts are considerably more expensive than the cost of conventional procurement using Treasury gilts at the current rate of 4.5%.

- The SPVs' post-tax returns on shareholders' funds are high and higher than elsewhere in the industry.

- The SPVs' total effective cost of capital was about 11% in 2002. Although the NAO believed that this additional cost of private finance (6 percentage points above Treasury stock) represented the cost of risk transfer (£56 m), it was difficult to see what risks the companies actually bore since their payments were guaranteed by the Government and based on shadow tolls, which in the context of rising traffic meant that they were insulated from downside risk at the Highways Agency's expense.

- In practice, the shadow tolls have led to a front-loading of the payment flows and the SPVs' profits.

- Without arrangements to ring-fence the post-tax profits, should the DBFOs fail for whatever reason later in the contract – despite front loading the payment stream to cover the future cost of maintenance – the Highways Agency could find that it has to bear the remaining and higher cost of private capital and the maintenance costs that it thought it had already paid for.

DBFO and roads

Although this contract and DBFO in general are perceived as 'successful', this operational success is viewed independently of the financial costs.

A roads case

This chapter considers how one of the Highways Agency's first tranche of DBFO projects is operating. Since there is a lack of 'hard information' available for use in the public domain, owing to reasons of commercial and Government sensitivity, the evidence presented here is based mainly on interviews. We interviewed people at the Highways Agency who are currently closely associated with the project, including, at the regional office, the Agency's departmental representative who is responsible for this first tranche project on a day-to-day basis and his line manager, the Agency's departmental manager. We also interviewed Highway Agency staff from head office in London. The Special Purpose Vehicle (SPV) preferred that its respondent should be of very senior managerial status, and although he was closely associated with the construction phase of this project, his involvement in the operations phase is less direct.

After outlining the key features of our case project, this chapter presents the perceptions of our interviewees about three issues that have become important in the assessment of PFI. As explained in Chapter 1, the interviews followed a semi-structured format and the questions asked – and hence the perceptions reported – were initially guided by our review of academic literature and of secondary sources specific to the sector and the case, but there was also opportunity for interviewees to provide additional information and for the researchers to pursue issues arising at interview.

Our initial review suggests that three issues are important for the assessment of PFI. The first of these is whether the project has achieved the objectives set for it; the second is the procedures (and their usefulness) that have been established for ensuring that the project delivers VFM over its life and for managing risk transfer (the key assumption upon which VFM is based); the third is whether the financial arrangements are working in practice.

In terms of the project's objectives, the Highways Agency is of the firm belief that the construction phase has been successful, and this is in line with the experience of other construction projects in this and in other sectors. Since the Highways Agency had used the services of private companies to construct roads for many years it was not a surprise that this project was completed successfully. Therefore our interviews focused on those issues that changed apparently because of PFI, for example, that the road had come in under budget and on time, and since one rationale for DBFO is that integration of all aspects of the project will enable long-term planning and cost reduction we also focused on the project's softer objectives, such as the use of innovative techniques. In practice, the most important change introduced by PFI is the long-term operational and maintenance provision by the private sector, which requires monitoring by the public procurer in order for payments to be approved. Since this was a new area of activity, much of our interview discussion related to how this worked in practice. In this area we were alerted to and report a number of problems or issues that lack clarity. Interviews necessarily focused on only some aspects of a complex project and, although whenever possible we have used direct quotes from the interviewees to report their perceptions fully, the choice of questions around which discussions took place was driven by the researchers and the academic literature. Much of the rest of this chapter raises concerns based on our interpretation of the interview material, but in essence it should be made clear that those with close oversight of the project fundamentally view it as a successful road.

THE DBFO PROJECT

Our case study is one of the first and largest of the eight roads DBFO projects intended to further the Government's Targeted Programme of Improvements. Like the other roads projects, although the Secretary of State for Transport was the signatory to the contract with the SPV, the Agency has executive responsibility for the administration of the contract, which is the principal legal relationship between the private sector and the Agency, with the Secretary of State retaining overall responsibility (Highways Agency 2003).

The ownership and operations of the contract are complex and have been subject to change. The SPV is owned by a holding company whose ultimate owner is a consortium of two organisations, Companies A and B. The SPV is a shell company that has no employees, and it entered into a joint venture with Company SA, a subsidiary of one of its parent companies, and Company C to provide the construction phase of the project. It has also subcontracted the operations and maintenance parts of the contracts to subsidiaries of its parent companies. With about 30 similar projects around the world, the DBFO company has considerable experience in this type of operation.

In essence, this project has three phases: construction, operations and finally handover to the Agency. The statutory procedures in relation to planning were complete by the time this scheme went out to tender. The new construction and improvement elements, which include over 150 structures along the route, were completed about three years after financial close, some months ahead of schedule. During the operations phase the private sector will maintain the road for 30 years, including a schedule of planned structural and replacement work, which to some extent at least will depend upon traffic volumes. At the end of the contract, the road and related structures will returned to the Highways Agency with an expected agreed residual lifetime.

The project is currently in the operations phase and so the main point of contact on a day-to-day basis between the public and private sectors occurs between the DBFO's general manager, who has responsibility for overseeing the operational phase of the project, and the Agency's departmental representative, who is charged with monitoring the service provision. As explained in the previous chapter, the public sector already had

considerable experience of contracting with the private sector for both the construction and maintenance of roads. One important consequence was that the Agency had already developed a three-volume Trunk Road Maintenance Manual (TRMM), which sets out the expected procedures for the care and maintenance of roads and provides the basis for the standards expected during the operational phase of the project.

Unlike PFI projects in other sectors, the payment mechanism is based on shadow tolls linked to volume, which means that the private sector carries demand risk. Shadow tolls, based on a payment per vehicle using a kilometre of the project road, differ from real tolls that are paid by the user in that they are paid by the Agency on the users' behalf. Tolls increase over time according to an indexation formula, but are profiled so that eventually they will fall after the third-party debt has been fully repaid – believed to be after 20 years – reflecting the fact that any excess of revenue over costs represents return on equity. The Agency needs to predict expected payments and to submit its claims to the DoT four years in advance for finance to cover actual payments to the DBFO companies. Recently, this process has become more complex with the transfer from cash to accruals accounting. It requires an estimate of traffic volumes to be made using a spreadsheet model provided by an independent adviser, which are reviewed on a six monthly basis. According to an interviewee, these estimates are generally accurate to within three per cent of the actual flows.

Two forms of incentive system operate. First, the Agency may award a bonus payment or impose a financial penalty. For example, bonus payments are used to encourage good safety performance and as a means of avoiding traffic congestion by basing payment on the relationship between traffic volume and speed of flow. Financial penalties, which cannot be regained by the contractor, may be imposed for events such as lane closures. Secondly, the Agency can also award penalty points to the DBFO company or its contractors, which have a finite life, for example for failure to administer the contract properly during the operations phase. Beyond a certain level, these penalty points trigger action that could lead ultimately to contract termination. The contractual arrangements also include the requirement that the Agency notify the DBFO's leading bank, in the event of any formal notices on the contract, including penalties. This contrasts starkly with the fact that the taxpayers have no similar right of access to contractual and financial information.

PERFORMANCE AGAINST THE ORIGINAL PROJECT AND POLICY OBJECTIVES

One important way of assessing a project is to consider whether it has achieved its original objectives. These included the requirements to construct a strategic route for traffic, bypassing a major city and easing congestion, by an agreed date; to construct new carriageway; to widen and upgrade existing roads; to construct a new interchange and new road links; to operate and maintain the route for 30 years; and to remove traffic from some local roads. To the extent that the road was designed and built to meet these objectives, it may be assumed that these objectives were met, and this was confirmed by the Agency interviewees, who indicated that the new construction and improvements were achieved ahead of the contractual schedule and were approved by the Agency. Although the final cost of this element is not in the public domain, it was said to be very close to target, which is likewise unknown. Other project objectives included: enabling innovative construction and maintenance practices and the softer objectives of safeguarding the environment and providing safer travel conditions and better information to road users, and delivering all these objectives in partnership with industry. Although the relative weight of these objectives in relation to the construction and logistical objectives is unclear, our interviewees raised a number of interesting points on these issues, which we consider in turn.

Innovation

Proponents of PFI have argued that the private sector would be more innovative than the public sector. Since the design, build and maintain elements of the project were controlled by one company there would be an incentive to design the road in order to minimise whole-life costs. Contractors would be allowed to use alternative approaches to both construction and maintenance as long as they delivered equivalent levels of service and durability. To consider innovation in construction first, the Department of the Environment, Transport and the Regions (DETR), in a review of all the first tranche projects, claimed that the use of DBFO

. . . provided opportunities to use innovative technical solutions and new materials to reduce the whole life cost of the road by reducing maintenance requirements and minimising disruption to road users. (DETR cited in NAO 2000c)

It argued that many amendments to design standards took place during construction of this case project and that these have delivered benefits to the project. However, the evidence is not clear cut. The Agency (Highways Agency 1997) has a different view, arguing: 'Although, in theory the DBFO Co could propose alternatives to the Agency's existing design, few bidders exploited the opportunity'.

Specifically with regard to our case, one Agency interviewee indicated that DBFO had led to some innovation during the construction phase in relation to the use of new materials and earth-moving techniques. Without the long-term savings to be gained on the operations contract, he argued that there would have been no reason for the private sector to carry the risk associated with innovative techniques of construction: 'Maybe if they built it in the ordinary way there wouldn't be the incentive to take that risk'.

The contractor needs to seek approval to use innovative techniques and this interviewee argued that DBFO provided the incentive to do that.

They need a departure from standard agreement and they've more incentive to seek departures from standard than perhaps the standard designer . . . they've got an incentive, a cash incentive, to do it quicker, a lot more quickly, in which case we get our benefit quicker.

This implies that in part such innovation was introduced for faster completion rather than lower maintenance costs. However, in contrast an SPV interviewee argued: 'I think the big issue on the DBFOs is that, in our experience anyway, as soon as we tried to vary the scheme that the Highways Agency had designed they vetoed it'.

This is possibly because the Agency's consultants had to approve all drawings and:

In our specific case the Highway Agency's adviser was the consultant they'd used when they prepared the scheme, and so when our designer came along with something that we felt was an improvement, it was two sets of designers arguing against each other. So I'm not saying we didn't get some things through but nothing like as many as we would have liked. (SPV interviewee)

An Agency interviewee argued that the Agency would refuse a particular construction type only if it believed there to be very strong safety reasons against it, because the Agency had no other reason to do so. Since the life expectancy of the road is greater than the contract period of 30 years, and provided that the road is returned in the condition expected by the contract, the use of new technologies should not have any adverse effects on the Agency.

Nevertheless, the Agency has acknowledged the validity of the SPV's general point by indicating that bidders must become involved in the outline design of underlying assets if greater innovation is to occur

(Highways Agency 2003). It recognises that the first tranche of DBFO schemes included specifications that prescribed how the service was to be delivered, rather than focusing on outputs, and this undermined the ability to introduce innovation.

In relation to maintenance, the Agency departmental representative argued that innovation was not very evident and a second interviewee agreed. The SPV perspective, especially in relation to maintenance work, is that the Agency will not allow divergence from the Agency standard maintenance manual. This interviewee recognised, however, that views differed within the Agency. He indicated that:

I think it is fair to say that the Highways Agency has a number of people, especially in their divisional offices, who would be quite keen to see work done in a different way, but the headquarters groups are somewhat remote and not in the real world, and they have their way of doing things and it's quite difficult to get them to change. (SPV interviewee)

Pressing for change is perceived as a time-consuming activity for which ultimately there is limited resource available. In another project with which the company was involved the organisation was different, so that the SPV was nominated as the technical improvement authority. Consequently it had considerable involvement in approving the design as well as drawing it, and found that 'this gave us a lot more freedom to change things'.

This analysis shows that, first, there are two aspects to innovation: construction and maintenance; secondly, despite the Agency's claim, it appears that there has been less innovation than expected or possible; and thirdly, the purpose of construction innovation – implemented or proposed – was partly faster completion and partly lower life-cycle costs. One final point is that the evaluation of innovative techniques is a long-term issue, and as yet it is too early to assess whether those innovative techniques that were adopted will deliver benefits over the whole life of the project.

Softer objectives

The Agency has environmental protection objectives and a key objective of reducing accidents on trunk roads, which apply to all projects, including DBFOs. In the context of DBFOs it argues that, in principle at least, these objectives are a potentially significant VFM consideration, although they may not be quantifiable and hence may not be included in the comparison between the PSC and DBFO options (Highways Agency 2003). Some environmental requirements were built into our case contract, and the perception within the industry is that serious efforts were made to protect the environment. One interviewee argued:

I think the DBFOs that I've been involved with – there's a lot of intention to protect the environment – what we would consider to be inordinate amounts of money have been spent in preserving it. On [this case road] we had to protect this plant. I've forgotten what this damn plant is but whatever it is has spread all over the place. So whatever conditions suit it there's more of it now than there was before.

This interviewee proved additional examples in relation to tree planting, collection of reeds and crayfish for preservation and the moving of a heath, all of which he argued might not have happened previously without, however, suggesting that this was connected to the use of DBFO as opposed to traditional sources of finance.

In our case project, safety payments may be made as bonus payments, which are intended to encourage the SPV to address safety issues. The SPV is concerned about the use of payments based on safety performance indicators because it perceives that it was refused permission to design the road in the way it believed would be safest, although it recognised that this was not a precise science. Consequently it is reluctant to accept responsibility for something over which it has no control.

Until very recently the Highways Agency would not have concrete barriers down the centre of a road – they insist on having a particular design of steel barrier – now most sensible people would say if you have a concrete wall down the middle of the road it'll stop traffic crossing over and that's where you get the worst accidents. So you know, different people have different ideas about what is safe and what is not safe.

The Agency has suggested that for future DBFOs there should be a five-year rolling operational plan that would include issues such as safety, facilities for pedestrians and environmental protection. In addition, payment criteria are to be strengthened so that the safety payment will be both a bonus and a deterrent. Performance will be tied into a comparison between national and local accident rates on the relevant stretch of road. Accidents are not a risk that this SPV wishes to carry, however, especially over relatively short stretches of road.

You've seen what drivers get up to on the roads – it's the luck of the draw. People have the most unbelievable driving habits and you're asking a company to take that sort of risk – I don't think that's a particularly clever idea. Part of the difficulty at the moment is that these DBFOs are relatively small stretches of road. I think a much more preferable situation would be to have much bigger stretches of road that would allow the concession company to be judged fairly.

There is an absence of quantitative information or evaluation of the achievement of these softer objectives at the Agency and no comparison of the relative performance between DBFO and conventional forms of contracting. However, these perceptions – taken at face value – imply that these factors can be addressed if there is a specific allocation in the contract and presumably, therefore, in the bid price. Despite the Agency's desire to use the DBFO payment mechanism to reduce accidents and thereby increase safety, this may not be a simple matter to achieve. Given that the evaluation of environmental and safety objectives is a long-term issue, as yet it is too early to assess whether these practices will deliver benefits over the whole life of the project.

Partnership and/or private road operators

One objective of the first tranche of DBFOs was to create a private road industry, so that companies can develop their expertise and bid for future projects both in the UK and overseas. The Agency does not appear to have evaluated whether DBFO has contributed to the achievement of this objective and its relative importance is unclear. Furthermore, in the previous chapter we found that there have been few new DBFOs after the first eight, thereby inhibiting the growth of expertise in the UK, although our case SPV has experience of bidding and winning contracts abroad.

A second objective of DBFO was to deliver the wider objectives of the Agency's mission in partnership with the private sector. Although the relationship between public and private sectors has been characterised as one of partnership, the interviewees were not clear that a partnership had been achieved on this project. An interviewee from the Agency said:

Not totally partnership. I think we try and bring them along with us – obviously we do have differences of opinion. I think the advantage of saying you're working in partnership is you both try to do it, but sometimes we might feel we're not getting the support or they seem to be intransigent about certain things. I think you have to respect that they have a different point of view, and I hope they do the same about me.

In summary, this analysis of the policy's success in relation to the Agency's softer objectives suggests that it has been limited. The very different views of the two sectors about innovation and safety suggest that the issues will not be easy to overcome. Whether the DBFO

in roads policy has created a sustainable private sector road industry can be judged only in the longer term, but in the foreseeable future it appears that there is work yet to be done in establishing stable partnership relationships between contractors and the Agency.

PROCEDURES FOR MANAGING THE CONTRACT

We consider the payment mechanism in some detail since this is crucial to understanding the contract monitoring regime. We then examine: the reporting and monitoring procedures that surround it; the sanctions that are available to the Agency to discipline the SPV; and the procedures for contract amendments and the end-of-project handover for their effect on VFM, since these are critical to an understanding of how VFM is to be delivered.

Payment mechanism

Although the payment is based on a shadow toll dependent on volume of traffic, it actually involves three criteria: availability of service; usage/demand; and performance, which includes safety performance and lane closure elements. First, availability of service payments begins on new constructions once the Permit to Use is issued for the road to open to traffic, and payments amount to 80% of the full level of traffic payment. 100% payments begin once the construction works are complete and the Agency issues the Completion Certificate.

Secondly, payments for usage are based on shadow tolls that represent a payment per vehicle using a kilometre of the project road within different traffic bands. Bidders were required to establish the parameters of traffic levels for a maximum of four and a minimum of two bands, based on their own assessments of traffic levels. Although the top band must have a toll set at zero so that the maximum liability under the contract is capped, there is no minimum safety net for the contractor. So, for example, incidents such as a fuel crisis or foot-and-mouth disease, which resulted in a significant dip in volume, represent risk to the SPV. Inside each band there are two rates: one for long and one for short vehicles. Vehicle length is used as a proxy for the more significant effect of weight, because there is no available method for differentiating between vehicle weights. It is also possible for the SPV to gain bonus payments, related to traffic speed, as an incentive to avoid congestion, for example, by ensuring a reasonable snow gritting policy. The payment mechanism is based on a flow/speed relationship, with speed linked to the relevant volume of flow.

Thirdly, performance has two key elements. The first relates to the Agency's key objective to reduce accident levels and it therefore encourages contractors to seek approval for safety improvement schemes. The SPV pays for these schemes but is compensated by a payment equal to 25% of the economic cost of personal injury accidents avoided in the following five-year period. This compensation is measured by comparing accident statistics for three years prior to the implementation of the scheme. In relation to the second element, a deduction is made from the toll payment when lanes are closed for reasons within the control of the SPV. Lane closure thus attracts a financial penalty, and the level of the deduction depends upon the number of lanes closed, the duration of the closure and, in order to provide incentives for closure at off-peak times, the expected traffic volume at the time of closure. Despite the first performance measure, however, it is assumed that closure by the police after accidents is not within the control of the contractor and is therefore not subject to penalties.

The Agency makes monthly payments of a constant value for a 12-month period to the SPV. It makes an estimate, based on the previous year's volume, to establish the size of the monthly payments for the year. 'At the beginning of each year the Highways Agency works out how much they paid us the year before, divides it by twelve and pays us that on a monthly basis'.

At the end of the year in March or April, an annual reconciliation is performed and adjustments are made for actual traffic volumes less any charges. In this contract there are sculpting factors to be applied so that the payment for an individual year may be higher than the norm to reflect the need for extensive planned maintenance in that year.

The reconciliation between estimate and actual usually results in a higher payment being required, because traffic volumes have outpaced predictions. Final payments for each year are based on a reconciliation report provided by the contractor, which is verified by the Agency using both manual calculations and a spreadsheet model provided by their advisers, so that the figures can be checked independently. This reconciliation has not always been agreed at the first attempt. 'There's been a change of personnel on their side, of the people who actually do the annual reconciliation, and we have to send it back, and then we've agreed the figures' (Highways Agency interviewee).

Data collection and reporting

The Agency makes the monthly payments on receipt of the SPV's report, which sets out information on traffic volumes, lane closures and a self-assessment of performance as specified by the contract. In addition to collecting and reporting data that feed directly into the payment mechanism, the SPV also has to collect and report on other aspects of its operational performance that are important for the Agency's work and yet do not appear to be included in the payment mechanism. For example, the SPV perceives the Agency as being very keen on the availability of emergency telephones, and measures this even though there is no availability payment for telephones. The most significant element is the traffic volumes, which need to be counted with great accuracy, given the nature of the payment mechanism.

The initial responsibility for counting traffic volume lies with the SPV and the data are then monitored by the

Agency. The SPV counts the traffic using loop technology under the road and 'most people wouldn't even know that their car is being monitored'. Traffic is measured at a number of points along the road on a continuous basis, and these raw traffic data are reported monthly.

There is a verification process, performed four times each year, during which a video is made of traffic flow at the same locations at which the counting equipment operates, so that this equipment can be checked visually. This is a time-consuming activity and its contribution to accuracy is unknown. An Agency interviewee indicated that the Agency was currently attempting to establish contact with a company in London to check these verifications because having people sitting watching a video was likely to be problematic. A similar argument was made by the SPV.

The loop technology is about ten times more accurate than we expected it to be, so you know we are within half a percent of actual, and the visual verification is a bit problematic – people are staring at a camera for a long time. I would personally take the loops as being a better measurement than the video, but the Highways Agency insist.

This insistence is based on a perceived need to ensure integrity of the process, although as an interviewee at the SPV argued: 'I suppose there is an opportunity for us to fix the data but I mean that's just something we wouldn't contemplate. It'd be too difficult anyway'.

The Agency believes that manipulation is in fact feasible even though the traffic counting is subcontracted to a separate company, which is not paid on volume. This means there would have to be collusion between one or more companies in order to manipulate traffic volume data.

I'm sure if you wanted to do it you could manipulate the technology. Basically you have to go back to the

binary file which is something inside the machine itself, and that would need the collusion of the people who actually do the traffic counting.

The Agency believes that the verification processes prevent manipulation and retains the data for a number of years so that audits can be conducted.

Self-assessment of performance includes evaluations of road availability based on times and durations of lane closures, response times in relation both to necessary repairs and to dealing with complaints from the public. There is a booking system for recording the notification of problems and the triggering of a response, so that it seems that the time taken to respond to problems is the crucial performance indicator, rather than performance itself. Yet, at least in the early phase of the contract, some difficulties were encountered.

When we started off we did have one or two hiccups. It's fairly onerous, depending on the grade of defect. If it's the worst type of defect you have to repair it within so many hours, and I mean, we've only got so many people. So if you've got too many of these you will have difficulty.

In general, while in the early stages of the project, the Agency was evidently unhappy with the information provided by the SPV and requested changes in its reporting system, the SPV believes this is now satisfactory.

It's fair to say that for six or nine months they were looking for a number of changes . . . so there was a certain amount of to-ing and fro-ing and there were certainly a number of things that took some time to tie up, which they weren't happy about, but I think now all are reasonably content with the way we report.

The nature of this reporting is critical, given the way in which the Agency monitors performance, a point which we take up in the next section.

Monitoring by the Highways Agency

With PFI the public agency moves from providing to procuring services and thus acquires new tasks and roles, the chief of which is monitoring, because it must ensure that it is receiving the services for which it is paying. Essentially, this monitoring function consists of auditing the SPV's reporting methodology, processes and systems and ensuring that it complies with its systems, rather than checking actual performance. That is, to use the language of financial auditing, monitoring is based on compliance assessment rather than substantive testing.

The Agency appoints representatives to monitor the contracts and ensure that the DBFO companies comply with their contractual obligations. An Agency interviewee whose role had changed because of DBFO said:

This is hands off. I would not query the work they are doing, you know, ask them to do less. You've got to let them use their expertise – you can ask them why they are doing something, but you can't say you won't do that or you will do this. That's a sort of fundamental change.

This project uses internal monitors, but in addition monitoring may be subcontracted to an external consultant, with oversight from the Agency. According to the departmental representative: 'Basically they [the senior managers] decided they needed external staff – we were short of civil servants so they brought in consultants to help us. Then they suddenly decided they didn't need the consultants any more'.

The NAO had criticised the Agency's monitoring procedures on the first four DBFOs, and an interviewee suggested that the underlying problem was a failure by the Highways Agency to train staff. As a consequence, the Agency introduced more formalised monitoring procedures, including a departmental representative's guide or manual on monitoring, staff training in negotiation and audit skills, and regular meetings of managers every two or three months to share best practice. This training included within it a focus on partnership relationships: 'We send staff on audit training straight away. Also we do negotiations. We try and generate a partnership approach'. The Agency staff can also draw on consultants' advice, especially 'if things get very technical on the financial side'.

The Agency espouses a desire to follow a 'hands off' approach to monitoring. A monitor reported that 'We've been told to keep a light hand on it – let them do the work.' In practical terms this means that the data from the contractors are monitored on a monthly basis with a formal auditing process three or four times a year. In addition to these checks by the Agency's internal auditors, an NAO team visited frequently, and perhaps more so on this PFI than for other projects (probably because of the size of the scheme) focusing on procedures and project management. 'They're checking our procedures and our documentation, and the way we manage the project.'

Despite earlier criticism by the NAO, especially in relation to maintaining a paper trail, more recently feedback was described as good because: 'In earlier audits they suggested that we perhaps should show that we've done things – as time has gone on we've improved . . . I mean we have a system now with our annual reconciliation and it's checked against theirs [the SPV's].'

However, one consequence is that administrative cost savings may not have been realised. The Agency's departmental representative, speaking of the monitoring learning curve said,

I think what we've learned is that you have to show that you've done something . . . . It's not that you've done it, it's a case of putting something on file saying, 'Route run completed and reported problems x, y, z,' just showing that you've done it. We're not brilliant but we're much better.

The purpose of the Agency's formal audit is to focus on the SPV's quality plan. This plan includes details of some 25 procedures, and appropriate sub-procedures, for all aspects of their role including, for example, issues such as winter maintenance, liaison and emergency procedures, emergencies in tunnels, etc. The Agency checks compliance with these procedures on a rolling basis, covering about four of these per year. The objective of the audit is to ensure that the SPV or its subcontractor is carrying out its activities in accordance with this written plan and the Agency's maintenance manual (TRRM). Although it would be possible for the Agency to monitor on a random basis without prior notification, the normal process is to agree a schedule of procedures.

We don't just descend on someone and say we want to look at this that and the other. We don't do that because I think what we try to do is work in partnership with these people. And if we did do that, I think we'd antagonise them because it's going to disrupt their day.

The lack of random checks in the formal audit processes is recognised by the SPV: 'I'm not sure if they [the Agency] do random monitoring. I'm not aware of them ever attempting to do that.'

In order for the Agency to monitor the SPV's monthly reports, a number of procedures are adopted. Traffic volume data are received in two formats: raw and processed data. These data are input to a spreadsheet of a traffic model that compares the data against the previous month's and the previous year's. The monitors will identify any blank periods in the data, when the loops have not been counting, since the SPV is entitled to insert estimated traffic flows during these periods to generate the processed data. Traffic counter availability is perceived as being better on this project than on other projects nearby and: 'Generally, yes, the counter availability has been there . . . . But recently we had a

problem with one of the loops and it took a long time to put it back in'.

In the event of non-availability, data are estimated from other counters on the road.

Basically we patch the data . . . we've got three counters, one, two, three, so if number 2 goes down you look at the two weeks before and the two weeks after [non-availability] *then you look at the first counter and the third counter and then at all three counters so the missing data is patched through by a method that's been agreed.*

In order to be able to monitor other monthly data, the Agency operates a system of day-to-day checks, the purpose of which is to monitor specific details. An Agency interviewee indicated that there is a route run on a monthly basis checking for lane closures, whether work is taking place at peak or off-peak times, and maintenance issues. This checking was described as 'random'. In addition, members of the public and the police are also potential sources of 'random' information about the road. Most contacts from the public are reported to be requests for information, however, especially in relation to an interchange junction, and the police have only ever provided information about road subsidence, which is related to a geographical feature of this road. These checks notwithstanding, the process is essentially based on trust in the SPV's report. Speaking about lane closures, an interviewee at the Agency said: 'To tell the truth we trust them on that one because usually all the lane closures go on overnight. I would expect if there'd been a problem I would get complaints. I've not had any complaints'.

Potentially there is one source of check data available to the Agency in relation to lane closures. In order to close a road the SPV must seek prior approval, through a temporary road traffic order, from the Agency, which approves times and locations for the closure.

Consequently, although there may be reasons for variations, the Agency could check these approvals against the contractor's report data. However, this is not done at present. 'I haven't checked one against the other, the notice against the report, because the report comes in later. We assume they use the closure because they need it to do the work'. In this case, the SPV indicated that lane closures normally occur at night when no penalty is payable because traffic is light.

At the end of each monthly reporting cycle a meeting is held between the Agency and the SPV's staff and a summary is prepared. At the end of each quarter there is a final agreement on the traffic flow figures for the previous three months. The SPV has a general manager, based on site, who was described as having day-to-day interaction with the Agency at the beginning of the project. More recently as 'things have settled down', however, the monthly meetings at the end of the reporting cycle are the more usual form of contact. Additionally contacts may be made between the Agency's representative and the SPV's managers and engineers and, on occasion, with technicians. The Agency's representative indicated that it is rare that he has contact with anyone of director status from the SPV. The SPV indicated that a head office representative was closely involved with the Agency during construction, but this degree of contact is now significantly reduced and normally takes place only if there is to be a variation to the contract.

Respondents from both sectors indicated that there was trust in the quality of the contractor's reporting. A private sector interviewee with experience of non-road PFIs that involved a cleaning contract said:

I don't think, at least in my experience, there's ever been any suggestion that we weren't reporting anything other than the truth. It's not quite like, well you know, whether there is dust on the table, and how many specks of dust – it's much more factual, so we don't have those sorts of problems.

To a large extent, this trust is likely to be a consequence of the objective nature of decisions. For example, a road's skid resistance fades over time and needs to be renewed. Because there is a regime under the Agency operating procedures that must be followed, it is relatively clear when a repair must be effected. That is, there is a technologically determined measure by which decisions can be justified.

Nevertheless there are some situations in which judgement is required and in these cases there is scope for differences between the organisations. Two examples were provided relating to the quality of the network, which is heavily dependent on the standard of maintenance. Interpretation of that standard now lies with the SPV. First, an example was given of a part of the road that runs over an opencast mining area.

We have had some problem with settlement in the road, and when that happens you get a slight wavy thing in the road and then it's a matter of judgement as to when it needs to be repaired, and we've had some differences of opinion.

The SPV indicated that normally, if the Agency becomes concerned about an issue, it is already under review by the contractor, but it could take some time to organise a response.

I'd have to say I'm not aware of any time when there's been a complaint when we haven't been in the middle of doing something about it, so the criticism might be that we haven't done it quickly enough . . . . But we have to go through a procedure of inviting tenders to do the work and it might take a month to six weeks to get that sort of work set up.

A second example of differences of opinion was given in relation to the timing of gritting to maintain traffic flow in the event of a snowfall. Network availability and quality are important to the Agency since it is responsible to the public for service delivery and is perceived to be responsible if roads are not gritted, although under PFI, this responsibility no longer comes under its direct control. Issues such as the timing of gritting, never an easy set of decisions, have now become entangled with the SPV's trade-off between the loss of revenue if traffic flow ceases versus the cost of the gritting operation, giving rise to potential disputes between the Agency and the SPV.

Despite these differences of opinion, however, the Agency's representative's impression is that generally: 'It's a very tidy road actually. We find very few things wrong with it'. In other words, in his opinion, after some initial changes to the reporting and monitoring systems these now work well to deliver the required standard of service, in this case.

Sanctions to deter poor performance: penalty points

The terms of the contract include a penalty system whereby the Agency can award penalty points for failure by the concessionaire to perform during both the construction and operational phases. It appears both from discussions with the Agency and from recent evidence about the Agency's maintenance contracts (PAC 2003c) that the penalties relate to the response time to rectify problems rather than actual poor performance. The allocation of points above a threshold allows the Secretary of State to take remedial action which would take the form of triggering increased monitoring by the Agency, the cost of which would fall on the concessionaire. In the event that non-performance continues, the Agency eventually has the right to terminate the contract. In practice, penalty points are issued only after a warning: 'You don't just impose them the first time something goes amiss. You ask them why it's amiss and it depends how important the transgression is – if that's the right word'.

Normally the intention to issue a penalty point triggers high-level negotiations: 'If you give penalty points directors suddenly talk to directors'. An excessive accumulation of penalty points could 'be linked to us

taking over the contract'.

The Agency has issued very few penalty points on this contract and the SPV indicated that they had found them 'pretty easy to avoid'. During the construction phase, a limited number of penalty points were awarded to the subcontractor but not to the concessionaire, with one interviewee indicating that there had been some reluctance within the Agency to issue penalties: 'I felt inclined during construction – but I wasn't allowed – partnership.'

Penalty points can be awarded also during the operations phase for failure to administer the contract properly, but an SPV interviewee said: 'We haven't had one penalty point during the operations phase'. He said that there had been very few penalties relative to the contractual targets that could trigger contract termination.

The number of points that you had to get to terminate the contract was so great that we never got anywhere near that. You have to have something like three hundred penalty points within twelve months. I don't think we ever got above 25 or 30.

A further 'incentive' to perform is provided by the requirement for the Agency to notify the syndicate's lead bank directly when it issues penalty points. Perhaps not surprisingly, the control exercised by the syndicate's bankers is a tougher target than that in the contract and both the Agency and the SPV perceived that the banks attach considerable importance to this issue. An Agency interviewee said: 'It's the banks that are worried about their investment – so contractors don't like getting penalty points – so they are a good incentive for them to do what they're required to do'.

The SPV confirmed this:

It was quite amusing really because they [penalty points] were the only thing the banks ever did get worked up about. In the planning agreement with the banks we got into severe difficulty if we got say 200 points. Even with those 20 or 30 points we got more enquiries about what was going on than anything else at all – it was totally out of all proportion.

Although the Agency representative acknowledged that another local SPV was less satisfactory, having incurred penalty points, he seemed to sum up the Agency's belief that the system seemed to be working well in this project, saying: 'I've never given a penalty point yet – they seem to do all right'.

Sanctions to deter poor performance: terminating a contract

As outlined earlier, the SPV is a shell company that works through a complex web of contractual relations: the SPV subcontracts work to a main contractor, who will appoint further subcontractors; it also appoints subcontractors for grass cutting, maintenance of the counting equipment, and for communications and electrical aspects. Consequently, the SPV must coordinate all its activities if it is to operate effectively and deliver the required level of service. This means that, where service delivery is unsatisfactory, it must be possible for the Agency to terminate the SPV's contract and for the SPV company to terminate the main contractor's and subcontractors' contracts.

Although in this project the SPV and its subcontractors have attracted few penalties, an SPV interviewee indicated, in response to a question asking whether it was possible to terminate the contract of any one provider, that its ability to do so is variable.

I would say it's to all intents and purposes impossible to get rid of the main contractor unless you're right at the beginning or right at the end. It's certainly possible to go to the main contractor and get him to get rid of one of his subcontractors, and certainly that, in my experience, has happened during the operations phase. The grass cutting is for three years – I don't

think there would be any difficulty in terminating that contract. We'd find it quite difficult to terminate the civil, the communications and the electrical, unless we were sort of doing it amicably.

In effect, termination of the main contract is problematic because it would leave the SPV, a shell company, responsible for the road and it would take time to organise a replacement contractor. Furthermore, although it could dismiss its own and the contractor's subcontractors, this is subject to the constraints of the industry itself. For example, the SPV is subject to a monopolistic supplier in relation to the specialist counting equipment.

The counting equipment is a nightmare because that's proprietary equipment and we are absolutely stuck with the people that supplied that equipment. This is one part of the industry that nobody's particularly happy with. There are only two or three people who do this sort of thing, in fact we may be down to two now, and they've got us over a barrel and they know it.

Similarly, it would be difficult for the Agency to terminate a contract for poor performance, because they would need to maintain the road until a replacement contractor was found. On this project, however, it was thought most unlikely that such an eventuality would arise because, if high levels of penalty points were reached: 'I would think not only we would be doing something, but their directors would be doing something.'

Because the current project has so few penalty points and consequently is a long way from such serious action, the Agency believed that it did not need a contingency plan in place to manage such an eventuality, but an interviewee said: 'We would get MAC [combination of the maintaining agent and the regional maintenance contractor roles that preceded DBFO] to take it over – the road is not very long'.

In summary therefore, it appears that the penalty points system does have the potential to deter poor performance by the SPV, especially because of the role of the financial institutions. Nonetheless, contract termination is perceived as a difficult if not impossible event and it is doubtful, therefore, whether it can serve as an effective sanction.

Contract amendments

PFI involves signing long-term contracts for the provision of services, typically for 30 years. Obviously, changes to the contractual specifications are going to be required for various reasons, including new legal requirements, especially in relation to health and safety; improving facilities; change of use of the infrastructure; and new technologies. The NAO (2003b) has warned that contract amendments offer the opportunity for the private sector to earn substantial additional revenue, with a consequent impact on the project's VFM. Indeed, the Agency became involved in a considerable amount of change very soon after implementation of this project.

The Agency described contract changes as 'one of the most difficult situations'. Although the contract documentation, when written in the mid 1990s, was described as very good, subsequently standards and requirements may change. The impact of any change has to be costed not only in terms of the immediate outlay, but also in terms of the annual cost over the contract lifetime. The Agency gave this example of an improvement.

We've put a new sign up – a big new electric sign – we pay for the improvement, the sign goes up, and then we've to negotiate with them and agree how many times that sign will need to be replaced in 30 years and I'll say five and he'll say three. They have to say how much cleaning it'll need, they might say, well, it'll get knocked down three times by motorists, we'll say well yes, but you'll get it on the insurance – although you have to catch them because they'll drive

away. So it'll wear out three times, get knocked down twice and we won't catch them, then we negotiate a figure for the change.

A second example was given in relation to standard response times, which were set out in the contract for serious maintenance problems but which then proved inadequate. Consequently, these were reduced from a 60-minute to a 30-minute response time in some circumstances, but this resulted in an additional cost to the Agency. This interviewee at the Agency stressed that 'the actual introduction of work's not difficult', but it was the consequences, or 'settlement of account' that causes the difficulties. Clearly, the outcome of these negotiations affects the project's VFM and, since there is no realistic alternative to using the SPV, the latter has a strong bargaining hand. Nevertheless, and by way of contrast with the trust case described later, the Agency interviewee believed that a reasonable outcome was likely since these negotiations occurred as between equals, 'they are chartered engineers and we are'.

Another example of contract amendment arose out of a regulatory change relating to discontinuing the use of concrete as a road surface. An interviewee at the Highways Agency said:

We've got this thing where the Government decide to resurface all the concrete sections of our road, and that'll be one of the biggest jobs. I wasn't aware that we would compare that with the public sector comparator – not for a Government initiative. I don't see it as part of my job to keep that up to date. If someone tells me it is I will – but I'll need a lot of training.

At the time of construction, concrete roads were permissible and met the statutory terms of the contract; however, the same interviewee continued:

We weren't very happy, but you know, they've met their requirements of the public enquiry and everything else – but now we've to pay for it being resurfaced and that'll absolutely tear apart their [the private sector contractor's] *maintenance strategy for the future – the concrete was there forever. Now we put some blacktop on top of that, which needs replacing every . . . we'll say ten years and they'll say seven – and there goes the negotiation.*

In the case of regulatory change, therefore, the Highways Agency bears the cost.

The road is also subject to a regional initiative for a driver information system, the capital cost of which is not part of the DBFO but which may have an impact on the maintenance of the road.

That's a contract that's been regionally let, but some of the works are going onto my road. The cost is not borne by myself – it's somebody else's budget, the only thing we're paying for is the maintenance. (Agency's departmental representative)

This change has not been input to the PSC and therefore over time the base case will lose its value as a comparator, reducing the usefulness of the PSC as a benchmark against which to measure VFM. The further into the contract the change takes place, however, the less difficult it becomes to cost change, because predictions of future cost have to be made for a reduced period of time.

When pricing amendments during the construction phase, the calculations were kept separate from the main contract, so that a price was agreed that did not affect the traffic parameters and the bands on which the shadow toll is calculated. It was argued, 'this would be a bit of a nightmare'. Such payments are an additional cost over and above the shadow toll. An SPV interviewee said that some likely future amendments might involve renegotiation of the toll but 'it's not a nice thing to have to do'. Such a fundamental change to the pricing of the entire project could have a significant impact on VFM.

The end-of-project handover

The actual lifetime of the road after the PFI contract is important because it will affect the eventual VFM obtained over the whole life of this project. According to the terms of the contract, towards the end of the 30-year contract, the Agency can withhold payments against the performance of necessary works, which will be agreed following a survey some five years before the contract ends. The Agency's acceptance of the road's return depends upon a final inspection of its condition. At this early stage in the project's life there is no clear plan as to how that process should be managed, although the Agency does maintain a risk register that records the relevant risks on each of its roads, which ought to provide information to guide the end-of-contract inspection. For example, a Highways Agency interviewee said:

We've got a culvert and there's aggressive ground there. You've got concrete, you've got steel and if you've got excessive sulphates in the soil it'll corrode the steel. So we've put in some electrical stuff that will repel the ions. Now that's one of the risks that will obviously affect the life of the structure. So hopefully the risk register would include that in the inspection.

The manager for this contract noted that: 'that will be an interesting time, when we come to negotiate the residual life, but there are conditions in the contract'. This is likely to be a complex process since the road and the various supporting structures may have different residual lives attached to them by the contract at the point of handover.

The Agency representative said: 'Before the road is handed back there's going to be an inspection, so I presume we're all hanging our hats on that inspection'.

In other words, although there will be an inspection prior to handover it is not clear that robust procedures have been put in place to ensure that the road is returned in good condition. Since staff involved in either the original contract negotiations or in the current phase in both the Agency and the SPV will no longer be employed at the point of handover, the wording of the contract is likely to be critical to the outcome.

Conclusion

In this section we have discussed some of the procedures for controlling and managing this contract. The nature of PFI is that many decisions have been transferred to the private sector and thus within the public sector the emphasis is on monitoring. At present, the focus is on the data collection and monitoring that surrounds traffic volumes, since these are a major driver of cost to the Agency and income to the SPV. In this area it is relatively straightforward to design an audit trail that is capable of detailed monitoring. Accurate traffic volume counting depends upon the accuracy of the loop counters and their availability, however, and changes to the monitoring of the loop-counting data are still being investigated several years after the opening of the road. Since much of this road is 'new build', currently there are relatively few issues surrounding repairs and (consequently) lane closure. Nonetheless, the interviewees indicated that where judgements need to be made about the timing of repairs or the gritting of roads there is scope for conflict, which is not easy to manage within the monitoring system. Thus the extent to which maintenance risk has been transferred is unclear. Since the contract is perceived to be operating well there is limited contingency planning in place.

RISK TRANSFER

With risk transfer being crucial to the VFM case, the Government sought, via DBFO contracts, to transfer a number of risks, including statutory procedures, protestor action, latent/inherent defects; design, construction, operation and maintenance problems; downside traffic volume; insurance and indemnity risks; and non-discriminatory legislative risk. This project has a risk register that sets out the probable risks at each

stage of the contract and this was used to determine which risks should be transferred.

In relation to the first risk, statutory risk, this project – like most of the first tranche projects – had planning permission before the contract reached financial close, and therefore the private sector did not carry any risk in relation to statutory procedures. On a later project, however, one SPV did take the project through these procedures. A number of our interviewees in both public and private sectors reported that their understanding from the sector grapevine was that this company would not do so again because uncertainty about the outcome represents too great a risk, and there may be a lack of expertise. An Agency interviewee also expressed his own opinion that this type of risk is probably too great for the private sector: 'Trying to get it through a public enquiry and ending up with nothing at the end of the day – you might get objections – you get protestor action – or maybe there is a delay and you have to look at an alternative route – it's too hard.'

Nevertheless, the Agency remains committed to the private sector's taking some of this statutory risk if the concept of construction design and innovation on the part of the private partner is to have any substantive meaning. It recognises that bidders would be unwilling to accept risk associated with large schemes at an early stage in the statutory process (Highways Agency 2003).

In relation to the second risk, protestor action, one aspect of private sector efficiency may be its ability to respond robustly to certain kinds of public activity. A story from an SPV interviewee illustrates this point.

When we were building [this project] *a chap parked a caravan on our land, and he made an illegal connection into the local grid and ditto to the water. The Highways Agency asked us to build around him. Our attitude was, 'He's parked illegally, let's get him towed away'. In the end some kind of compromise was reached. We moved the road slightly, because there was plenty of land to do it, but I mean the whole thing was ridiculous – the chap had no right to be there, he was stealing electricity and water, and here they were sort of standing back. I mean it was just crazy.*

Our raconteur indicated that the SPV would be happy to take much more of a 'hard nosed' attitude towards this kind of behaviour. An Agency interviewee disputed the feasibility of taking a more forceful attitude:

I don't see how they can. I mean the Highways Agency does get people down from trees or has dug them up from the ground. Usually we get another firm in to actually do that work. Also the DBFO will have the Highways Agency on their back to make sure they are seen to be fair, just and things like that.

This interviewee argued that SPVs are better at dealing with bricks and mortar than the interpersonal aspects of road development, and in effect acknowledged the Agency's continued role in such incidents, owing to reputational risk.

Initially, the Agency was unclear about whether private sector bidders would be prepared to accept the third type of risk, latent defects associated with existing stretches of road that the SPV would become responsible for maintaining. Consequently bidders were asked to present prices for each of three potential scenarios in which these risks were transferred, shared or retained by the Agency. Agency interviewees believed that bidders were generally very willing to accept latent defect risk, because of their previous experience of dealing with the Agency, and it is therefore likely that bidders will be expected to carry this risk in full, as opposed to sharing it, in future contracts.

This contract clearly transferred risks associated with the fourth set of risks, design, construction, operation and maintenance, so that the perspective of the Agency's departmental representative is that: 'We don't have problems where we have to, say, renew a bridge in, say, 15 years.'

Unlike many projects in other sectors, the Highways Agency does seek to transfer the fifth risk, demand risk, to the private sector, and in our case this was particularly attractive to the SPV: 'Our shareholders are interested in taking volume risk. So, for example, we don't have investments in hospitals or school buildings and so on because it doesn't provide the sort of risk share that we're interested in.'

The DBFO consortium is experienced in carrying volume risk on projects it invests in around the world and consequently: 'We think we have some understanding of how traffic grows in different circumstances and the risk is, we feel, one we understand so we're prepared to take'. This is tantamount to admitting that since traffic volumes are rising, particularly in Britain, there is little or no downside risk. The SPV uses industry-recognised models to estimate traffic volumes in order to make a bid, since the Agency does not make its own predictions known to bidders. In this project, which involved new build, the volume risk was greater than for widening or improving existing roads and for which existing volume levels are known. Since the bidders had to estimate new traffic rather than just growth rates in this case: 'It's quite possible that the various bidders had quite different traffic figures, which were probably different again from the Highways Agency'.

In Chapter 5, we presented information about the percentage of risk as a proportion of the total project cost. In relation to this project, an SPV interviewee indicated that the figures seemed improbable because the SPV had passed all the risk to the contractor.

In the [SPV] company there was no risk money at all. When I say there was no risk money I mean there was no contingency in risk. The contractor had a risk element because he was taking basically all the risk in completing the project on time, but I really doubt if his risk would be more than about ten per cent of his price.

Given that our figures are drawn from public domain information this is an interesting perspective, which we pursue further in our discussion chapter.

Although the transfer of traffic volume risk is crucial to the VFM case it is not yet clear how the costs to the Agency and the costs and income of the SPV will work through in the long run. The payment mechanism ensures that the greater the usage the greater the cost to the Agency, although the mechanism does set an upper limit on the volume-related payment. At present, traffic volumes are running ahead of expectations, but have not reached the upper limit cap. To the extent that design decisions and maintenance costs are volume related there is no reason why this mechanism should not be capable of delivering VFM. To the extent that costs are fixed and volume is greater than expected but not capped, however, the project might not achieve VFM. If volumes rise above the level of the cap then the implication for the SPV is that it receives no additional income but is likely to face higher maintenance costs, since these are correlated with volume. In this latter scenario the model is capable of producing VFM for the public sector. If this scenario causes maintenance costs to become so large in relation to income that the SPV becomes loss making or fails to carry out maintenance, then risk could revert to the Agency and the Government. Consequently although apparently demand risk has been transferred to the private sector, uncertainty over traffic volumes implies that some risk may remain with the public sector.

In relation to other types of risk there is a lack of clarity about whether risk has been transferred in fact. The Agency gave two examples, the first relating to a possible serious accident.

If the contractor does what it says in the TRRM manual, the road should operate safely. If he doesn't do that then obviously we would see that the contractor was liable. But if he does do that then the duty lies with the Highways Agency. I'm not quite certain where we lie. I mean we're their [the victims'] first port of call, and we would have to see what the contract says . . . . We'll either have to apportion blame and say you were deficient in this and therefore you need to reimburse us – for the sake of argument.

The second example relates to an actual incident at a place where the road is too high relative to the bridge. It has caused serious problems for high-sided vehicles that have led to legal action and raises issues about the additional risks posed by PFI. 'I mean, the design was down to the DBFO company, so we expect them to pay everything, but we're sort of joint defendants for some reason. Instead of going for the person who designed it they've gone for us as well because we are the statutory body'.

This highlights the fact that, although under PFI the SPV is responsible for service provision, the public agency is responsible for service delivery, a point which was also made by the NAO (2000a) in relation to problems that occurred at the Public Health Laboratory. When there are problems, the general public believes the Agency is responsible and directs any complaint or claim against it. In other words, as the NAO (1999d) noted in relation to the delays at the Passport Agency, the public agency cannot avoid political or reputational risk, and PFI may actually increase this. For example, in relation to neighbours affected by a DBFO road, complaints ought to be directed to the contractor. However, although the Agency interviewee indicated that the contractor was good at dealing with complaints, his experience was that: 'People who have a complaint – the [SPV] are very good. They do take it very very seriously, but people who live alongside the roads still feel sometimes they have to come to us because they are not getting the required response – and we have to be involved'. Such involvement clearly adds cost to the Agency.

In summary, this project involves a number of different risks. For some of these the impacts are well known and therefore the likely outcomes are capable of prediction, while for others the impacts are as yet unclear. It will be especially important, from a public accountability perspective, to monitor the impact of rising traffic volumes on costs. This will deliver evidence as to the affordability to the public sector of this and other projects with similar payment mechanisms, taking the related maintenance costs and performance of the private sector into account.

THE FINANCIAL COSTS

The financial arrangements that surround DBFO contracts introduce a number of new aspects to the provision of a roads service. First, there is an impact on the way that the Agency's budget is allocated. At present this project is experiencing more demand than was expected by the Agency but has not reached the level at which it is capped. Therefore the payment mechanism means that the Agency's costs and the SPV's revenues are running ahead of expectations. Irrespective of whether the project turns out to be VFM, to the extent that this is costing more than expected, it must affect the Agency's budget as a whole, limiting the cash available for other work. On the other hand, to the extent that higher volumes must lead to higher maintenance costs, one important aspect of PFI contracts is that these monies are ring-fenced and must be paid, thereby ensuring that the maintenance will be carried out. As the SPV interviewee explained:

The difference is, we maintain it properly, and the Highways Agency very rarely does. It's a sweeping statement but the Highways Agency, I'm afraid, suffers from not having money. Every time there's a problem with the Treasury the first place to go is the Highways Agency. You find we take over bits of the Highways Agency's road and it simply hasn't been maintained in the way that it should have been. One of the advantages of DBFOs is that the Government owes us so much money, and you know what it is used for. This is a big plus because the roads do get maintained properly, which in the long run has to be a good thing.

Secondly, although public sector procurement processes are normally intended to achieve purchase at the lowest bid price, which ought to ensure affordability, under conventional procurement this ignored the reality that it was normally possible to renegotiate the price upwards after closure.

I would argue that one of the biggest problems in government procurement is that they go for the lowest price, and they put people on the bid list that shouldn't be there . . . but the chairman knows the minister. Then because they've put in the cheapest bid they have to give them the job. Then a year or two later they're giving them 30% more. I think the PFI system is better. The contractual structure makes it much more difficult for a successful bidder to increase his price.

Although the reasons for such price inflation may be disputed, that contract price inflation occurs is not. The NAO has indicated that additional costs after financial close under traditional procurement may add on average 28% to the final cost (NAO 1988). The nature of PFI contracts, by way of contrast, is that there will be no price increases after financial close other than those specified by the contract, eg inflation, volume, and amendments to contract. Although the final costs of our case project were said to be close to the bid price, the bid price necessarily included an element for unforeseen contingencies, as the SPV interviewee acknowledged:

We really didn't have any inflation of the price. Now it's certainly true that the contractor [to the SPV] included in his bid some amounts for contingency – it certainly would not have been 25%. I'm absolutely certain of that. It might have been 10%. So I would have said at the very least there is a saving there.

One such contingency relates to the risk that the project may be delayed, which under PFI is likely to have serious effects on the contractor: 'In my experience of PFI you don't get delays because the penalties on the contractor are so great, so it's probably true that the initial price is somewhat higher' (SPV Interviewee).

This raises important financial issues since it is difficult to quantify the benefit of finishing on time and to assess this against the increase in price that the contractor demands in order to carry the risk of timely completion. Also, there appears to be no reason why similar contractual arrangements could not be used for conventionally financed projects.

Third, the view of the SPV lends another interesting perspective to the question of whether these deals are cheaper than conventional procurement and constitute VFM. An SPV interviewee argued that the private sector's interest costs and legal fees are significant and likely to be greater than if the government borrowed the money directly:

I'd have to say the comparisons that I've seen are not very clever, and they don't look in too much detail at what the concession company's costs are, and how they're built up. It's something that could be improved, but it's certainly true that the cost of doing something via a PFI is going to be significantly more expensive than it is if the government did it, if the government could do it as efficiently as the private sector, which usually they can't. But if they could, it would be much cheaper for the government because the government can borrow money at whatever the long-term loan rate is. Whereas these days we are

paying at least three maybe four per cent over . . . . On some debt we were paying seven or eight per cent over. Then [there are] the legal fees which [on this project] were a significant sum of money.

Clearly, such fees add to the cost of PFI and since these are now well recognised within the contracting industry, future contracts are likely to be less affordable as companies seek to cover these fees in the contract price. Also, there may be contracting costs associated with contract cancellation. Since the first round of projects in 1996–7, there has been relatively little interest in DBFOs, as evidenced by the number of contracts signed or under consideration, and a number of projects for which companies were in the process of tendering bids were cancelled. The SPV interviewee said that this caused much concern in the industry in Scotland, because companies were not reimbursed for costs already incurred. 'Everybody spent a lot of money and then they got cancelled. Some people got more upset than others, particularly as we got no compensation, so I mean we just refused to bid in Scotland after that'.

The Scottish experience was in contrast to the situation in England.

We were in the middle of bidding for jobs. However, they did agree before we bid that in the event the government changed and the whole bidding process was cancelled that they would reimburse people for their bidding costs and to give them their due they did actually do that.

This interviewee described the more recent projects available for tender as 'glorified leasing deals' that downgraded volume-based payments in which his company had no interest. Nonetheless, the costs associated with these outcomes imply first that the supply of competing bids may be reduced in the future, and secondly that the reimbursed costs for failed bids provide no VFM and need to be considered in a holistic evaluation of the PFI policy.

A fourth area of interest surrounds maintenance costs that the NAO and PAC have investigated (NAO 2003c, PAC 2003c). The PAC (2003c, para. 13) noted that unit costs of maintenance work of all the Highways Agency's roads that are maintained by the private sector on long-term contracts have risen substantially in recent years, from £34 per square metre in 1997/8 to £42 per square metre in 2000/1, an increase of 24% in real terms. This is contrary to the notion that private sector efficiency would reduce costs, but the Highways Agency told the PAC that it had contracted for quality not cost. The SPV interviewee was unfamiliar with this report but argued that this is likely to be a consequence of conducting maintenance properly, because: 'Ultimately maintenance comes back to haunt you if you don't do it and you know the reason the infrastructure in this country is in such a mess is because this sort of money hasn't been spent in the past'.

Similarly, the Agency representative on this project was not able to relate to the £42 cost per square metre for maintenance quoted by PAC, because the payment he authorises represents a combined payment to cover capital and maintenance costs: 'I can't relate to a cost per square metre. We're paying tolls and they're also paying off the capital costs. We have an idea what it costs to maintain the road, but we don't split the payment . . . . I'm sure it can be done'.

In response to a question about the split between contract costs for construction and operation, another Agency interviewee indicated that in the contract the Agency had agreed not to release any commercially confidential information, and that it would not separate out the different contracts: 'That's one of the promises we made . . . . If we did give figures it would be a package'. This commercial and political sensitivity makes it difficult for external interests to form an opinion on VFM, but may also have an impact on the ability of government agencies such as the NAO to report publicly on specific areas of concern. An

interviewee indicated that the Agency does check the accounts of the SPV each year and a short report is made available on these to the Agency representative, but admitted 'Whether it [the SPV] is making a profit or not doesn't really affect us – well, I mean it will affect us ultimately'.

This appears to be the crux of the regional Agency's assessment of this project. Providing the SPV maintains the road to the contractual standards and in accordance with the TRRM, the project is perceived as successful. Any costs or indeed benefits associated with the payment mechanism fall on the remainder of the Agency's budget. In other words, 'success' at an operational level is viewed independently of the financial costs.

The representative in the Highways Agency's head office was very satisfied with the way that DBFOs were working and the efficiencies that had been achieved. Although he believed that, under DBFO, expenditure is predictable and largely in line with expectations, he opined that if a financial review were undertaken, it was very likely that DBFO would turn out to be a more expensive way of doing things. He acknowledged that the reduction in the Treasury's test discount rate from 8% to 6% in 1997 made it more difficult to demonstrate that DBFOs delivered VFM (HM Treasury 2003a). This has now been exacerbated by the further reduction to 3.5%.

SUMMARY AND CONCLUSIONS

The Highways Agency awarded four projects during the first quarter of 1996 and an additional four projects between May and October of the same year, and we have examined one of those projects as our case project.

In terms of the policy and project objectives, the road was built to budget and slightly ahead of schedule. Since the contract included heavy penalties for late delivery of the road, it is not a surprise that it was delivered on time. Although there was some innovation during the construction phase, this was only to ensure faster completion not to reduce future maintenance costs. Its efficacy can only be assessed later in the project. There was little evidence of innovation in operation and maintenance. In relation to the other softer objectives, there is a lack of quantifiable information, or they have not been evaluated, or it is too soon to know whether they have been achieved.

We found that although this system is described as operating effectively, it is not without problems. For example, the vehicle-counting equipment is not always functional and there is very limited random monitoring. The standard of service, about which there are currently generally favourable reports, relates to a project which involves substantial new construction in an environment where there are agreed and well recognised and understood industry standards. Any issues of conflict reported to us refer to instances where judgement may vary between the relevant negotiators, and such situations may be expected to increase as the road ages. In addition, performance measurement is sometimes measured in terms of response time to solve problems, rather than directly in relation to the underlying quality of performance. Such an approach generates the possibility of reputational risk to the Agency. Both these issues suggest the need for future research. The Highways Agency is reluctant to make deductions for poor performance and few penalties have been incurred. The SPV's bank arguably has a more crucial role in enforcing service standards, since it must be informed of any penalties incurred. Taken together, it is unclear how the payment mechanism provides incentives for the SPV.

Good quality procedures for enabling amendments to contracts are essential in an industry where technical specifications and standards are continually improving and changing. The financial settlements that surround such changes have been described as difficult in practice and in future should such changes involve amendments to the toll, as agreed in the original contract, the complications are likely to increase. Similarly, it appears that it would be very difficult in practice for the Highways Agency to terminate its contract with the SPV or its contractors, or indeed for the SPV to terminate its contract with its main contractors.

Despite the fact that the project is perceived as an operational success, it is perhaps surprising that there is no clear contingency plan in the event that the private sector organisations should fail. Similarly, although it is still in the distant future, there appears to be limited understanding of how the handover phase will be controlled and it is unclear that robust procedures are in place.

Projects in this sector differ from many other sectors in that the intention is to transfer demand risk to the private sector, with the payment mechanism closely linked to demand. Since traffic flows have increased, payments based on shadow tolls have risen and have not yet reached their cap. Thus, the payment mechanism, far from transferring risks, has created additional costs for the Highways Agency. In relation to other risks that the Agency had sought to transfer, the effects of some of them are known or quantifiable but others are unclear.

Several further points should be made about the cost of DBFO. Although this contract and DBFO in general are perceived as 'successful', this operational success is viewed independently of the financial costs. The SPV acknowledges that financing costs are typically three to eight percentage points more than public sector borrowing costs. How all these additional costs affect the Highways Agency's budget and its other activities is unclear.

Finally, although it is too early to determine the whole-life costs of this project, PFI has introduced some predictability into project costing in relation to the design and construction phases, but there is no reason why similar incentives could not operate under traditional procurement routes. Under PFI, the payment mechanism means that road maintenance is assured. This means that more money may be spent on the maintenance of PFI roads than non-PFI roads, thereby distorting national priorities. It is important to recognise also that there are additional costs within the system, in both the public and private sectors, that would not occur under conventional funding routes.

Our analysis of the cost of PFI suggests that the emphasis on expected VFM may be misplaced. . . . At the very least, the experience of PFI does not sit comfortably with the general aim of controlling public expenditure.

This chapter presents a sectoral analysis of PFI for new builds in the acute hospital sector. It is organised in several sections. The first explains the origins, development, scope and objectives of PFI in the context of hospitals. The second section reviews the research literature, official reports and other commentaries as they relate to the evaluation of PFI in hospitals, and the NHS's response. The third section presents the publicly available financial information as it relates to the way PFI operates in hospitals, its costs, VFM, risk transfer and accountability, based on official publications and the trusts' and the private sector's annual reports and accounts.

HISTORY AND DEVELOPMENT OF PFI IN HOSPITALS

The use of private finance in hospitals marked a complete change in hospital financing. Since the inception of the NHS in 1948, hospital building had been financed by central government grants and funded out of general taxation and national insurance contributions, occasionally supplemented by private endowments and fund raising for specialist facilities such as children's services and equipment. There was little hospital building until the 1960s as investment in public services focused on housing and education. Only one third of the 1962 hospital plan for 224 schemes was implemented before public investment was curtailed in 1976. Between 1980 and 1997, only seven public schemes costing more than £25 m were completed (House of Commons 1997), leaving the NHS with an outmoded and worn-out estate, a significant part of which predated the First World War, and a backlog of maintenance. However, it should be noted that although hospitals were built with public finance, after 1973 regional health authorities were allowed for the first time to use the proceeds from land sales for investment, and land sales became an increasingly important source of capital funding, masking the decline in new funding for investment (Meara 1991). In other words, NHS capital expenditure

was, to some extent at least, self-financed.

The first hospital to be built with a significant private contribution in recent times was the Guy's Hospital Phase III Development. The private partners were not the commercial sector but charities and other public sector agencies that would use the facilities. When the scheme was signed in 1986, the intention was that the non-NHS partners would provide 45% (£16 m) of the total £35.5 m costs. However, costs soared to £152 m. This was due to the failure to freeze the design and significant subsequent design changes, changes in statutory requirements and building regulations, a new liability for VAT, inflation, delays to the building works, a large number of disputes and claims associated with the construction works, changes to the design team's fee rates, and the insolvency of works package contractors (NAO 1998b). The partners failed to maintain their contributions in line with the overall escalation in costs and the NHS was forced to foot the bill. Ironically, the cost escalation in this innovatory scheme was used to criticise the NHS's cost containment and justify the turn to private finance in health.

With the introduction of PFI in 1992, the newly established hospital trusts were required to find a commercial partner to design, build, finance and operate the non-clinical services, if they wished to replace or enhance their buildings and equipment. Although there are many similarities with DBFO in roads, one of the first private finance programmes to get off the ground, there are also some differences. In effect, instead of commissioning their own hospital, the trusts would lease their new or refurbished facilities for 30 years. In return, they would pay a two-part annual fee to the private company, usually a consortium made up of finance, construction and facilities management companies and known as a special purpose vehicle (SPV), which provides the hospital and non-clinical services. First, there would be an availability fee for the capital element or rental charge and secondly, a service charge for the facilities management. The charges would be linked to performance to provide incentives for the SPV. Should some services become unavailable or fall below the level stipulated in the contract, then the payment would be reduced, although usually not below the level needed to service the SPV's debt. Although the capital element was new, the service element of PFI represented an extension of the compulsory contracting out of manual services to a wider range of clinical and, in some cases, non-clinical-related services, and thus could be construed as an operating lease. Hence, PFI functions as both a finance and an operating lease. At the end of the 30-year contract period, the hospital would either revert to the trust or the contract could be renewed.

The move to PFI followed a change in the hospitals' financial regime. Under the 1990 Health and Community Care Act, the trusts were required to pay for the cost of capital by means of what became known as the capital charging regime. It became a statutory obligation for the trusts to make a surplus of their income over expenditure, including a charge for depreciation, equal to a 6% return on their assets, valued at current replacement cost. The 6% on past capital was repayable to the government in the form of Public Dividend Capital (PDC), equivalent to the government's equity stake and interest-bearing debt. This meant that trusts had an incentive to move to leasing, since this moved assets off the balance sheet and hence reduced capital charges, and provided, all other things being equal, a revenue stream for the availability fee.

Although the Conservative Government was keen to extend the use of private finance to the health sector, PFI proved slow to take hold, in part at least because it was not clear that the NHS hospital trusts had the legal power to enter into such contracts. Furthermore, whereas for roads the purchaser was central government, the trusts did not have a proven financial

track record. Indeed, within a few years of moving from being directly managed by the NHS, many had financial deficits (Shaoul 1998). In 1997, the incoming Labour Government resuscitated the policy and got PFI hospital projects off the ground by removing the requirement for universal testing of all capital projects for their 'PFI-ability' and by prioritising projects. The NHS (Private Finance) Act 1997 helped to persuade potential bidders and the financial backers that NHS trusts not only had the power to enter into such contracts, but that the payments to the consortia were in effect underwritten in the event of a financial crisis within the trust. Additional funds were provided in some cases to make the plans affordable. Ten PFI schemes in the first round were awarded subsidies totalling £7.3 m for the first year, under a smoothing mechanism intended to reconcile the different pattern of costs that emerge from a contract period of 30 years under a PFI deal (during which the private sector expected to recover its costs) and the normal accounting life of an NHS hospital of 60 years (Gaffney and Pollock 1997).

Following these measures, the Labour Government approved several waves of large hospital projects under PFI. It signed the first health PFI contract in 1997 and the first PFI hospitals were completed in autumn 2000. By May 2001 six projects with a capital value of £423 m were in operation and a further 17 schemes with a value of £1.6 billion were under construction (Audit Commission 2001). Since 1997, some 85% of the NHS capital investment projects have been financed under the PFI, with a focus on larger new-build investments (Sussex 2003). The National Audit Office (NAO 2003d) reported that in the year ending March 2002, there were 102 NHS trusts in England with PFI schemes including community, mental health and ambulance trusts as well as acute and specialist hospital trusts. Ninety-five NHS trusts reported off balance sheet schemes with an estimated capital value of £3.6 billion, while seven trusts reported on balance sheet schemes with a capital value of £185 m (NAO

2003d). By December 2002, 25 large hospital schemes had reached financial close. By November 2003, there were 49 signed hospital PFI schemes in England with an individual cost of more than £15 m, the total cost of which was some £3.4 billion (PPP Forum 2003c). The PFI hospital programme is now routinely described as 'the largest building programme in the history of the NHS'.

If this is confusing it is because collecting data on Department of Health annual capital expenditure, both for PFI and for non-PFI projects, is not straightforward. Data are provided for England not the UK. There is no longer a clear statement setting out the annual capital expenditure. Instead, it is aggregated in ways that make a clear summary of capital spend on a consistent

12-monthly basis impossible to compile. HM Treasury's list of PFI projects shows a complete listing, noting the date of financial close and the capital value, without recording any construction dates. The Department of Health shows a running total of major projects, both PFI and publicly funded (see Table 7.1), but again it is not possible to disaggregate this on the basis of annual spend. More helpfully, the DTI Construction Statistics and its predecessors show live construction projects over a number of years (Table 7.2 on page 138), although there is some overlap in the figures from year to year as some large projects may take more than one year to complete. Over the years, the amounts shown for specific major PFI projects vary, owing to changes in the contract value, again making it difficult to draw sensible conclusions about the total capital spend.

Table 7.1: Capital schemes (over £10 m) approved – May 1997 to December 2003

	Number	Capital value (£m)	Capital value as % of total
PFI schemes			
PFI schemes which are complete and operational	21	1,527	
PFI schemes in negotiation but not yet reached financial close:			
2nd wave schemes prioritised	3	1,692	
3rd wave schemes prioritised	4	682	
4th, 5th and 6th wave schemes which have placed OJEC adverts	18	2,957	
4th, 5th and 6th wave schemes which have not yet placed OJEC adverts	12	2,758	
Total PFI	**64**	**11,008**	**84%**
Non-PFI schemes			
Publicly funded schemes which are complete	3	132	
Publicly funded schemes with work started on site	1	50	
Total non-PFI	**4**	**182**	**16%**
Total capital investment given go ahead	**68**	**11,190**	

Source: DoH (2004).

In short, although it is difficult to get precise figures on the total spend on PFI in hospitals, it is clear that significantly more than half of all capital expenditure on schemes with a value greater than £2.5 m is being financed under PFI and this is increasing. Secondly, PFI is also being widely used in other parts of the NHS: in primary care, community and mental health hospitals and ambulance trusts.

The evaluative literature

We first review briefly the main findings of the appraisal literature in the health sector as it relates to the anticipated VFM, since it provides pointers to the kinds of issues relevant to evaluation. We then consider such literature as exists on the implementation phase, VFM, risk transfer or the procedures for managing risk transfer and accountability. The literature relating to PFI in hospitals and its evaluation derives from several sources: official reports, research papers and commercial consultants. We consider each in turn.

Appraisal literature

Prior to the new builds for hospitals, the full business cases (FBCs) to support PFI projects were not placed in the public domain. Indeed, it has been only in the case of health and education that the FBCs have entered the

Table 7.2: Department of Health PFI and non-PFI building construction projects

Live schemes of capital value	PFI		Non-PFI	
Year	Number	Capital value £m	Number	Capital value £m
Nov 1995 > £1 m	16 schemes published in OJEC	723	108	765
June 1996 > £1 m	150 schemes between OBC and FBC	2,188	69	496
June 1997 > £1 m	98 schemes between OBC and FBC	2,028	37	515
March 1999 > £1 m	26	1,080	34	560
March 2000 > £2.5 m	31	1,542	33	534
March 2001 > £2.5 m	43	1,812	46	489
March 2002 > £2.5 m	48	1,982	50	667
March 2003 > £2.5 m	31	1,604	72	1,126

Sources:

DoE (1995, 1996, 1997); DETR (1998, 1999, 2000); DTI (2001, 2002).

Notes

1. 1995–97 data relate to all schemes in progress.

2. From 1999 onwards, data relate only to projects in the course of construction and therefore some projects will appear in several years.

public domain, and even then only in particular instances and after financial close. This information is limited, however, by the fact that other supporting information and the contracts are not released. These limitations notwithstanding, PFI hospitals were particularly important because the publication of their FBCs made it possible for the first time for researchers to examine systematically the financial case and wider issues raised by PFI. In other words, the policy has been subject to detailed scrutiny only after deals were signed, rather than before, and in the context of specific projects rather than that of the policy or programme for the country as a whole.

Following the release of the FBCs, there have been a number of empirical studies examining the anticipated VFM in specific hospital projects (Gaffney and Pollock 1999a; Price et al. 1999; Pollock et al. 2000) and in the health service (Hodges and Mellett 1999; Gaffney and Pollock 1999b; Gaffney et al. 1999a, 1999b, 1999c; Sussex 2001). For three PFI new hospital schemes for which information about the cash costs were available (Gaffney and Pollock 1999a; Price et al. 1999; Pollock et al. 2000), the cost of raising finance averaged 30% of construction costs.

These financing costs are costs that conventional public procurement does not incur, or at least not to the same degree, for several reasons. First, there is the higher cost of private finance that is likely to be four or five percentage points higher than the rate for public finance under Treasury gilts. Secondly, the amount of capital to be raised through loans or equity under PFI is inflated by financing charges that include the not inconsiderable professional fees and the 'rolled up interest' derived from the construction period before the trusts begin their payments. Finally, there are the transaction costs associated with preparing the bid and contract negotiations, typically running into millions.

Pollock et al. (2002) show that, in every case, the Net Present Cost (NPC) of a publicly funded hospital was

lower than a PFI one before risk transfer was included in the VFM analysis. It was only after including risk transfer that the NPC of PFI hospitals was lower than the PSC. In other words, the VFM case rested upon risk transfer. The advantage, however, was only marginal. Although most projects seemed to value risk transfer at around 30–35% of construction costs, there was a wide variation in the discounted value of the risk transfer, ranging from 17% to nearly 70% of construction costs. Given that most risk is construction risk and the projects all involved new hospital builds, it was difficult to see why they should vary so much unless the high-risk hospitals were taking on very different, costly and inappropriate risks, such as demand and political risks. At the very least, this suggested that the risk assessment methodology was somewhat arbitrary. It was difficult to avoid the conclusion that the value of the risk transfer had been deliberately calculated in such a way as to close the gap between the PSC and PFI. From the perspective of a study concerned with VFM in the operational period, this means that the VFM case rests upon evidence of actual risk transfer. The absence of real risk transfer in practice would mean that the trusts have paid a higher price to little effect.

These studies question the economic case for PFI and whether the projects demonstrated VFM compared with conventional procurement, and raise other issues of concern, particularly their affordability. The latter issue has largely been ignored both in the appraisal process and in the wider public debate. They noted that the high cost of PFI meant that the first wave of PFI hospitals were smaller than the ones they replaced as trusts adjusted their plans downwards. The affordability gap was further reduced by subsidies from the Department of Health, land sales, a shift of resources from within the local healthcare economy to the PFI hospital, and 'challenging performance targets' for the trusts' reduced staff complement. Thus, PFI also comes at the expense of capacity and access to healthcare treatment. Froud and Shaoul (2001) question both the process of appraisal and the interpretation of the full business cases used to support the VFM case for the procurement of new hospitals under PFI. Shaoul (2005) raises questions about the validity of the VFM methodology and shows empirically that it is a far from neutral technique: it serves as a mechanism for legitimising the higher cost of PFI. All this suggests that the emphasis on relative VFM may be misplaced. This, plus the increasing emphasis on PFI in health, makes it all the more important to assess whether the operation of PFI can or does deliver VFM.

Official reports
Of the 20 or so reports produced by the National Audit Office on the anticipated VFM case, two have considered specific hospital projects, the Dartford and Gravesham and the West Middlesex University hospitals (NAO 1999b, 2002f).

In relation to the Dartford and Gravesham Hospital, the NAO (1999b) found that the estimated non-financial benefits were likely to be greater than under traditional procurement, but there was uncertainty as to the level of savings. Indeed, there might be no savings, as a miscalculation in the PSC had overstated estimated savings by £12.1 m and sensitivity analysis indicated that a 10% reduction in costs in real terms would lead to PFI being more expensive than traditional public procurement. The NAO reported that despite the extra financial support of £4 m a year required to pay for the scheme, the Health Authority and the NHS Executive were satisfied that the scheme still remained good VFM. The NAO did not comment on their optimism or itself explicitly draw any conclusions about the overall VFM of the project based upon its own work. The PAC, on the other hand, was rather more critical than the NAO and said in relation to the affordability issue that it was 'not convinced' that the use of public finance had been considered as a serious option for Dartford and Gravesham (PAC 2000c). The NAO recommended that the following issues should be better addressed: flexibility in long-term service planning; the

consideration of affordability of schemes within the context of the overall local healthcare strategy; and the rigorous review of calculations and procedures to reduce bidding costs. Subsequently, the NHS Executive and the Treasury amended their guidance relating to PFI and a new standard PFI contract was developed.

Three years later the NAO (2002f) examined the redevelopment of the West Middlesex University Hospital in the context of reporting on how the findings from Dartford and Gravesham had been applied and how VFM was established in this case. It found that the trust had run an effective procurement, using the new guidance including the new standard contract. The bidding competition had been effective and included a faster bidding process. Once again the financial comparison was 'not clear-cut', however, with the size of the risk adjustment in the PSC being crucial. In the end the trust lengthened the contract to 35 years in order to keep the annual cost down to an affordable level. The trust went ahead with the deal on the grounds that the unquantifiable benefits (price certainty, incentives for service delivery and transfer of responsibility for assets) of doing the project as a PFI outweighed the disadvantages. The NAO recommended that this broader approach to VFM should be taken in all PFI cases. In other words, the Government's criterion for establishing the superiority of PFI versus the PSC was not sustainable and should be replaced. The NAO did not draw out the implications of this for the policy as a whole. It concluded that the deal was affordable provided that running cost savings were achieved.

The West Middlesex report also identified some points relevant to post-project evaluation. The payment mechanism incorporated incentives to ensure that Bywest, the SPV, provided services as agreed in the contract. For example, if an operating theatre were unavailable for 24 hours on a weekday there would be a deduction of approximately £1,400 (NAO 2002f, p. 20). The contract also contained safeguards to control the rate of return Bywest could make in relation to contract variations. In addition, net savings of £1.6 m from the running costs of the trust were required, arising from the increased efficiency of the new building design and a reduction in the duplication of administration created by a fragmented site layout. The range of these issues demonstrates the level of complexity in evaluating PFI projects as it is very difficult to obtain the necessary figures to assess what cost savings are being achieved.

The NAO's and PAC's reports on the construction performance of all projects completed by summer 2002, including 11 NHS hospitals (NAO 2003b, PAC 2003d), showed that hospitals, along with other assets such as roads and prisons, were now being delivered early or at least on time, to budget and specification. They did not, however, carry out a survey of users' opinions of the buildings, something that the Audit Commission (2001) had highlighted as an important aspect of a performance review. Certainly, in that respect, the NAO's report does not sit well with a study in which staff and patients at nine PFI hospitals were interviewed (Lister 2003). That survey noted that the hospitals were riddled with structural and design faults. There were criticisms about the poorly designed fire doors, the lack of space and ventilation at several of these hospitals, one where corridors are too narrow for more than one trolley, and another where the plumbing was so bad that the pathology laboratory was flooded with raw sewage (Lister 2003).

It is important when considering the speed of project implementation to consider evidence about the total delivery time. The performance measures above suggesting a PFI success story measure the time only from financial close to implementation. This needs to be linked to the time taken for the PFI selection/bidding and contract negotiation process, which takes months, or even years – longer than that for Exchequer-financed schemes. Meara (1997) argues that for each of five

major London hospital PFI schemes the PFI procurement procedures added two years to the process.

Significantly, the NAO (2003b) indicated that it was not able to judge whether these projects could have achieved these results using a different procurement route. Indeed, Sussex (2003) quotes a memorandum from the NHS Executive to the PAC about improvements in performance of conventionally funded NHS projects:

The overall performance of the NHS [on major capital projects] *has shown a long-term improvement. The three-year moving average for 1988–91 showed a time over-run of 14 per cent and a cost overrun of 13 per cent. The figures have steadily declined to about 8 percent and 7 per cent respectively.* (Public Accounts Committee 1999c)

He went on to argue that certain risks, such as those related to construction time overruns and availability, could in principle be transferred under a publicly financed design, build and operate contract.

There is, however, another perspective on the success of the construction phase and the emphasis on building to time and budget. The Commission for Architecture and the Built Environment has argued that the design standard of the first wave of PFI hospitals does not match the high aspirations of the building programme (letter to the *Financial Times* 26 November 2003). Although the design quality in the second wave was improving, this was still problematic. The Commission believed that many designs failed to consider the long-term implications of better environments on healthcare needs. There was an over-emphasis on construction time and budget at the expense of design quality, despite the evidence that good design aids patient recovery and saves on hospital operational costs across their building lifespans. Similarly, the Building Futures Group (Worthington 2002) argues that the 70-plus hospitals being built under the PFI could become obsolete long before the contracts expire, yet the NHS would have to continue paying for them. More immediately, if there were medical or technological advances or shifts in demand/need, changes in the infrastructure and service provision would be required. A recent review of the Government's health policy over the last five years makes a similar point when it concludes that the Government: 'has rushed into a massive building programme without any collective or central reflection as to precisely what type of facilities it ought to be investing in' (Appleby and Coote 2002).

As noted in Chapter 5, the VFM case largely rests upon risk transfer, the main component being the cost and time overrun on construction. The NAO and PAC reports raised two issues in relation to risk transfer. First, the PAC was concerned that construction companies may be earning over twice the rate of profit for construction services compared with what they earn on conventional projects, and called for more thought to be given to the most appropriate measures for monitoring returns of private sector participants in PFI projects (PAC 2003d). The available information on the level of rewards to construction companies from PFI work is limited and rather mixed (NAO 2003b), leaving unanswered questions about whether VFM really exists, ie whether the cost of building to time and budget is worth the additional cost.

There is no legal requirement to disclose information on separate contracts in published financial statements, so construction companies typically supply very little. The PAC (2003d) Supplementary memorandum supplied by the NAO) asked the NAO if it was possible to identify the amount of capital employed by building contractors and their rates of return. The NAO was able to supply detailed figures only for Balfour Beatty, which appeared to show 'a substantially higher profit margin on PFI work compared to all business carried out (in 2002 an operating profit margin of PFI business of 50% compared to 4.3% on all business)'.

Secondly, the PAC was particularly concerned that the inevitable changes to the service element of the contract in future years would not yield the VFM achieved under the initial competitive pressure. The PAC noted that the public sector frequently makes changes or additions to facilities within a few years of letting the PFI contract, with the NAO stating that one in five public authorities do this. As the work relating to these changes and additions may be given to the existing service providers, there is a risk that VFM may be lessened, unless market testing or benchmarking is carried out. The NAO estimated that benchmarking had taken place in fewer than half the cases it examined (NAO 2003b, para. 7). The Audit Commission (2001) reported, however, that market testing was common and the OGC's 2002 guidance does require benchmarking of any additional works.

Hospitals must monitor the operational services in order to ensure that the service stipulated in the contract is being provided. The NAO has not yet reported on operational performance of PFI in hospitals for, as noted earlier, the first schemes have not been operational for long enough to make a worthwhile study. Evidence on monitoring of performance therefore exists only as snippets across a wide range of sources. Trusts have criticised the performance of some contractors. For example, at the Queen Elizabeth Hospital, Woolwich, there were teething problems with catering and portering, and a need for more initial training (PPP Forum 2003a). Carlisle reported teething problems with cleaning and: 'some weaknesses in the Contract particularly in relation to the Payment Mechanism, service performance penalties and operational costs that affect all parties.' (Health Committee 2002, Appendix 6).

South Manchester reported continuing problems with support services not delivering agreed quality standards (Health Committee, 2002, Memorandum PS 52). This memorandum further argued that management had found it hard to apply the concession agreement to ensure that problems were put right and significant management time, contrary to expectation, was still being still spent on monitoring performance.

The Audit Commission (2001) reviewed ten completed schemes in local government and health. Although it neither endorsed the PFI nor examined the underlying fundamental assumptions, it made some useful points. First, there was the excessive amount of senior management time spent on the PFI procurement process because of its complexity, leading to adverse but largely uncosted effects on existing services, with 'client-side' resources consistently underestimated. Secondly, the specification of long-term service requirements was found to be problematic, particularly in relation to the operation of long-lived assets. The lack of certainty regarding delivery of health and social services made planning particularly difficult. Thirdly, it found that good practice to ensure continuing VFM allowed for a review of 'soft' services such as cleaning, catering, etc and one-off contractual amendments. Fourthly, although there were some good examples of continuous service improvement through the use of challenging performance targets, there was not enough sharing of experience and learning from early schemes among project managers. In addition, for these early schemes, external audit was used in the scheme review, but some project managers had a poor perception of the quality of such external audit. The report found that local government, with its established Best Value reviews, was ahead of the NHS in terms of performance management.

Research literature

As yet there is very little systematic research evidence in the UK relating to post-implementation experience in hospitals from sources other than the National Audit Office and Select Committees of the House of Commons. Such research that is available is inconclusive and notes both the difficulty in isolating the effects of PFI from other simultaneous changes and the lack of appropriate comparative data.

Sussex (2003) reviews the literature to compare the costs and benefits of PFI and conventional public financing in the public hospital sector. He finds that PFI may or may not offer design improvements and lower construction costs; probably does not lead to more cost-effective support services; may involve higher costs of borrowing, even after accounting for risk; and will probably lead to more projects being completed on time and better maintained hospitals. He concludes that the overall advantage of PFI procurement is unclear.

In their case study of a PFI hospital, Grimshaw et al. (2002) show that it is difficult to disentangle PFI cost savings from savings associated with the simultaneous closure of one of the hospitals that is part of the trust. The absence of prior measures of productivity and performance, difficulties in ensuring equivalence between the specification of tasks in the formal contract and the actual tasks undertaken, and incomplete provision of information on the invoices presented for payment make evaluation difficult if not impossible. They argue that a large part of the savings have come from reductions in labour costs. Similarly McKendrick and McCabe (1997), in their study of a Community Hospital in Scotland, note that there had been no PSC against which to compare the expected benefits of PFI. They question whether the alleged operational efficiency of the PFI project came from the concentration of services on one site, an option which had not been available to the public sector, rather than the use of the PFI. In addition, Pilling (2002) found it difficult to construct the PSC to take account of technology refreshment, the cost of which is unpredictable.

Broadbent et al. (2003) has studied eight post-project evaluation systems in trusts and reports that they concentrated on the design and working of the facilities management (FM) systems, which in the case of Dartford and Gravesham accounted for only 43% of the transferred risk. Such systems are silent on the remaining 57% of risks. Fifty per cent of these related to design and construction, where typically there were difficulties over handover arrangements and signing off, situations occurring before the FM systems commence. The FM systems focus on the performance of 'soft' facilities, and do not monitor shared non-quantified risks such as contract renewal, the likelihood of SPV corruption or hospital obsolescence. They conclude that post-project evaluation systems are very limited in scope and it is 'extraordinarily difficult' for a trust to make availability deductions; rather, the trusts use the systems more as 'symbolic threats'. They recommend that post-project evaluations should be largely proactive in nature, should incorporate non-financial as well as financial aspects, and should relate to PFI issues only.

Although the evidence from the UK is limited, Australia embarked upon the private management of hospitals somewhat earlier than the UK and can provide some insights. Again, as in the UK, there is no systematic evidence across the sector and such as there is largely derives from official reports, which have been critical. Indeed, Australia's experience with the private management of public hospitals has been so fraught with problems that a Committee of the Australian Parliament recommended that: 'No further privatisation of public hospitals should occur until a thorough national investigation is conducted and that some advantage for patients can be demonstrated for this mode of delivery of services' (Senate Community Affairs References Committee 2000).

The state of Victoria, Australia, was one of the first public agencies to consider the use of a form of PFI for new hospital building. Its experience is instructive. The first hospital, La Trobe Regional Hospital, had to be taken into public ownership at substantial cost within a few years of opening, after the company made huge losses largely due to incorrect cost estimates. The second, Mildura Hospital, required increased annual payments to prevent the private operator from making losses. As a result of these experiences, Victoria

abandoned the attempt to seek a private operator for a third project, the Mercy Hospital in Melbourne. Similarly, in South Australia, the state Government was forced to amend its contract for Modbury Hospital so as to increase its payments to Healthscope Ltd, the contractor, and ensure that the company could continue the contract. Despite these additional payments, the Australian Nurses Federation expressed concern about the level of services provided, as emergency services had been reduced to save money (Senate Community Affairs References Committee 2000).

In 1997, the Western Australian Auditor General, in its report on a contract between the state government and a private company to manage the Joondalup Public Hospital, found serious limitations in the quality standards employed within the contract (Auditor General Western Australia 1997). Not only might the contract not deliver the required quality of services, the private company could limit the quantity of services provided if it was in its commercial interests to do so, discharge patients early to minimise operational costs, and increase its own payments from the state government by 'coding up' the treatments. In relation to risk transfer, the Auditor General believed that far from transferring risk to the private sector, the contract had created extra risks, including limited financial control over the quality of services; financial incentives for the company to influence admission, treatment and discharge patterns; and potential overpayments because of incorrect coding of treatments.

In New South Wales, the State Auditor General was highly critical of the BOO (build, operate and own) contract to run the Port Macquarie Base Hospital, questioning the capacity of government to negotiate acceptably balanced deals with the private sector. His report criticised the financial arrangements that ensured that the state paid for the cost of capital construction twice over through an annual availability fee and the set fee for service payments, thereby paying A$143.6 m through this service charge (New South Wales

Auditor General 1996). Collyer (2001) cites a newspaper report based on figures published by the Department of Health that showed that it was costing 30% more to run Port Macquarie than its own public hospitals.

In short, there is very little evidence in the academic literature about the post-implementation phase of hospital projects in the UK and such as exists is inconclusive. In Australia, where similar arrangements to PFI exist, these have proved problematic. Although there may be more positive experience in Australia to report, this has not come to our attention.

Commercial reports
There are two additional sources of reports on PFI, the credit ratings agencies and the PFI corporate press. We consider each in turn.

The credit ratings agency, Standard and Poor's (2003), provides a useful assessment of PFI in general and hospital PFI projects in particular. It has rated and assessed more than 30 PFI projects, including eight hospital projects, from the standpoint of investors and the capital markets. Its key ratings factors include credit rating of the public body, construction risk, contractual and revenue structure, operating risk, financial structure and legal issues.

First, it notes that since NHS trusts are independent bodies, the Secretary of State for Health, unlike the Secretary of State for Transport, will not guarantee the performance of the contracts, and hence NHS trusts are not AAA rated government-guaranteed debt. Although the underlying projects have been rated at BBB+, they have received AAA ratings on the basis of insurance wrapping. This is because, as Standard and Poor's recognises, high levels of direct and indirect government support and control mean that the trusts' poor creditworthiness is not a problem in practice.

Secondly, although in general PFI construction risk is low compared with other infrastructure projects,

hospitals tend to be more complex than office accommodation projects. Nevertheless, all rated PFI projects have been built to time or early and within budget. Indeed, the Carlisle project finished six weeks ahead of schedule.

Thirdly, hospital PFI projects lack volume and market risk, with PFI revenue largely based on the asset being available for use. Standard and Poor's notes that availability income has been very stable thus far. Although Carlisle PFI hospital has suffered three unavailability incidents, only one led to a deduction and that was less than £100. Other rated projects have not suffered any deductions.

Fourthly, in the context of performance risk during the operational phase when payment streams are dependent on performance reaching agreed service levels, a risk held by the service provider, Standard and Poor's notes that the performance monitoring regimes are generally complex and untested. Many are too complex to be applied effectively and their subjectivity could lead to disputes. Consequently, the reality has been that there have been few deductions thus far. Standard and Poor's reports that even in the case of Carlisle Hospital (where there have been well publicised difficulties), despite disagreements in 2000 over catering services creating difficulties for the SPV, there were no deductions for poor service, as there was a ramp-up period before the penalty regime took effect. In areas of soft-cost risk such as cleaning and catering, benchmarking around years five to seven is likely to lead to an increase in the service element of the PFI tariff, thereby cushioning the SPV and mitigating risk. The most important risks are likely to be in the hard services, such as maintenance, that will be necessary half way through the contract, since this element of the tariff is fixed. Only then will it be clear whether in fact the original estimates and reserves were accurate.

Standard and Poor's believes that the PFI market will grow and undergo further innovation, including a greater operational role in core services and a corresponding increase in risk. This is likely to be mitigated in ways that ensure that most projects remain investment grade, because if ratings were to fall below investment grade, this would push up finances charges and thus the cost to the public purse.

Standard and Poor's therefore concludes that PFI projects provide a relatively stable income stream and limited operational risks. The above-mentioned factors plus the ability of the SPVs to structure the deal in ways that push risk down to the subcontractors mean in effect that the SPVs carry little risk. Nevertheless, the high levels of debt, low debt service coverage and the single asset nature of PFI projects mean that most PFI projects fall within the low investment grade of BBB+, unless they are insurance wrapped. They warn against projects with increasingly risky services, especially those that are highly geared and over-reliant on poor subcontractors, volatile income streams and onerous performance regimes. As will be seen, however, hospital projects contain many of these characteristics.

The second source of information about the performance of PFI hospitals is derived from the PFI corporate press. *PPF Focus: Health* reported that although the design and construction of three PFI hospitals, the Norfolk and Norwich, Barnet and Chase, and Calderdale were good, the trusts suffered from a shortage of capacity that adversely affected their performance (PPF 2001). All the hospitals were operating at above desirable capacity levels, normally believed to be about 85%. This has several interrelated implications: first, service levels fall, waiting lists lengthen and income falls as the primary care trusts send patients elsewhere; and costs rise sharply because of additional PFI payments when activity rises above the contractual 'normal' level. Calderdale has had to refurbish some of its old estate that it had hoped to close. Barnet and Chase failed to achieve a single star in the star rating system, with the local PCT being

reported as saying it was considering avoiding it altogether, while Norfolk and Norwich actually dropped a star. Thus PFI has the potential to destabilise the trusts financially.

There are several implications of this literature review for the present study.

- Numerous studies question the economic case for PFI, the appraisal methodology, interpretation of the projects' full business cases, the high cost of using private finance and the implications for affordability and service provision, suggesting that the emphasis on VFM may be misplaced.

- Most of the risk transfer relates to the construction phase, which has been successful in delivering new hospitals on time and to budget. Although the system of incentives has worked, it has come at a cost and it is unclear why similar objectives could not be achieved by appropriately designed construction contracts.

- Not all the hospitals have been trouble free and concerns have been raised about their conception and design.

- The operations phase is believed to be more problematic. Given the early stage of the policy, little is known about whether the system of incentives and penalties can and will deliver in the operations and maintenance phase.

- Similar hospital projects in Australia have turned out to be more expensive than expected and in one case had to be taken back into public ownership.

The NHS's response to the official reports
Although the NHS has provided guidance on PFI procurement issues since inception (NHS Executive 1994, 1999a, 1999b), it provided limited guidance on project evaluation as the emphasis in the early years for

PFI was rather on the forecast procurement requirements. We noted above that there was patchy provision of systems of performance monitoring and benchmarking in the NHS, making it difficult to assess whether the trusts achieved VFM.

In recent years the NHS has introduced a number of procedures designed to improve performance monitoring and review across the board, for both procurement and operational performance. It has addressed the more general capital procurement issues with the development of the ProCure21 initiative (NHS 2003) described as a 'dynamic benchmarking and performance management system'. ProCure 21, launched in April 2000, has brought together the recommendations of a number of government reports, including the adoption of partnering arrangements in accordance with the Achieving Excellence in Construction initiative launched by the Treasury in 1999, and the use of benchmarking and performance management to raise standards in response to the Egan Report *Rethinking Construction* (1998) and the report *Sold on Health* (DoH 2000). The aim of these requirements was to save the cost of legal advice and tendering time. This appears to have been very successful as the *NHS Estates Annual Report and Accounts 2002/03* (NHS Estates 2003c) states that it reached its target procurement time of four years for £300 m worth of projects in just six months.

In 2002, the Department of Health issued new practical and evidence-based guidance to improve post-project evaluation with its *Learning Lessons from Post-project Evaluation* (DoH 2002a) which replaced the guidance given in the *Capital Investment Manual* (NHS Executive 1994). As the reports emanating from this process are not in the public domain, it is impossible to draw any conclusions about post-implementation performance of NHS PFI projects or even to find out whether such reviews have been carried out. Broadbent et al. (2003) criticise this guidance because it applies to all NHS capital projects, irrespective of whether they are PFI or not, and therefore does not address the features specific to PFI evaluation.

Only some of the 13 trusts in our study have carried out a post-project evaluation. We have obtained a copy of the post-project evaluation for one trust (Queen Elizabeth Hospital 2003). The fieldwork for this was carried out in mid-2002, with the report finally being issued in December 2003, thus demonstrating the long time lag with such reports. Although it followed the DoH's *Learning Lessons from Post-project Evaluation* it made two significant changes, thereby highlighting potential shortcomings of this guidance. First, following the suggestions of the trust's director of modernisation, it surveyed all trust staff rather than the 100 recommended by the guidance and it held significantly more workshops and meetings. Secondly, the consultants who compiled the report changed the format of the standard contents and headings to produce what they thought was a more readable report. A significant portion of the report concentrates on issues prior to the service phase, where the lack of guidance and previous PFI experience caused problems in the procurement, contract negotiation, construction and equipping phases, with the trust having to commit a greater level of resources than anticipated.

With regard to the services phase, there were criticisms of many aspects of the facilities management services provided by the private sector partners, including portering, catering, cleaning, security, car parking and estates management. The report states:

Although it is acknowledged that day-to-day relationships have been good there are many significant contractual and practical dimensions of the facilities service provision that attract vociferous criticism and considerable frustration amongst trust staff that there is insufficient resources or staffing to fulfil the FM function to a satisfactory standard. (Queen Elizabeth Hospital NHS Trust 2003, para. 4.7.1)

There is clearly a need for post-implementation review to be carried out on a regular basis over the life of the PFI contract. The NHS has addressed this by adopting the Gateway Process in 2003 (outlined in Chapter 2), although, given the time lag experienced on the above post-project evaluation case, it is too early as yet to see any evidence of its implementation.

Regarding the sharing of operational performance experience, NHS Estates have developed a database system for the electronic collection and provision of information and benchmarking in line with e-government principles (NHS Estates 2003a, 2003b). Its purpose is to enable information to be shared across NHS trusts, so that service and maintenance costs may be compared, and hence allow an evaluation as to whether VFM is being achieved. However, as yet there is no publicly available evidence relating to the usefulness of this system.

In summary, in recent years the NHS has expanded and standardised its systems of performance evaluation for both capital procurement and operational activities. The use of database systems accessible by all trusts suggests enhanced opportunities for benchmarking and comparative performance evaluation, while the greater standardisation and increased requirements for post-project evaluation mean that more analysis should be taking place that would also aid cross-project learning. From the public perspective, as very little information is in the public domain, it is not possible to assess in any way whether VFM is being achieved. Official reports do no more than comment in very general terms on aggregated performance. The veil drawn across all detailed performance outcomes necessarily means that any analysis is limited to the much less detailed published financial statements of the NHS acute hospital trusts.

PFI: FINANCIAL PERFORMANCE

Table 7.2 (see page 138) shows the number of PFI projects that have reached financial close or are in progress. Of these, while 21 PFI hospitals were open by December 2003, only 13 were operational during the financial year 2002/3, as reflected in the trusts' accounts. The subject of our analysis is therefore the first 12 PFI hospitals in England and one in Scotland that are now operational. We examine the 13 trusts' expenditure on PFI and how this is reported, the structure of the deals, the PFI companies' income, costs, including the cost of capital and returns to shareholders, to provide evidence about the actual VFM, risk transfer and how PFI projects are reported and accounted for.

For our evidence base, we use the trusts' annual report and accounts for the years up to 2003, not the summaries shown on their websites. In the case of North Durham, however, we use only the accounts up to 2002. This is because the trust merged with South Durham Healthcare Trust in October 2002 and we were able to obtain only the 2003 accounts for the six months October 2002–March 2003, not the full year. It must be said that it required considerable persistence to obtain the full set of accounts from some trusts. In one case, we were even asked to pay for the accounts, something that is allowed by the NHS *Trust Manual of Accounts* (NHS Executive 1999c, para. 4.2).

In the case of the PFI companies, after identifying the consortia from information provided by the trusts, we used the FAME database of company accounts to identify the company, its parent and related companies, and then obtained all the PFI companies' accounts from inception up to their most recent filing from Companies House. Since as private companies the SPVs are not required to file their accounts for up to eighteen months after financial close, the most recent accounts relate to 2001/2. This means we have fewer financial data for the SPVs than for the trusts.

Table 7.3: First 13 new build hospital PFI projects to reach completion

Hospital	Capital cost (£m)	Total cash cost over contract period (£m)	Contract length (years)	Project details	Sign date	Construction completion /fully operational
Barnet and Chase	54	448	Implies 31–35	Redevelopment of Barnet General Hospital	02/99	Completion late 2002
Bromley	155 on balance sheet scheme	559	30	Rationalisation of several sites, two-phase project including (i) mental health and (ii) acute hospital, plus services at another three hospitals (maintaining four hospitals in total)	11/98	Part opened 03/00, and complete 12/02
Calderdale	76 refinanced	474	30	Centralisation of acute hospital services at new hospital, merged with Huddersfield Acute Trust	07/98	03/01 and full services 06/01
Carlisle	67	366	45 originally stated as 30	Rationalise three sites, refurbish and new build of acute hospital services at new site, trust merger	09/97	Operational during year ending 12/00
Dartford	133 refinanced	450	67 originally stated as 60	New general hospital replacing three old hospitals	07/97	07/00
Edinburgh	Not stated but approx 200 on balance sheet scheme		30	Reconfiguration of acute services from four sites onto one new greenfield site	08/98	07/07 provision of services 10/01 phase 1 new build. 07/02 services at medical school. 09/03 project completion
Greenwich	94	523	60 originally stated as 30	Rationalisation, new build and some refurbishment	07/98	Hospital completed 03/01
Hereford	65	310	30	New district general hospital replacing three older hospitals	04/99	Completion 04/02
North Durham	92	380	30	New district hospital at Dryburn. N and S Durham Healthcare Trusts merge to form Co Durham and Darlington Acute Hospitals Trust with a PFI project at S Durham (later)	03/98	Completion 04/01
Norfolk and Norwich	229	1,163	60	Rationalisation and new hospital on one site, two phases/contracts	01/98 07/00	Main hospital complete 08/01. Extension 10/02
South Manchester	67	450	35	New build and centralisation of acute and mental health services at suburban site plus maintenance of all services	12/98	Phased completion and fully operational by 08/01
South Bucks	38 on balance sheet scheme	328	30	Site rationalisation and new wings at two sites	12/97	Phased completion 03/00 and 11/00
Worcester	106	517	30	New district general hospital on greenfield site, replacing three sites	03/99	12/01

Sources: annual reports and accounts (various years); PPP Forum.
Note: capital value financed by private sector, excluding NHS contribution.

THE TRUSTS' EXPENDITURE ON PFI

Estimating the value of PFI hospital projects

The 13 PFI hospitals that are the subject of our study are listed in Table 7.3 (see page 149). As the first PFI deals, signed between 1997 and 1999, they have been at least partly operational since April 2001. As noted earlier, it is difficult to get consistent information about the projects as various sources cite different figures. First, there are different estimates of the capital costs of the new builds. Although this may reflect different definitions, eg the private sector's contribution as opposed to the total capital cost, which may have included a contribution from the NHS, land sales, etc, it makes accuracy, transparency or accountability somewhat problematic. Secondly, even the length of the contract period does not appear to be fixed. Not only did the various sources show different contract periods, but the trusts themselves are also reporting different contract lengths. For example, three trusts (Carlisle, Dartford and Greenwich) reported a longer contract period in 2003 than they did in earlier years (Table 7.3 on page 149), without providing an explanation for this change.

There is a further indication of the confusion and lack of clarity that surrounds the reporting of PFI. According to the DoH, as reported by the Health Select Committee (2000), the total expected cash cost of the Hereford PFI project was about £310 m at 1996/7 prices (Table 7.4 opposite). This implies a Net Present Cost of about half that, assuming a 6% discount rate, over the expected 30-year life of the contract. Yet the DoH reported an NPC of £685 m – more than the presumed cash cost (£620 m) over the project, shown as having a life of 60 years. The DoH claims that this is slightly lower than the PSC, raising questions about the accuracy of the data it provided to the Health Select Committee and whether the projects were indeed VFM.

According to the trusts' accounts, the capital costs of these 13 PFI hospital projects in England and Scotland

were £1,376 m (column 1 of Table 7.4, see page 151). Thus, the first wave of 12 PFI hospital projects in England accounted for only £1.2 billion of the £3.7 billion PFI projects in the NHS (NAO 2002f), implying that the more recent contracts are much bigger and that some of the PFI projects relate to community and mental health hospital trusts. The projects involved some element of new build, often rationalising facilities on several sites in one location, either as an additional hospital on an existing location or on a greenfield site. Most of the schemes were not particularly large as reflected in construction costs, with only five hospitals costing more than £100 m. When the total costs of operations and maintenance over the contract life are considered, however, it can be seen from Table 7.4 that the 13 trusts are committed to a total expenditure of nearly £6 billion (at 1997 price levels) and annual payments of about £208 m, as reported by the DoH to the Health Select Committee (2000).

In the absence of specific information on these projects about the value of risk transferred to the private sector, we have assumed conservatively that the discounted value of risk transfer was equal to about 30% of construction cost based on evidence submitted to the Health Select Committee (HSC 2000). This implies that about £420 m (30% of the total £1,376 m construction costs) relates to risk transfer. Since most of the risk relates to construction risk, which occurs in the first few years of the project, the discounted value of the risk may not be very much less than the cash value of the risk. This means that the trusts have paid the best part of £420 m to get the hospitals built to time and budget. The evidence shows, however, that the average increase in cost over approved tender sums for NHS capital projects has been between 6.3% and 8.4% in the 1990s (NAO 1998b). Assuming that the capital costs under conventional procurement are £1,376 m less the cost of risk transfer at £420 m, ie £956 m, then one might expect a total cost overrun of £76 m (8% of £956 m for the 13 hospitals). Although one can vary the assumptions, this does suggest that

Table 7.4: PFI project costs

Hospital	Capital value (£m)	Expected total service charge for contract (£m)	Expected total availability charge for contract (£m)	Expected total cost for contract (£m)	Expected annual availability fee in 2002/3 (£m)	Expected annual service fee in 2002/3 (£m)	Total Expected annual cost in 2002/3 (£m)
	Col 1	Col 2	Col 3	Col 4	Col 5	Col 6	Col 7
Off balance sheet projects							
Dartford	133	150	300	450	12	6	18
Greenwich	94	174	349	522	12	5	17
Hereford	65	138	172	310	6	5	11
Norfolk and Norwich	229	329	834	1,163	28	11	39
South Manchester	67	225	225	450	8	8	15
Worcester	106	300	217	517	8	10	18
Off balance sheet projects – trust mergers							
Calderdale	76	200	274	474	10	7	16
Carlisle	67	159	207	366	7	5	12
North Durham	92	159	221	380	8	6	14
On balance sheet projects							
Barnet and Chase	54	310	138	448	5	10	15
Bromley	155	241	318	559	4	2	6*
South Bucks	38	186	141	327	5	6	11
Edinburgh	200	177	550	727	12	4	16*
Total	**1,376**	**2,571**	**3,396**	**5,966**	**125**	**85**	**208**

Sources:

Hospital accounts for capital values in col 1.

Health Select Committee Memorandum (2000) for expected charges for hospitals in England (cols 2–7).

Royal Edinburgh Infirmary full business case for expected charges for Edinburgh (cols 2–7).

Note

* Expected annual cost in 2002/3 is not necessarily steady state cost, particularly for Bromley and Edinburgh, which were not fully operational.

On balance sheet schemes: payments include payments as stated in Note 25 to the accounts plus imputed interest on finance lease.

Sums may not add up owing to rounding.

the trusts are paying a very high cost of risk transfer to get the hospitals built to time and budget.

In three cases, PFI was accompanied by trust mergers and corporate restructuring. In most cases, there was extensive reprovisioning of healthcare facilities within the local healthcare economy. PFI was usually accompanied by asset sales (or transfers) of land and buildings, sometimes to the PFI company or related parties. The replacement facilities (old and new) typically resulted in smaller hospitals with fewer beds and less capacity than those they replaced, with implications for revenue and costs. The significance of all these concurrent changes is that it necessarily makes it difficult to isolate the impact of PFI on the trusts.

Accounting for PFI

In order to analyse the cost of PFI to the trusts, we consider its accounting treatment since this determines how the substance of the transaction is reported. This requires an analysis of the relevant risks and rewards which each party will bear, in order to determine which assets and liabilities will or will not be recognised in the relevant financial statements. ASB (1999) sets out guidance as to how such an analysis should be carried out. The general rule is that if demand risk is borne by the trust, key operational features are determined by the trust, there is little or no opportunity for financial penalty and the trust bears the cost of obsolescence, then the hospital will be regarded as on balance sheet. In other words, it is necessary to show that risk transfer has taken place if schemes are to be recorded as off balance sheet. This in turn would have seen many PFIs remain on balance sheet, contrary to the wishes of the Government. Broadbent and Laughlin (2002) have analysed the technical and political trade-offs that took place with regard to acceptable accounting treatment for PFI assets. This resulted in the publication of an addendum to the main reporting standard (ASB 1998) and a revision to the Treasury guidance (Treasury Taskforce 1999a).

The effect of this accounting regulation was to increase pressure to transfer risk into the private sector despite the fact that the contracting party best able to manage it ought to hold the risk. Indeed, Standard and Poor's (2002) confirm that the private sector has been asked to take more risk in more recent schemes than in earlier projects and imply that the Government has been willing to pay for this.

If it is determined that the hospital is an asset of the trust, then it is treated under the rules for a finance lease as laid down by SSAP 21 *Accounting for leases and hire purchase contracts* (Accounting Standards Committee 1984). It should be recognised in the trust's balance sheet at fair value when it becomes operational, and depreciated over its expected useful life. A liability for the corresponding obligation should also be shown. The unitary payment should be split between a capital repayment of the obligation, a related finance charge (based on a property-specific rate) and a service charge, which is recorded as an operating cost. As the asset is on the trust's balance sheet, it will incur capital charges under the NHS's capital charging regime.

If it is determined that the trust does not recognise the hospital as an asset, then the unitary payment should be recorded as an operating expense. Some assets and liabilities may still need to be recorded, as in many cases the trust has contributed some assets to the scheme. In addition, the trust will have an interest in the residual value, because at the end of the contract term the asset will be returned to the trust.

Since conformity with FRS 5 would require the assets to be on balance sheet unless sufficient operational risk has been transferred, the fact that four of the 13 trusts now show the contracts on balance sheet indicates that the determination of risk transfer is not straightforward. These four trusts evidently consider that they still retain a large element of risk in relation to the contract and therefore under the accounting regulations they must keep the full assets on balance sheet together with the related financial obligations. As there is no requirement in the accounting standards or Treasury guidance for the public or the private sector to disclose details of their risk assessment it is impossible to understand the basis for their decisions.

Although the different accounting treatments create budgetary uncertainty for the trusts, their significance for analysis purposes is limited. Higher asset values are recorded for on balance sheet schemes and offset by the corresponding financial obligation. Over time, the assets will be reduced by the accumulating depreciation and the finance obligation will reduce owing to increasing capital repayments (there will be a timing difference between straight-line depreciation charges and increasing capital repayments). In the profit and loss account, off balance sheet schemes will record the full charge under operating costs. On balance sheet schemes split the charge in the profit and loss account between the service element (operating costs) and the imputed finance charge. An additional depreciation cost is charged against operating costs. These three elements should be roughly equivalent to the total unitary charge of the off balance sheet schemes (although as noted there will be timing differences). As a result of both the different accounting treatments and the trusts mergers, there are three groups of hospitals which we will treat separately for analytical purposes: the six off balance sheet hospital schemes, the three off balance sheet merged trusts and the four on balance sheet schemes.

Reporting PFI payments
The visibility and transparency of the information about PFI is very poor. The trusts do not normally provide financial information about their PFI payments in their annual reports and summary accounts, produced for the wider public and available on the trusts' websites. The information relating to PFI is given in two notes to the accounts. First, and most importantly, Note 25 gives details, usually very brief, of the PFI scheme in

accordance with the disclosure requirements of FRS 5. It reports the full sum paid in relation to the PFI contract for the off balance sheet contracts and expected payment in the following year (which may differ considerably from the actual payment as shown in Note 25 to the accounts in the following year), future payments, the capital value and contract period. For the on balance sheet schemes, additional disclosure is given in the notes in accordance with the disclosure requirements of SSAP 21 in relation to finance leases.

The second potential source of information is Note 5 to the accounts. This provides a somewhat limited breakdown of operating expenses, in accordance with NHS guidelines. Since there is no explicit heading for PFI payments under operating expenses, however, trusts simply allocate their payments between the various headings. An examination of the trend of operating costs indicates that elements of the PFI service charge are generally included within the headings of 'premises' and 'clinical supplies/services', with the availability fee usually allocated to the 'other' heading. This varies from trust to trust, with some trusts merely allocating the whole payment to 'other' with no further breakdown. In only two cases is it possible to calculate or see the split between the availability fee and the service charge and that is because extra information is provided as an addendum to Note 5.

It is unclear whether this lack of clarity is deliberate obfuscation or occurs simply because the NHS trust standard templates for the preparation of accounts do not permit the information to be shown in any more distinct way. The reporting of PFI payments in annual accounts is still relatively new and it may be that individual trusts do not yet realise that more information about the split of PFI payments is necessary to permit an informed analysis in relation to VFM and accountability to be carried out. Furthermore, an examination of the contents of Note 25 indicates that there is some confusion as to what the NHS requires the trusts to provide. As it stands, therefore, it is impossible to carry out very much financial analysis.

At the very least, in the interest of clarity and accountability, the notes to the accounts should show the split between the availability fee and service charge, how the payments are allocated between the various expenditure categories in Note 5, performance deductions on each element of the payment mechanism, and should explain the reasons for the difference between the previous year's expected payment and the amount actually paid.

PFI charges

Table 7.5 (see page 155) shows the payments made by each of the trusts to the SPVs since 2000, when the projects became operational. In the early years, payments were small as projects were phased in, with the consortium taking responsibility for services of existing facilities before each new hospital was completed. Payments increased as the new buildings were completed. In most cases, the projects appear to have become fully operational by 2002/3 since the expected payments in the next and future years were of the same order. The chief exception to this is the Royal Infirmary at Edinburgh (RIE), where the new hospital was not expected to be fully operational until October 2003, half way through the financial year 2003/4. According to Table 7.3 (see page 149) , it is likely that a further three schemes (Norfolk and Norwich, Barnet and Chase, and Bromley) became fully operational only later in the financial year 2002/3 and thus their payments may rise in 2003/4 to reflect this.

Table 7.5 also presents the expected payments at 1996/7 price levels as set out in the trusts' full business cases (Health Select Committee 2000). Considering the off balance sheet schemes first, it can be seen that the pattern of payments has not been exactly as expected. First, payments started earlier than expected, probably because the SPV took over service provision at the existing hospitals before completion of the new facilities and/or the construction element of the project was completed ahead of schedule. Secondly, once the projects were up and running, some hospitals seem to have been paying more than expected. For example, in 2002/3 Greenwich paid 36%, South Manchester paid 34%, Carlisle paid 5%, and Calderdale and Worcester paid 4% more than expected. Such increases could be due to price inflation as set out in the contract, volume increases, contract changes and unexpected increases due to failure to identify and/or specify requirements in sufficient detail in the contract. In two cases, Dartford and North Durham, payments seem to be slightly less than expected. In principle, this could be due to penalty deductions for poor performance. None of the trusts, however, sets out expected payments as per the FBC and/or explains why outcomes have varied. Neither do they explain why the payments turned out to be different from their estimates made only the year before. Considering next the level of payments in 2003/4, four expect to pay significantly more than they paid in 2002/3, again without any explanation of why this may be.

Considering next the on balance sheet schemes, it can be seen from Table 7.5 that these also seem to have become operational – at least in relation to the service element – earlier than expected. One scheme, Edinburgh, was costing more than expected at financial close, even though it was not fully operational, but the other three schemes were costing slightly less than expected at financial close. This is likely to be because they were not fully operational in 2002/3. Considering next future payments, Barnet and Chase and Bromley do expect to pay slightly more in 2003/4 than anticipated in their FBC. Their imputed interest will decline in the future, however, in theory reducing their actual payments. Edinburgh, on the other hand, does look set to pay significantly more than expected in the FBC. Thus, although the picture is, to some extent at least, confused, as PFI is still new and payments have not settled down, at least one of the off balance sheet schemes is also likely to pay more than expected at financial close.

Table 7.5: Trusts' PFI payments

Hospital		2000/1 (£m)	2001/2 (£m)	2002/3 (£m)	Expected in 2003/4 (£m)
		Col 1	Col 2	Col 3	Col 4
Off balance sheet projects					
Dartford	Actual	11.67	17.35	16.05	16.80
	Expected in FBC	0.00	18.00	18.00	18.00
Greenwich	Actual	0.00	18.11	23.17	19.44
	Expected in FBC	0.00	17.06	17.06	18.07
Hereford	Actual	0.00	5.99	10.75	11.38
	Expected in FBC	0.00	4.64	10.56	10.56
Norfolk and Norwich	Actual	0.00	20.73	38.55	40.70
	Expected in FBC	0.00	26.15	39.23	39.23
South Manchester	Actual	13.50	19.79	20.47	About 20.00
	Expected in FBC	0.00	7.64	15.28	15.28
Worcester	Actual	2.46	5.20	18.63	21.94
	Expected in FBC	0.00	0.00	17.83	17.83
Off balance sheet projects – trust mergers					
Calderdale	Actual	0.00	15.23	17.10	17.10
	Expected in FBC	0.00	13.71	16.45	16.45
Carlisle Actual		11.54	11.86	12.78	12.60
	Expected in FBC	0.00	12.40	12.20	12.20
North Durham	Actual	0.00	11.06	13.74	About 14.00
	Expected in FBC	0.00	13.50	14.10	14.10
On balance sheet projects					
Barnet and Chase	Actual	7.56	12.26	14.83	10.98 plus an estimated imputed interest on finance lease of 4.60 (15.58)
	Expected in FBC	0.00	12.34	15.04	15.04
Bromley	Actual	3.27	3.06	5.61	7.87 plus an estimated imputed interest on finance lease of 12.00 (19.87)
	Expected in FBC	0.00	1.10	5.80	19.70
South Bucks	Actual	8.63	9.73	9.90	4.86 plus an estimated imputed interest on finance lease of 4.70 (9.56)
	Expected in FBC	0.00	10.92	10.92	10.92
Edinburgh	Actual	0.00	10.31	27.80	36.37
	Expected in FBC	0.00	1.98	11.67	31.48
Total	**Actual**	58.63	160.68	229.42	255.34
Total	**expected in FBC**	0.00	139.44	204.14	238.86
Difference		58.63	21.24	25.28	16.48

Source: Annual report and accounts (various years).
Notes
Actual, as stated in the accounts.
Expected in 2003/4 as stated in the accounts.
Expected payments in Full Business Case in 1997 prices as reported in Health Select Committee HC 882 Session 1999–2000 for hospitals in England.
Year end 31 March.
On balance sheet schemes include payments as stated in Note 25 plus imputed interest on finance lease.
Edinburgh not fully operational in 2002/3.

Taken together, this means that the PFI contracts turned out, in some cases at least, to be more expensive than expected and that therefore the total costs of the projects over their 30-year lifetime are likely to be much more than that expected at financial close (£6 billion). The reasons for this are developed with our case hospital in the next chapter, and illustrate that the nature of the contracts means that the PFI payments determined at financial close may change.

The trusts' financial performance

To understand the impact of PFI and the new facilities on the trusts' financial position, it is necessary to consider the trusts' asset base, since this determines the charges payable on their Public Dividend Capital (PDC) to the Treasury, as well as the PFI payments. Table 7.6 (see page 157) shows first that most (an exception is Worcester) of the off balance sheet PFI schemes resulted in estates of lower or at least similar value, because trusts sold or rationalised their estate as their new PFI build came on stream. Secondly, some of the trusts, as a result of mergers, reconfigurations and rationalisations, saw a significant increase in – in some cases a tripling of – their asset base. Thirdly, the on balance sheet schemes resulted in a significant increase in the value of the trusts' estate, up to threefold in the case of Bromley, because the projects involved a new hospital costing more than the previous value of the asset base, plus the retention of some of their existing facilities. Considering the trusts as a whole, their asset values rose from £892 m in 2000 to £1,434 m in 2003, an increase of 61%.

Although any new hospital will necessarily have a higher book value than the heavily depreciated one it replaced, irrespective of how the new hospital is financed and who is the owner, this higher capital value carries the penalty of higher capital charges (dividends to the Treasury on Public Dividend Capital and depreciation), currently 6%. This can be demonstrated by comparing the dividends on the PDC of the old estate in 2000 with an estimate of the PDC for the new estate in 2003, calculated for simplicity as 6% of fixed assets (which is slightly higher than the average relevant net assets actually used). Column 3 of Table 7.6 shows that the estimated capital charge (dividend payable on the PDC) for the new hospitals and the retained estate for 2003 is indeed considerably higher than for the old estate as it existed in 2000. The cost of capital more than doubled (£145.73 m in 2003 compared with £57.94 m in 2000). The size of the increase varied considerably depending on the net increase in the value of the estate. In fact this underestimates the impact of the new hospital on capital charges since, as the appraisal literature reviewed earlier showed, the cost of the new hospitals upon which the capital charges are based was up to 30% higher under PFI than it would have been under conventional procurement.

The availability fee for the new facilities under PFI is higher than the Government's 6% dividend on the PDC as it must cover several extra costs: the cost of private finance – both debt and equity – that is necessarily more expensive than public finance; the high transactions costs involved in the bidding process; the cost of risk transfer (approximately £420 m as we have earlier estimated); and an element for premises and maintenance, previously an operational expense for the trusts if carried out at all, although as a new hospital this is unlikely to be significant until later in the contract. This means that the trusts will face an even greater increase in the cost of capital for the new estate under PFI. Column 4 demonstrates this by comparing the cost of capital (dividends on the PDC and the availability fee) in 2000 and 2003, before and after PFI became operational. It shows that there was on average a threefold rise in the cost of capital after PFI (£190.28 m in 2003 compared with £57.94 m in 2000). This rise was larger for the off balance sheet schemes than the on balance sheet ones, although this was to some extent because the latter were not all fully operational throughout 2002/3.

Table 7.6: Trusts' capital charges and PFI payments

Trust		Total Fixed assets (£m)	Capital value of new hospital (£m)	Estimated capital charge on old and new hospitals under capital charging (£m)	Actual capital charge plus PFI availability fee (£m)	Actual capital charges plus depreciation and PFI availability (£m)	Income (£m)	Actual capital charges plus depreciation and PFI availability /income
		Col 1	Col 2	Col 3	Col 4	Col 5	Col 6	Col 7
Off balance sheet projects								
Dartford	2000	25		3.57	3.57	4.63	61	5.01%
	2003	6	133	9.50	13.52	14.50	84	17.31%
Greenwich	2000	47		2.83	2.83	4.78	96	4.71%
	2003	38	94	8.10	14.66	15.42	126	12.27%
Hereford	2000	14		1.24	1.24	3.39	53	5.05%
	2003	14	65	4.63	6.68	8.07	68	11.82%
Norfolk and	2000	14		0.95	0.95	4.52	145	3.08%
Norwich	2003	32	229	15.49	29.98	34.40	217	15.83%
South	2000	118		8.57	8.57	16.92	178	7.99%
Manchester	2003	116	67	10.13	13.75	19.46	194	9.99%
Worcester	2001	75		5.64	5.64	9.70	160	3.59%
	2003	94	106	11.07	12.19	16.56	182	9.08%
Off balance sheet projects – trust mergers								
Calderdale	2000	32		2.25	2.25	4.36	89	4.68%
	2003	97	76	11.18	16.14	21.16	197	10.74%
Carlisle	2000	9		1.22	1.22	3.04	58	4.21%
	2003	51	67	6.75	9.63	12.79	146	8.74%
North Durham	2000	19		1.70	1.70	4.22	90	4.47%
	2002	35	92	7.13	7.60	12.21	114	10.69%
On balance sheet projects								
Barnet	2000	179		11.61	11.61	16.52	146	11.29%
and Chase	2003	235	54	18.23	19.67	25.69	198	13.00%
Bromley	2000	67		4.67	4.67	7.92	123	5.41%
	2003	189	155	14.08	12.27	17.95	118	15.21%
South Bucks	2000	88		4.53	4.53	8.27	93	8.79%
	2003	100	38	5.64	12.57	15.97	96	16.64%
Edinburgh	2000	205		9.16	9.16	21.37	319	6.69%
	2003	427	200	23.80	21.62	35.27	416	8.47%
Total	2000	892		57.94	57.94	109.64	1,611	6.81%
	2003	1,434	1,376	145.73	190.28	249.45	2,156	11.57%
Difference attributable to new hospital and restructuring of assets					132.34	139.81		

Sources:

Annual report and accounts (various years).

Capital value of new hospitals as stated in accounts.

Health Select Committee for estimates of availability fee (see also Table 7.4 on page 151, column 5).

Royal Infirmary of Edinburgh full business case for estimate of availability fee.

Notes

Income has been adjusted downwards where appropriate to take into account the additional income received to compensate for fixed asset impairment.

Capital charges include payments on Public Dividend Capital and interest on public debt (largely phased out by 2000) as stated in accounts.

Estimated capital charge at 6% of assets, ie assuming conventional procurement at the then prevailing 6% capital charge rate.

Edinburgh not fully operational in 2002/3.

In order to compare like with like, since PFI usually resulted in lower depreciation charges – although not for those trusts that merged or had on balance sheet schemes – column 5 of figures in Table 7.6 (see page 157) shows the total cost of capital, including depreciation, before and after PFI. It shows that the average increase was two and a half, rather than three fold (£249.45 m in 2003 compared with £109.64 m in 2000).

In other words, as a comparison of the totals for columns 3 and 4 in 2003 shows, PFI is costing at least £45 m a year more for these 13 hospitals than conventional procurement, albeit including an allocation for maintenance in later years. Furthermore, this is set to rise because not all the projects are fully operational. This must have an impact on the trusts' budgets. In column 6, we show the trusts' income before and after PFI, adjusted downwards where appropriate to take into account the extra (nominal) income received to compensate for fixed asset impairment, and, in column 7, the total charge for capital as a proportion of income. It can be seen that taken as a whole, the capital/income ratio almost doubled. It rose from 6.8% of income in 2000 to 11.6% in 2003, with some considerable variation between the trusts. In the case of the off balance sheet schemes, it rose from about 3% of income pre-PFI to at least 9% of income post-PFI, rising to 12% of income at Greenwich, 16% at Norfolk and Norwich and 17% at Dartford. In the case of the merged trusts, the cost of capital rose from 4% to 9–10% of income, as rationalisation provided some cushion against PFI. For on balance sheet schemes, the picture is more confused as these schemes are not yet fully operational. In the case of Barnet and Chase, the total cost of capital rose from 11% to 13%, whereas for Bromley and South Bucks it trebled and doubled respectively. Edinburgh's total cost of capital has already risen from 6% to 8% and can be expected to rise much further.

Thus, although trust income as a whole rose by £545 m or 34% between 2000 and 2003 to meet new Government initiatives, fund salary increases, and compensate for lost income from car parking, canteen, patients' telephone and televisions, etc in 2003, 26% of that increase went on the extra capital costs (£139.81 m as shown in the bottom line of column 5 of Table 7.6 on page 157) for new hospitals that were smaller than the ones they replaced, rather than for front line services. This was generally higher in the off balance sheet schemes and lower in the merged trusts and on balance sheet schemes, although the latter is likely to rise as the hospitals become operational. Some of this increase quite explicitly recognised the extra costs of PFI. For example, although the trusts must pay the 6% capital charges on its deferred assets, the Treasury had agreed with the Department of Health that first wave PFIs would be reimbursed for this. Thus, to cite but one example, Greenwich Hospital Trust's income for 2001/2 contains £1.5 m to offset its PDC dividends.[5]

This higher cost of capital, both in absolute terms and relative to income, necessarily has implications for patients' access to healthcare and affordability for the trusts: four of the nine trusts with off balance schemes and two of the trusts with on balance sheet schemes had net deficits of more than £500,000 after paying for the cost of capital (column 4 in Table 7.7 on page 159). Six out of 13 trusts (54%) have a net deficit in 2002/3, and this is a much higher proportion of *all* trusts (including community, mental health and ambulance trusts) than the national average. The NAO (2004) reported that 50 trusts (18%) had a deficit in 2002/3. According to recent press reports (*Observer* 14 March 2004), the number of financial deficits among PFI trusts has increased. Although it is unclear why the trusts were in deficit, and therefore further

---

[5] Letter from Greenwich's finance director to John Austin MP.

Table 7.7: Trusts' financial performance

Trust		Income (£m)	Operating Surplus (£m)	Operating surplus/ income	Net surplus after paying capital charges (£m)	% increase in income spent on extra capital charges/PFI
		Col 1	Col 2	Col 3	Col 4	Col 5
Off balance sheet projects						
Dartford	2000	61	3.016	4.90%	−0.152	
	2003	84	−1.238	−1.48%	−2.710	43%
Greenwich	2000	96	−6.125	−6.25%	−7.909	
	2003	126	9.596	7.63%	7.213	37%
Hereford	2000	53	1.120	2.08%	0.114	
	2003	68	0.749	1.10%	0.017	33%
Norfolk and Norwich	2000	145	0.757	0.53%	0.126	
	2003	217	1.599	0.74%	0.032	42%
South Manchester	2000	178	8.336	4.60%	0.016	
	2003	194	−0.689	−3.50%	−6.980	19%
Worcester	2001	160	4.830	3.02%	0.009	
	2003	182	−5.391	−2.96%	−9.926	23%
Off balance sheet projects – trust mergers						
Calderdale	2000	89	1.847	2.08%	0.000	
	2003	197	6.625	3.36%	0.013	16%
Carlisle	2000	58	1.063	1.7%	0.022	
	2003	146	0.697	0.48%	−5.733	12%
North Durham	2000	90	1.558	1.77%	0.050	
	2002	114	−2.739	−2.40%	0.030	33%
On balance sheet projects						
Barnet and Chase	2000	146	9.495	6.49%	−1.776	
	2003	198	13.414	6.77%	−2.376	10%
Bromley	2000	123	3.252	2.50%	1.128	
	2003	118	4.343	3.68%	0.507	—
South Bucks	2000	93	3.703	3.93%	−0.567	
	2003	96	5.432	5.65%	2.974	100%
Edinburgh	2000	319	8.623	2.70%	0.030	
	2003	416	15.641	3.76%	−6.892	14%
Total	**2000**	**1,611**	**41.474**	**2.57%**	**−8.999**	
	2003	**2,156**	**48.039**	**2.23%**	**−23.831**	**26%**

Source: Annual report and accounts (various years).

Notes

Income has been adjusted downwards where appropriate to take into account the additional income received to compensate for fixed asset impairment.

Edinburgh not fully operational in 2002/3.

Column 5 is calculated as the difference between the 2000 and 2003 values of capital charges plus PFI availability fee and depreciation (Col. 5 of Table 7.6 on page 157).

research is needed, it is noticeable that the trusts with the largest deficits had the smallest increase in income. As the corporate press cited earlier reported (PPF 2001), a number of the new hospitals, being smaller than the ones they replaced, suffered from a lack of capacity and this had affected their performance.

In summary, PFI has increased the cost of providing a hospital over and above the cost of building the same new hospital under conventional procurement. Within just a few years, the contracts have turned out to be more expensive than some trusts had expected at financial close. This raises questions about the reliability of an appraisal process that depends so crucially upon accurate forecasts of costs under conditions where the differences between the publicly and privately financed options were very finely balanced (Health Select Committee 2000). The escalation in charges also makes it more difficult in practice for PFI to deliver the anticipated VFM.

Since the additional costs of the new hospitals, particularly under PFI, must be met out of a limited budget that cannot easily be increased, this is likely to give rise to cost cutting elsewhere. With most of the trusts' non-PFI expenditure now relating to core services, this must mean reducing the cost of clinical staff. The fact that so many PFI trusts were in financial difficulties does raise questions about the degree to which the plans were 'economically sound', the trusts' longer-term financial viability and the implications for the rest of the local healthcare economy, since the trusts are committed to long-term payments. The implication for the future is that the primary care trusts may have to increase their purchases from the PFI hospitals at the expense of their own budgets and other hospital trusts elsewhere, so that PFI payments affect not only the procuring trust but also other parts of the local healthcare economy. Taken together, our analysis of the cost of PFI suggests that the emphasis on expected VFM may be misplaced.

PFI COMPANIES

PFI company structure and activities
The trusts pay the annual tariff to the PFI partner or concessionaire, which is typically a consortium or SPV made up of a bank or finance house, a construction company and sometimes a facilities management company that invest up to 5% (typically less) of the SPV company's capital. A consortium has no recourse to its parent companies but raises the rest of its finance from the banks, its parent finance house or the bond market. Figure 7.1 shows the structure of one such hospital SPV and its financial arrangements: the Meridian Hospital Company Plc, the Queen Elizabeth Hospital Trust, Greenwich's PFI partner, which is fairly typical of hospital SPVs.

As noted previously with regard to roads, the SPV's only activities and income relate to its contract with the trust. According to the accounts, the SPV is a shell company which has no employees but serves as a conduit to channel the payments received from the trusts to its subcontractors, typically subsidiaries of the SPV's parent companies. This complex structure and elongated chain of command could lead to communications problems, extra monitoring costs and disputes, as evidenced by the experience of the privatised rail infrastructure company (Shaoul 2004a) and these are issues that we develop later. It also creates the possibility of transfer pricing, with profit being recorded in a related party's accounts rather than the SPV's. Furthermore, should the contract with the SPV be terminated, for whatever reason, the trust may find that not only does the contract require it to honour the SPV's debt but also potentially to honour long-term contracts with the subsidiaries of the SPV's parent companies. We cited earlier the example of La Trobe Regional Hospital in Victoria Australia, which found itself locked into long-term contracts when it was forced to take the privately financed and operated hospital back into public ownership.[6]

Figure 7.1: The anatomy of a PFI hospital project: Meridian Hospital Company Plc

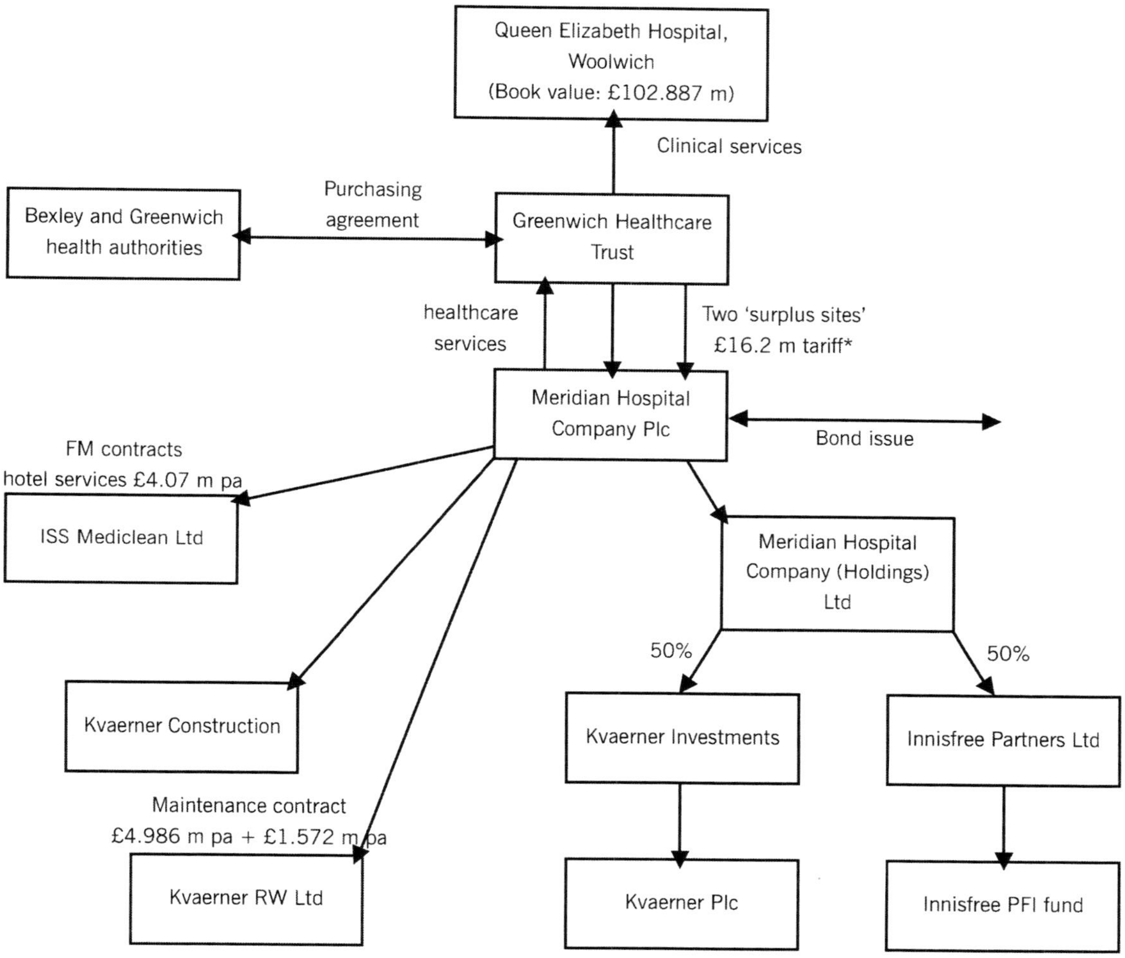

* Tariff comprises:
  Availability payment = £12.596 m in the first full contract year
  Service fee = £ 5.1 m in 2000/1.
Source: Barclays Capital (1998).

Project finance	£000
Shareholders' equity	50.0
Shareholders' subordinated loan stocks	10,089.2
Trust contributions	13,590.0
Bonds	91,200.0
	109,929.2

In contrast with roads contracts, there are other potential sources of income from the PFI hospital contracts: receipts from the trusts' visitors and patients, eg car parking charges, catering sales, patients' television and telephone charges, retail concessions, etc. It seems unlikely, however, that these payments will be recorded in the SPVs' accounts as opposed to those of their subcontractors. Similarly, it is unclear to which party any land sales are made, although it is known in the case of the Royal Infirmary at Edinburgh (RIE), for example, that the land was sold to a related party of the SPV. The chief executive of the RIE said that the land, from three surplus sites which the hospital plans showed were about 70 acres (RIE 1997), were sold for £12 m to the construction arm of one of the SPV's parent companies, although he sought, somewhat disingenuously, to give the impression that the two were not related (Owens 1999). This was about one third of the then-prevailing rate for residential land in less desirable areas. Thus, the parent companies may profit from the PFI contract in several ways: their equity stake in both the SPV and in subsidiaries that carry out work for the SPV, interest on any loans to the SPV, income received directly via the payment mechanism and user charges to the public, and the proceeds from land sales.

Operating as close companies, the SPVs are not required to disclose the amount of payments made to related parties. None of the consortia's accounts that we examined disclosed the size of such payments. Only in the case of Meridian Hospital Company Plc, the consortium supplying Queen Elizabeth Hospital Trust, Greenwich, was it possible to establish the network of relationships and the expected flow of funds, shown in Figure 7.1 on page 161, since Meridian disclosed this

---

in its bond offer document (Barclays Capital 1998).

The fact that our most recent accounts for the hospital SPVs are for financial year 2001/2 (compared with 2002/3 for the trusts) has some significance for this study. Whereas the roads projects had been in steady state since 1999, the hospitals were only just coming on stream and were in different stages of implementation. This means the SPVs are less homogeneous as a group, making the interpretation of the financial data, particularly when aggregated, more difficult. For example, in the case of tax, those SPVs with losses for the year, typically during the construction phase, generally did not record tax relief, while those SPVs that recorded profits also recorded tax charges. From the perspective of trying to understand their financial position, it would be useful to continue this study for a few more years, by which time all the SPVs will be in steady state.

Accounting treatment for PFI

Before presenting the SPVs' income from their PFI contracts, it is useful to consider the accounting treatment for PFI transactions, since this determines what should be classified as income from the trusts and sheds light on the issue of risk transfer. FRS 5 (ASB) 5 and its related amendment (ASB 1998) on PFIs require consideration of who bears the risk, typically the demand risk, in order to establish the appropriate accounting treatment. The party that bears the risk will be deemed to have control of the fixed asset and to show them on their financial statements. Where the SPV does not bear the demand risk, then it is deemed to have entered into a financing arrangement, and is acting as a financier to the trust. For hospitals, schools and prisons, since the SPV is unlikely to bear demand risk, the asset becomes a finance debtor on the SPV's balance sheet. This means that the trust's payment to the SPV must be split between a capital payment – reducing the SPV's finance debtor – an interest payment on that finance

Table 7.8: SPVs' turnover and interest receivable

SPV and year end	Payments recorded (£m)	2000 (£m)	2001 (£m)	2002 (£m)	Health Select Committee estimates for 2002 (£m)
		Col 1	Col 2	Col 3	Col 4
Off balance sheet projects					
Dartford	Turnover	2.67	7.02	7.76	6.00
(Dec 31)	Interest receivable	10.19	13.64	12.83	12.00
	Total	12.86	20.66	20.59	18.00
Greenwich	Turnover	0.00	1.73	11.48	5.04*
(March 31)	Interest receivable	0.00	2.26	8.93	12.02
	Total	0.00	3.99	20.41	17.06
Hereford	Turnover	4.29	5.13	4.85	4.63*
(March 31)	Interest receivable	0.04	3.27	4.65	5.95
	Total	4.33	8.40	9.50	10.58
Norfolk and Norwich	Turnover	0.00	0.00	25.30	7.40
(Dec 31)	Interest receivable	0.12	6.23	15.71	18.75
	Total	0.12	6.23	41.01	26.75
South Manchester	Turnover	5.92	12.74	14.75	7.64*
(March 31)	Interest receivable	0.03	0.05	4.70	7.64
	Total	5.95	12.79	19.45	15.28
Worcester	Turnover	2.43	2.49	19.43	10.35*
(Sept 30)	Interest receivable	0.00	0.00	4.78	7.48
	Total	2.43	2.49	24.21	17.83
Off balance sheet projects – trust mergers					
Calderdale	Turnover	0.00	0.00	21.68	5.78
(March 31)	Interest receivable	0.00	0.00	6.60	7.93
	Total	0.00	0.00	28.28	13.71
Carlisle	Turnover	5.97	6.48	7.11	5.50
(Dec 31)	Interest receivable	4.72	6.00	5.94	6.90
	Total	10.69	12.48	13.05	12.40
North Durham	Turnover	0.71	5.41	6.67	5.90
(Sept 30)	Interest receivable	0.79	6.29	11.31	7.60
	Total	1.50	11.70	17.98	13.50
On balance sheet projects					
Barnet and Chase	Turnover	10.03	13.00	14.24	10.02
(March 31)	Interest receivable	0.03	0.02	0.02	2.32
	Total	10.06	13.02	14.24	12.34
Bromley	Turnover	0.00	0.00	0.00	0.30
(March 31)	Interest receivable	0.32	0.25	0.21	0.80
	Total	0.32	0.25	0.21	1.10
Edinburgh	Turnover	0.34	1.67	17.08	Not available
(Sept 30)	Interest receivable+cap repayable	1.63	1.83	6.40	
	Total	1.97	3.50	23.48	31.48
South Bucks	Turnover	4.49	8.99	6.23	6.22
(March 31)	Interest receivable+cap repayable	0.03	0.59	0.84	4.70
	Total	4.52	9.58	7.07	10.92
Total	**Turnover**	**36.85**	**64.59**	**156.58**	**74.78**
	Interest receivable+cap repayable	**17.90**	**40.43**	**82.92**	**94.09**
	Total	**54.75**	**105.09**	**239.50**	**200.35**

Source: annual report and accounts (various years).
Notes
*2003 estimates used as being more appropriate comparators.
Carlisle, Worcester, Norfolk and Norwich's turnover adjusted downwards for movement of assets.
No data available to show expected split between turnover and interest for Edinburgh.

debtor, and a payment for services. In practice, because the schemes are still young, there are almost no capital payments; the availability fee is recorded as interest receivable and the service fee is recorded as turnover.

Treating the asset as a finance debtor means that the SPVs consider that relatively little risk has passed from the trusts to the private sector. It also means that in the case of the trusts' off balance sheet schemes, the assets are not shown as tangible fixed assets on either the public or the private sector's balance sheet, in contrast to roads, which are on both. Indeed, Catalyst Healthcare (Worcester) Holdings Ltd (2002) explains its accounting treatment thus: 'Applying the guidance within the Application Note indicates that the project's principal agreements transfer substantially all the risks and rewards of ownership to the Worcestershire Acute Hospitals NHS Trust'.

This provides an interesting contrast to the Government's justification for PFI, particularly as the trust also treats the project as being off balance sheet. Such treatment raises concerns as to whether the nine off balance sheet trusts are recording fairly the substance of the transaction and hence their future obligations.

Again, as with the roads projects, we are unable to answer the substantive question, the degree to which risk has actually been transferred, as it must be finely balanced for the different parties to arrive at asymmetric accounting treatments.

PFI receipts and financial performance

Table 7.8 (see page 163) shows these two sources of income, as represented by turnover and interest receivable in their accounts, for each of the SPVs for the years 2000 to 2002, the latest year for which their accounts were available. Thus, without taking interest receivable into account, the use of the turnover figure alone would seriously underestimate the amount of income received. Generally, income rose as most of the

hospitals became operational, rising from £55 m in 2000 to £240 m in 2002. The last column of Table 7.8 shows the PFI tariff as set out in the trusts' full business cases (Health Select Committee 2000) for 2002 for all the trusts except the Royal Infirmary at Edinburgh, for which such detailed information was not available. In a few cases, we have used the expected payments in 2003 as being more appropriate. A comparison of the bottom line of columns 3 and 4 of Table 7.8 shows that actual income was greater than expected. In seven out of 13 cases, their income for 2002 was substantially greater than the business cases had expected, although in a few cases their income was less.

Table 7.9 compares the accounts of the trusts and SPVs. The final two rows of the table show that in every year, the trusts appear to be paying less than the SPVs record as having received, which is in contrast to roads where the Highways Agency appeared to be paying more than the SPVs received. For example, in 2002, the trusts were paying a total of £160.7 m while the SPVs were receiving £239.5 m. The difference may be partly because they took responsibility for the soft services before construction was complete and partly because of timing differences, as in six cases the SPV's year end was not the same as the trust's. Although in those cases it may be more appropriate to compare the SPV's income in any given year with the trust's payment in the following year, there are still some differences that we are not able to explain. These differences notwithstanding, under UK GAAP, symmetry between the two sets of accounts is not required because both entities have to make their own decisions.

Table 7.10 (see page167) shows their aggregate financial performance, including their turnover, interest receivable, total income, profits before interest, surplus, and tax and profit margins over the life of the contracts thus far. Turnover rose from £3 m in 1998 to £157 m in 2002 as the projects became operational, transforming a deficit of £3 m in 1998

Table 7.9: Comparison of trusts' payments and SPVs' receipts from PFI

Hospital	1999/2000 (£m)	2000/1 (£m)	2001/2 (£m)	2002/3 (£m)
	Col 1	Col 2	Col 3	Col 4
Dartford	0.00	11.67	17.35	16.05
SPV (Dec 31)	12.86	20.66	20.59	
Greenwich	0.00	0.00	18.11	23.17
SPV (Mar 31)	0.00	6.20	20.41	
Hereford		0.00	5.99	10.75
SPV (Mar 31)	4.33	8.40	9.50	
Norfolk and Norwich	0.00	0.00	20.73	38.55
SPV (Dec 31)	0.12	6.23	41.01	
South Manchester	6.90	13.50	19.79	20.47
SPV (Mar 31)	5.95	12.79	19.45	
Worcester	0.00	2.46	5.20	18.63
SPV (Sep 30)	2.43	2.49	24.21	
Off balance sheet projects – trust mergers				
Calderdale	0.00	0.00	15.23	17.10
SPV (Mar 31)	0.00	0.00	28.28	
Carlisle	0.00	11.54	11.86	12.78
SPV (Dec 31)	10.69	12.48	13.05	
North Durham	0.00	0.00	11.06	13.74
SPV (Sep 30)	1.50	11.70	17.98	
On balance sheet projects				
Barnet and Chase	N/A	7.56	12.26	14.83
SPV (Mar 31)	10.06	13.02	14.26	
Bromley	0.00	3.27	3.08	5.61
SPV (Mar 31)	0.32	0.25	0.21	
Edinburgh	0.00	0.00	10.31	27.80
SPV (Sep 30)	1.97	3.50	23.48	
South Bucks	0.00	8.63	9.73	9.90
SPV (Mar 31)	4.52	9.58	7.07	
Total trusts	**6.90**	**58.63**	**160.70**	**229.95**
SPVs	**54.75**	**107.30**	**239.50**	

Source: Annual reports and accounts (various years).

Notes

N/A = Not available

SPV year end is same as trust's unless stated.

Final column shows payments expected for 2003/4 in 2002/3 accounts.

into an operating profit of £27 m in 2002, by which time the profit margin was 13%. Since total income from the trusts includes interest receivable as well as turnover, however, a more useful way of understanding the SPVs' costs and financial performance is to examine their total income and operating surplus. Total income rose from £11 m in 1998 to £240 m in 2002. The surplus before interest payable and tax rose from £5 m in 1998 to £104 m in 2002. Although their surplus to income ratio varied from year to year, it was 43% in 2002, the average for the whole period. Thus, it is apparent that while the trusts' position has deteriorated, that of the private sector has improved.

Since the SPVs have no employees, almost all their operating expenses, except depreciation and a management fee to their parent companies, represent payments to their subcontractors, often related parties. This rose from £6 m in 1998 to £136 m in 2002. This means that in 2002 when most of the projects became operational, just over half the income (57%) received from the trusts was paid to their subcontractors, typically subsidiaries of their parent companies.

The cost of private finance

A surplus of income over expenditure is necessary to cover corporation tax on profits and the cost of capital, made up of interest payments on debt and returns on shareholders' funds to the parent companies.

We consider first their tax position. The SPVs' corporation tax payable increased over the period from zero in 1998 to £11 m in 2002. This represented an effective corporation tax rate of about 41% on £21 m in 2002 and 61% on £28 m of operating profits for the whole period, compared with the current tax rate of 30%. On a technical note, since there are also some non-trading activities, the post-tax profits do not necessarily equate to operating profit before interest and tax, less interest and tax, and in any case are non-material from the perspective of this particular analysis.

This apparent high rate of taxation is largely the result of aggregating SPVs whose construction is at different stages of completion when these accounts were prepared, and combining profit-making and loss-making enterprises. SPVs with losses for the year, typically during the construction phase, generally did not record tax relief, while those SPVs that recorded profits also recorded tax charges. In the terms of the calculations, therefore, the figure for tax used as the numerator includes only tax charges while the denominator includes profits less losses. Thus compared with roads, it is still too early to know what their real rate of tax is because the SPVs have not reached steady state, although we can expect the effective rate of tax to decline. It does not, therefore, undermine our earlier point in relation to roads, where the SPVs were paying a low effective rate that challenged the Treasury's assumption of a 22% tax rate for calculating the PSC (HM Treasury 2003c).

We turn next to the cost of capital: debt and equity. Table 7.10 shows that debt had risen from £197 m in 1998 to £1,212 m in 2002, compared with the £1,376 m capital costs shown in Table 7.4 (see page 151), although this is likely to rise as construction is completed. Total interest payable on their loans, including capitalised net interest,[7] rose from £11 m in 1998 to £96 m in 2002, equivalent to an 8% interest rate on their long-term debt, several points higher than the cost of Treasury stock, currently about 4.5%.

With respect to equity finance, Table 7.10 on page 167 shows that after two years of losses, the companies were reporting post-tax profits of £9 m in 2000 rising to £27 m in 2002. The surplus that remains after servicing debt is available, in principle at least, as

---

[7] Companies have capitalised interest during the construction phase of the projects as permitted by accounting regulations. This has declined as the buildings come on stream.

Table 7.10: Aggregate financial performance of 13 SPVs

(£m)	1998	1999	2000	2001	2002	Total
Turnover	3	11	37	67	157	274
Interest receivable	8	9	18	40	83	158
Total income from trusts	11	20	55	107	240	432
Payments to subcontractors	6	14	36	54	136	246
Operating profit before interest and tax	–3	–3	1	12	21	28
Operating surplus including interest receivable	5	6	19	52	104	186
Interest payable	8	11	22	39	77	157
Capitalised net interest	3	20	40	49	19	131
Total interest payable	11	31	62	88	96	288
Operating profit after interest payable	–3	–5	–3	13	27	28
Tax payable	0	1	1	4	11	17
Profit after tax	–1	–1	9	25	27	59
Dividends payable	0	1	0	0	0	1
Debt	197	631	945	1,158	1,212	
Shareholders funds	–2	–6	8	5	26	
Total capital	195	625	953	1,163	1,238	
Key ratios						
Profit/turnover	–118%	–23%	2%	17%	13%	10%
Operating surplus/total income	45%	30%	35%	49%	43%	43%
Total interest rate on debt	6%	5%	7%	8%	8%	
Effective tax rate	0%	–20%	–33%	31%	41%	61%
Gearing ratio	100%	100%	100%	100%	100%	
Post-tax profit/shareholders funds	—	—	113%	500%	104%	
Total effective cost of capital	5%	5%	7%	10%	10%	

Source: Annual reports and accounts (various years).

Notes

Payments to subcontractors = total income less operating surplus, management fee and depreciation.

Effective tax rate = tax payable/operating profit after interest (calculated as operating surplus including interest receivable less interest payable).

Gearing ratio = debt/(debt + shareholders' funds).

Effective total cost of capital = (total interest payable plus post-tax profit)/(long-term debt and shareholders' funds).

Profit after tax is affected by other income.

dividends to be paid to the parent companies. Dividends were paid once in 1999. After negative shareholders' funds in the early years due to losses, shareholders' funds, which include both the original equity stake and accumulated profits, rose to £26 m in 2002. This means that after negative returns in the early years, they earned a post-tax return of 113% in 2000, 500% in 2001 and 104% in 2002.

The cost of debt and equity therefore provides a way of understanding and estimating the SPVs' total cost of capital and hence the cost to the public purse of private finance and the price paid for risk transfer – the risk premium. That is, it serves as a proxy for the trusts' cost of finance under PFI. This gives figures of total interest payable in 2002 of £96 m plus post-tax profits of £27 m, totalling £123 m, the public sector's cost of capital under PFI, equivalent to 51% of income received from the trusts. The total effective cost of capital employed (the bottom line of Table 7.10 on page 167) rose from 5% in 1998 to 10% in 2002. If the experience of DBFO in roads is relevant, this will probably increase. That said, however, it may not rise as much as in roads (11% cost of capital and 68% surplus on income), in part at least because of the need for higher maintenance expenditure and because the level of risk, including demand risk (the justification for higher profit rates, although there is in fact little downside risk as we have shown) is higher in roads.

Two further points should be made. First, in the three most recent years when the schemes were largely operational, this is higher than the average return on capital employed implicit in the Government's 6% capital charging regime and the use of its 6% test discount rate used in the financial appraisal of the public and private finance options and even higher than the new rate of 3.5%. Secondly, since the difference between the actual cost of capital and the cost of sovereign debt is attributable to the cost of risk borne by the project companies (NAO 1999a), this must represent the cost of risk transfer and suggests that the

risk premium is slightly more than five percentage points (the difference between the effective cost of capital and the cost of sovereign debt). This translates into £62 m a year cost for the risk premium and £1.86 billion over 30 years, if this were to continue. There is, however, no yardstick against which to evaluate whether this cost constitutes VFM.

Returning to the issue of the SPVs' rate of return on shareholders' funds, the only evidence we have against which to benchmark this is that given on 'normal' post-tax return on PFI projects by the National Audit Office to the PAC, citing the Office of Government Commerce (PAC 2003d, Figure 2). The normal rate of return (post-tax) on the construction companies' investments (not defined) in PFI companies was 8–15% for 2001. Thus our data very clearly show that the actual returns on shareholders' funds from these projects are higher than 'normal'.

Although the hospital SPVs' financial models, submitted as part of the tendering process, are not in the public domain, their bond offer documents to the capital markets provide a means of comparing their actual performance with expectations. Meridian, the private sector partner to Greenwich Hospital, was one of the few hospital SPVs to issue a bond that was not insurance wrapped and thus showed their expected cash flows from the project (Barclays Capital 1998). It noted that investors were partly protected by a 'letter of support' from the Health Secretary, which provided bondholders with 'additional comfort' (Barclays Capital 1998) and the bond was rated a BBB+, two notches above the investment grade threshold.

From an original value of £100 m, the 30-year bond yielded £91 m. In other words, the fees associated with launching the bond cost £9 m (Barclays Capital 1998). Table 7.11 (see page 170) shows the expected revenues and costs based on 3.5% inflation per year. Of the £20 m annual fee income from Greenwich, Meridian expected that after paying operating costs, there would be £10–11 m a year to support debt servicing, dividends and future growth. Debt servicing was scheduled to rise annually, taking an increasing proportion of the free cash flow. Nevertheless, the project would be able to generate a post-tax profit of £273,000 in 2007 for the first time and, potentially at least, pay dividends to the parent companies. This was set to increase to £807,000 the following year and to continue rising as debt servicing declined (Barclays Capital 1998).

The interest on the 30-year bond, at 4.19%, is similar to Treasury stock (then about 4%) but lower than the 6% discount rate used in the NPC analysis that was assumed to be the marginal opportunity cost of capital. Debt servicing, including the cost of the bond and the shareholders' subordinated loan stock, would account for more than 30% of revenues. The free cash available for dividends and other forms of investment was expected to be about 12–15% of revenue, or about half that for debt finance, despite the fact that equity capital was £100,000, although the accounting profit necessarily will be lower than the free cash. Post-tax profit was estimated at £273,000 in 2007, rising to £2.3 m in 2011, £6.9 m in 2020, and £13.3 m in 2029. The Meridian analysis is important because the bond, at BBB+, is only a few points above investment grade, and Standard and Poor's (2003) believes that this is representative of the underlying risk for all PFI projects, nearly all of which are insurance wrapped and rated as AAA. Thus in 2003, 46% of Meridian's estimated income represented financing and other charges that would not have been incurred under conventional procurement, a sum equal to at least 7% of Greenwich hospital's actual annual income in that year, raising questions about the implications for affordability.

In the event, as Table 7.12 (see page 171) shows, Meridian's total income rose from nothing to £3.99 m in 2001 to £20.41 m in 2002. After paying its subcontractors about £9 m a year once the hospital was fully operational, considerably more than the estimated £7.5 m for 2002, its operating surplus rose to £11.18 m, compared with an expected £10 m, in 2002. In 2002, it made a post-tax profit of £2.47 m, ie five years earlier and ten times the amount expected, and followed in 2003 by a small post-tax loss. In every year, the income, costs and the operating surplus were higher than expected. As the trust explained,[8] it is likely that, since the trust's payment had increased in line with volume, the SPV had arranged a fixed-price contract with its subcontractor and was thus able to keep the additional revenue from the trust without passing it on to the facilities management company. In other words, the SPV has gained at the expense of its subcontractors. This is important because in the absence of information showing how much the SPVs are paying their subcontractors for each of the various services, the SPVs, after market testing in year five, could increase their charges to the trusts because of increases in their subcontractors' costs, thereby maintaining their own profit margins.

Although it is possible that the SPVs have gained at the expense of some of their subcontractors, the reverse is also possible. Indeed, this analysis of the SPVs' finances as a proxy for the trusts' cost of using private finance tells only part of the story. As Figure 7.1 shows (see page 161), the SPVs typically subcontract all the facilities management, construction and maintenance work to subsidiaries of their parent companies. As close companies, there is no requirement for the SPVs to disclose the value of such transactions and not one of the SPVs in our study chose to do so. Even then, it is possible to make a meaningful analysis of the profitability of such a contract only if the company concerned is servicing only one project. As a result we were unable to examine the other potential sources of income for the SPVs' parent companies, including

---

[8] Interview with the finance director of the trust.

Table 7.11: Meridian's projected revenues from Greenwich Trust

	March 2002	March 2003	March 2004	March 2005	March 2006	March 2007
	£000	£000	£000	£000	£000	£000
Cash flows						
Availability fee	12,169	12,596	13,036	13,492	13,964	14,454
Service fee	5,125	6,020	6,231	6,449	6,674	7,169
Other income	291	301	312	323	334	346
Total revenue	**17,585**	**18,917**	**19,579**	**20,264**	**20,972**	**21,969**
Less operating and maintenance costs	7,546	8,677	9,087	9,502	9,611	10,250
Operating cashflow	**10,039**	**10,240**	**10,492**	**10,762**	**11,361**	**11,718**
Net interest, fees and repayments	4,664	5,756	6,106	6,302	7,706	8,063
Net cashflow	**5,375**	**4,484**	**4,386**	**4,460**	**3,655**	**3,655**
Profits						
Operating profit	**6,967**	**7,266**	**7,388**	**7,690**	**8,520**	**9,159**
Net profit after tax	−2,780	−1,077	−1,233	−791	−203	273
Debt	97	99	100	101	100	100
Shareholders' funds	6	1	−3	−6	−6	−6

Source: Meridian Hospital Company Plc Offering Circular for Bond Issue (Barclays Capital 1998).

Note: Costs and revenues assume 3.5% inflation per year.

Table 7.12: Meridian's income from Greenwich Trust

(£m)	1999	2000	2001	2002	2003
Turnover			1.73	11.48	12.17
Interest receivable			2.26	8.93	N/A
Total income			3.99	20.41	N/A
Expected revenue (Bond IPO)			2.30	17.59	18.92
Payments to subcontractors			0.25	9.23	9.94
Expected payments to subcontractors				7,546.00	8,677.00
Operating profit before interest and tax			0.31	2.25	2.23
Expected operating profit (Bond IPO)	0.06	0.14	1.75	6.97	7.27
Operating surplus			3.74	11.18	N/A
Expected surplus				10.04	10.24
Interest receivable			2.26	8.93	Not shown
Capitalised net interest	0.98	3.10	6.00	0.00	
Interest payable			1.85	8.11	10.74
Total interest payable	0.98	3.10	7.85	8.11	
Tax payable	0.00	0.00	0.19	0.59	0.40
Profit after tax			0.53	2.47	−0.13
Dividends payable			0.00	0.00	0.00
Debt	88.00	100.00	115.00	98.00	95.00
Shareholders' funds	0.05	0.05	0.05	3.05	2.92
Total Capital	88.05	100.05	102.05	101.05	97.92
Key ratios					
Profit/turnover			18%	20%	18%
Surplus/income			94%	55%	N/A
Effective tax rate			61%	26%	18%
Interest rate on debt	1%	3%	7%	8%	11%
Gearing ratio	100%	100%	100%	97%	97%
Post-tax profit/shareholders' funds			1060%	81%	-4%
Total effective cost of capital	5%	5%	8%	8%	11%

Sources

Annual report and accounts (1999–2002).

FAME database for 2003.

Meridian Hospital Company Offering Circular for Bond Issue (Barclays Capital 1998) that assumes 3.5% inflation in costs and revenues per year.

Notes

Payments to subcontractors = total income less operating surplus, management fee and depreciation.

Effective tax rate = tax payable/profit before interest and tax.

Gearing ratio = debt/(debt + shareholders' funds).

Effective total cost of capital = (operating profit less tax)/(long-term debt and shareholders' funds).

refinancing, land sales and gains from the disposal of their equity stakes in the SPVs, or to discover the value of direct user charges for catering services, car parking, and patients' telephones and televisions to the subcontractors. It is worth noting in this context that Catalyst, the Calderdale Hospital SPV, the first hospital consortium to seek refinancing, made a gain of £12 m (16% on a £76 m hospital), of which it awarded £3.6 m to the trust (PPF 2001). This provides evidence that construction risk is indeed the main source of risk and that the trust has paid dearly to get the hospital built to time and budget.

As well as the cost to the trusts, it is important to consider the cost to the public purse as a whole. Under conventional public sector procurement and the capital charging regime, the cost of capital is in effect recycled back into the healthcare economy. Under private finance, a sum equivalent to the PFI availability payments to the SPVs 'leaks' out of the healthcare budget, requiring additional inputs to the healthcare budget at Treasury level every year. (Although we estimated earlier that the cost of the new hospitals added an extra £139 m to the trusts' costs in 2003 compared with the cost of the old hospitals in 2000 and that that took 26% of the increase in income over the three years since 2000, that was a different calculation and underestimates the annual cost to the Exchequer.) In the context of the capital charging regime, HM Treasury will have to find a sum equivalent to the trusts' annual payments to the SPVs for the cost of capital (ie the availability fee) every year if the hospitals are to deliver the same level of service. Although at financial close the trusts had expected that this would cost £125 m in 2003 (bottom of column 5 in Table 7.4 on page 151), PFI payments have risen as we have shown and the exact amount due to any increase in the availability fee is unknown since the trusts do not show the split between the capital and service elements of their PFI payments. At the very least, therefore, the Treasury must input an extra £125 m a year (the

expected availability fee) just to keep the system in steady state. Thus the net result is that the cost of PFI has an impact at both trust and Treasury levels.

The next step is to consider the implications of all this for using the private sector as a financial intermediary. The £123 m cost of capital attributable to the interest payments on debt and returns to shareholders after tax payable, equivalent to 51% of the income received from the trusts, plus the profits of the parent companies' construction, facilities management and finance subsidiaries, profits on refinancing, etc, means that less than half the payment made by the trusts actually goes on the construction, operation and maintenance of the hospitals. However, we were unable to identify these additional costs of private finance. It should be recalled, moreover, that since these PFI hospitals are up to 30% smaller than the ones they replace, in part because of the high cost of private finance (Gaffney et al. 1999a), their high cost is not the result of greater capacity. At the very least, this difference between the public and private cost of capital constitutes a drain on public resources that could have been spent on front line service.

In summary, this raises questions, first, about VFM under PFI. At least in principle it should be possible to assess the actual VFM by comparing the costs and SPVs' returns against the financial models submitted as part of the bidding process. However, the bidders' financial models are not in the public domain. The results of such a comparison have not been published, neither is it known whether the NHS has indeed carried out such an analysis. A second, interrelated and more concrete point that our analysis raises relates to affordability, the implications for the rest of NHS expenditure, and the extent to which the use of private finance is a good use of the taxpayers' money. At the very least, the experience of PFI does not sit comfortably with the general aim of controlling public expenditure.

In summary, our analysis of the literature relating to PFI in hospitals has shown that:

- there has been little empirical financial research into the cost and effectiveness of private finance in hospitals after implementation

- there is a lack of consistent and useful data about the extent of private finance in health, making it difficult to analyse the use of private finance and estimate the exact extent of the liabilities being incurred by various parts of the public sector

- more information appears to be made available to the capital markets than to the public at large, despite their interests as both taxpayers and users

- although the NAO is generally satisfied with the construction phase of the hospital projects, this conflicts with professional and press reports of problems with design and construction in a few hospitals

- as yet there is little evidence about the operational phase of PFI contracts

- the National Audit Office does not as yet appear to have exercised its 'right to roam' through the books of the complex web of PFI hospital companies to ascertain the full cost to the public of the use of private finance.

Our financial analysis was complicated by the fact that, first, it was carried out at a very early stage in the operation of PFI in hospitals, before they were in steady state, and secondly, numerous other changes have taken place making it difficult to isolate the impact of PFI. Despite these limitations, this study of the trusts has shown that:

- the trusts' financial reporting of their PFI contracts is limited and opaque

- despite annual payments of about £205 m by the hospital trusts, there is little information in the public domain

- given the cost of risk transfer, largely for construction risk, the trusts paid a high premium to ensure that the hospitals were built to budget and on time and much more than the average cost overruns in the 1990s

- nine of the trusts report off balance sheet schemes, as the Treasury had originally intended, implying that most of the ownership risks have been transferred to their private sector partners, but as none of the corresponding SPVs reports its hospitals on balance sheet either, this creates uncertainty as to who has ultimate responsibility

- within just a few years of financial close, some of the trusts have reported significantly higher payments than expected at financial close without any explanation; this raises questions about the reliability and validity of the VFM case that was used to justify the decision to use private finance

- from 2003, PFI has added about £45 m a year to the cost of new hospitals, smaller than those they replaced, over and above the cost of such hospitals when conventionally financed; this £45 m is an underestimate since the capital value of the new hospitals incorporates an additional amount for private finance (25% of the total value)

- the extra capital cost of the new hospitals has taken 26% of the increase in the trusts' budget in 2003, compared with 2000

- six of the PFI hospital trusts are in deficit, which has implications far beyond the trusts for the provision of and access to healthcare. Although it is impossible to attribute causality, the percentage of trusts in deficit is higher than the national average.

Our analysis of the private sector partners has shown that:

- the SPVs operate in a complex and opaque web of contracting that increases the costs and makes it impossible to assess their returns and thus the cost of private finance to the public purse

- there is a lack of disclosure of related party transactions

- about half the income received from the trusts is paid to the SPVs' subcontractors (typically sister companies) for construction, maintenance and services

- subcontracting in this way makes it difficult to isolate the cost of services in PFI contracts since subcontractors are likely to have multiple sources of income, putting the public sector at a disadvantage when market testing some years into the contract

- the SPVs are paying an effective cost of capital of 10%, about five points higher than the public sector's cost of borrowing

- the SPVs' high effective cost of capital means that PFI contracts are expensive and considerably more so than the cost of conventional procurement

- the SPVs made a post-tax return on shareholders' funds of more than 100% in each of the three years 2000 to 2002; this is higher than elsewhere in the industry and in the case of Meridian was more than expected

- this financial analysis is likely to underestimate the total returns to the parent companies because the SPVs subcontract to their sister companies and some of these subcontractors benefit from additional income via user charges, eg for car parks, canteen charges, etc

- £123 m or 51% of the income received from the trusts relates to the cost of capital

- since the SPVs are paying five percentage points above Treasury stock for the cost of capital, this reflects the cost of risk transfer or the risk premium, approximately £62 m in 2002; it is unclear whether this is money well spent

- the cost of PFI creates affordability problems not only for the trusts and potentially for the local healthcare economy, but also for the Treasury since the PFI payments for the hospitals 'leak' out of the system of capital charges that are recycled back to the Treasury; a conservative estimate suggests that at least £125 m a year has to be put into the NHS budget to keep it in steady state in relation to the capital charging regime

- this analysis is consistent with the research literature that suggests that the emphasis in appraisal on VFM at the expense of affordability is misplaced.

8. An NHS trust case

There are some huge holes in [the concession agreement] – *things that weren't covered – some are very silly, but the concessionaires work to the contract. So, you know, we forgot to put in marmalade, so patients don't get marmalade for breakfast, so we have to pay extra for that. Same with litter, we have to pay extra for litter, because nobody actually stated litter collection.*

An NHS trust case

In this chapter we present our NHS trust case. As with roads, the private sector had been building hospitals for many years, and in general terms our initial investigations showed that the perception was that the PFI's hard objectives, in terms of constructing a hospital on time and close to budget had been met. Therefore, as with roads our focus is on those aspects of the project that differ between PFI and traditional procurement. As in Chapter 6, we examine here the original project objectives, focusing again on the softer elements. In particular, our discussions with interviewees focus on the monitoring and payment approval systems associated with the provision of services. Thus, our focus is on the post-implementation phase of the PFI contract.

Our material is based on the perceptions and experiences of interviewees, who include trust and private sector employees. It is important to recognise that our interviews were conducted with people currently associated with the project, many of whom have seen a change in their role following implementation. These are not necessarily the same people as those who negotiated the contract, because only a relatively small number of people were closely involved with negotiations and there has been considerable staff turnover, a common feature of hospital trust PFI projects. Consequently, the prior expectations of many of the people we spoke to were formed without any close association or familiarity with the contracting process, and in the early stages of the post-implementation phase many trust employees lacked detailed knowledge of the concession agreement. Similarly, there have been staff changes and new appointments made within the private sector organisations. All the information has been modified to preserve anonymity. All our interviewees are referred to in the masculine gender to protect the confidentiality of individuals and the trust and for reasons of commercial and clinical sensitivity.

The rest of the chapter is organised as follows. In the next section we provide background information about the PFI and the organisational structures of the trust. We then examine interviewee perceptions about the post-implementation phase of this PFI by focusing our questions and our presentation here on the four criteria identified in our review of the literature on PFI:

- achievement of original objectives

- VFM

- risk transfer, and

- affordability.

As we noted in Chapter 6, the questions asked and responses given were driven by the researchers' review of the academic literature, although interviewees were offered the opportunity to provide any additional information they wished. Again, our presentation examines only some aspects of a complex project, and we have quoted directly from the interviewees in order to present the information given to us accurately. The concerns we raise come from our interpretation of that information, nevertheless, we should be clear that although opinions given to us were more mixed than was the case at the Highways Agency, in essence many interviewees were certainly content that this PFI provided new facilities that operated much as intended.

Although VFM, risk transfer and affordability are interrelated aspects of PFI, we examine each of these in a separate section. The chapter ends with a summary and conclusions.

BACKGROUND TO THE TRUST AND ITS PFI

This project started life in the 1990s as a traditionally funded scheme to amalgamate and rationalise hospital services on two existing sites into one. During this process, however, it was suggested that the scheme should become a PFI project. When the incoming

Labour Government of 1997 announced a significant review of health policy, the project was delayed. Eventually towards the end of the 1990s, and some five years from inception, the trust signed a contract with a special purpose vehicle (SPV) company (Company X) for a new build involving over £100 m of private and public funds. The trust that is the subject of our case study thus became one of the first wave of hospitals to sign a PFI agreement.

Figure 8.1 shows the structure of the private sector consortium. The SPV X has four equal shareholder companies V, W, Y and Z that are the syndicate members involved in the building, financing and servicing of the PFI. Company X designed and built, through its construction company W, the new units, which were completed to schedule. Company X also has responsibility for delivering building and non-clinical services through its two service providers. Company Y provides the estate service, building

maintenance and switchboard functions and company Z, which had experience of offering these services elsewhere under CCT, provides laundry, linen, catering, domestic services and portering. Finance came from company V, and two household-name banks, U1 and U2, which are not shareholders. The SPV company X has two employees, who are the general manager and a secretary, and a small number of staff on secondment from its consortium partners maintain an office on site. The general manager has responsibility for ensuring that the contract is delivered and the intention is that this role should be seen as independent of the service providers. Companies Y and Z run telephone-based help desks, which are the intended first point of contact between the trust and the service provider when assistance is required.

The staff who provide the services are employed by these companies. Many of the staff transferred from the trust to the companies when the PFI was implemented.

Figure 8.1: The private sector consortium

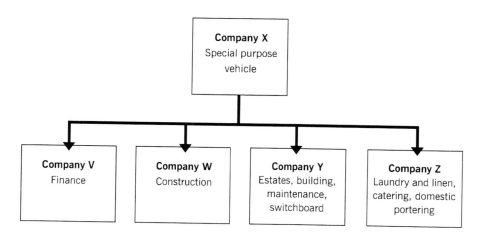

Although, since then, there has been a considerable turnover in areas such as domestic services, in others such as portering many of these employees are still covered by Transfer of Undertakings (Protection of Employment) Regulations (TUPE).

This trust is a large teaching hospital with geographical dispersion of its facilities, many of which were old, so there was an urgent need for new buildings and rationalisation, compelling reasons why the project should receive approval to proceed. The trust had no previous experience of outsourcing services under CCT, which perhaps makes it an unusual choice for the location of a first-wave project. Its organisational structure reflects its size and it is currently managed in six divisions, one of which is the corporate division, described as holding 'very big budgets'. The corporate division has responsibility for therapy services, recently transferred from the clinical support area, as well as a range of management functions, including human resources, finance, and estates and facilities. The estates and facilities division holds the budget for the whole of the PFI tariff and it provides the monitoring managers who monitor the work of the PFI contractors. The new director of estates, who took up his role during our research, is responsible for site strategy and planning, PFI, facilities and 'the things that go with having land as opposed to having a team of workmen doing repairs'. This post was described as having been reinstated after the trust realised that it had downsized too much following the initial implementation of PFI. The trust intends to integrate the management of areas that had previously been the responsibility of three separate managers who 'were all working a bit with their own agenda'. These areas included capital projects, which are the responsibility of a project manager, estates strategy, land, incineration, health and safety, backlog maintenance, facilities and hotel services, residential accommodation, security, transport, car parking and anything on site 'that was a problem really'.

The trust has recently seen a number of changes in its organisational structures and although these have led to some frustration among administrators, the view from within the finance area was that, as a consequence of these changes, 'hopefully we'll get a bit better communication between the parties in the PFI' and 'it's in some ways indicative of the fact that the trust needs better management of PFI.'

THE ACHIEVEMENT OF ORIGINAL PROJECT OBJECTIVES

One important way of assessing the outcomes of a project is to determine whether it has met its original objectives. The trust was involved in planning this project under both traditional procurement and PFI over a long period. During that time various trust staff gained perceptions about what was to be delivered. Ultimately, however, not all these expectations formed part of the PFI contract. A member of the finance team indicated that the trust had probably failed to communicate adequately the final objectives of the PFI to managers who were not closely involved in the contract negotiations, so that different perceptions about objectives were possible. The contract involved a number of building-related objectives as well as a number of other business case objectives, described as 'soft objectives,' as follows:

- two new units for clinical care

- rationalisation to reduce duplication of facilities

- a reduction in beds, in line with a planned reduction in case load, of about 18%.

- the provision of a critical mass for research and medical training accreditation

- a reduction in junior doctors' hours

- attention to the quality issues associated with dual approaches to clinical practice

- more effective management of emergency care

- improvement in relationships with neighbouring hospitals, community units and general practitioners

- the provision of estates and ancillary services for 35 years, not only in the new PFI buildings but also in pre-existing buildings.

The rationalisation and reduction in case load was intended to save about £20 m per year, updated for inflation. This was because reorganisation and rationalisation within the region meant that the trust had expected to lose about £27 m of its annual income to other hospitals, but in the event it lost only about £11 m. The Estates department estimates that the trust had a maintenance backlog of some £20 m when the PFI reached financial close. After financial close, a number of variations to the new building were agreed. Later a large variation, to provide an additional 12-bed facility, was agreed. Further contract variations have been made in respect of the provision of estates and other services.

Considering first the building – although this research study did not independently confirm the perceptions of users – trust interviewees agreed that the new building was delivered on time and broadly speaking operates as expected.

We know the facilities are good, we know that just walking around them, you can see there's appropriate privacy and dignity and the rooms feel large enough. You can get a bed round the corners; you can get a bed through the door. These are silly things but some PFIs were criticised for not being able to do that. We know from the feedback and from conversations with the staff that the facilities work generally very well.

In addition, the design and build phase came in at just less than one per cent over cost. Consequently the perception of the project manager is that 'the hard objectives, the project management objectives were achieved very well.' In relation to the softer objectives the following information has been provided. Junior doctors' hours have been reduced in line with legislative requirements. The reduction of two sites to one has eradicated some duplication and has helped to create the critical mass needed for research and education: 'There's a critical mass of services to promote specialism[s] and to encourage independence of clinical specialties – so improved clinical effectiveness, I would say has been achieved – I couldn't put a percentage or numbers on that'.

Although the improvement in clinical effectiveness may be unproven, relocation to one site has helped to remove some of the dual approaches to clinical practice previously in evidence. In relation to the effective management of emergency care, perceptions are that this has improved: 'We've gone from two A and E's and the staff being spread between them, down to one in a state-of-the-art new department.'

Although some of the strategic plans for re-allocating case load between this trust and other local hospitals have been implemented, there has been additional stress on bed provision, since the case load reduction was less than planned. The failure to reduce case load was attributable in part to new initiatives that carried additional case load. A project coordinator in the hospital's Estates department also attributed this to the failure of the primary care trust (PCT) to persuade local GPs to change their traditional pattern of referral. Nevertheless, an interviewee argued that the trust had seized the opportunity to avoid duplicating expensive provision both at this trust and at other neighbouring hospitals. In relation to the rationalisation of the provision at two sites, the expectations about savings proved optimistic, not only because of the failure to reduce case load, but also because of unrealistic assumptions about the trust's ability to reduce patients' lengths of stay: 'Some of the lengths of stay and the throughput with the case load that we were retaining were very heroic assumptions'.

Since the initial public consultations about the plans to co-locate on one site, there have been changes to guarantees that were given to residents about the nature of provision at one site, which was to be kept open as a community hospital. In fact, part of the site is to be closed down and the community hospital has been described to us as 'more like a treatment and diagnostic centre'.

The PFI also had objectives relating to the provision of the outsourced support services, but there are mixed perceptions about the achievement. Although trust staff have expressed concern about the quality of domestic services and there have been issues associated with estates, portering and switchboard, broadly they perceive them as functioning adequately. Linen was described as a success story:

Prior to the transfer of the linen service the trust had literally let the linen just run down. We had threadbare sheets – it was awful. Company Z came along and there was a massive injection of linen. So almost overnight new linen was into the system, stocks were up and of course it was a success story.

In general terms, therefore the PFI has provided the much-needed investment for buildings and linen.

VALUE FOR MONEY

One underlying rationale for PFI is a belief that the private sector can provide services more effectively and efficiently than the public sector, which is perceived as unduly bureaucratic and therefore expensive. Consequently VFM would be achieved because the same service could be provided at less cost, or a better

service would result for the same cash outlay. In general terms, Government advice is that VFM may be measured against a number of proxies, including the business case, the public sector comparator (PSC) and by benchmarking costs.

To measure whether or not VFM has been achieved implies a comparison of cost and quality before and after PFI implementation. It has proved impossible, however, to obtain this kind of evidence for this individual case. Interviewees from both the public and private sectors agreed that there is a lack of information, in a suitable form, about quality of performance before the implementation of the PFI against which to measure the quality of the service now. From the private sector's perspective, this is unfortunate:

I think there is a level of expectation that wasn't there before. I think you can look back through rose-coloured spectacles and think that the service was better before. I think there has been an acknowledgement – not from the people who ran the service before – but an acknowledgement that the issues that came up before are the same issues that come up now.

Comparing costing information before and after the PFI is further complicated by the fact that this project involved two separate hospital sites with two budgets. In addition, a member of the finance team indicated that because there were many changes in the period from inception of the PFI to service handover, they would have had to freeze the budgets and then to follow every number through the system to make a reasonable comparison. This was not practicable.

A representative from the finance area indicated that the trust had never compared actual VFM with the business case. Furthermore, our literature review has suggested that the use of the PSC is problematic either because a PSC is not always produced, or because sufficient resources may not have been allocated to working through the assumptions and calculations to ensure that the PSC is a reasonable base for comparison, in terms of accuracy and sufficiency of detail. In addition, the original contract and hence the PSC may quickly become out of date, unless they are revised as changes to the contract are negotiated. The initial evidence on operational services indicates that many contracts are subject to additions or improvements within the first few years (NAO 2003b), and PAC (2003d, para. 14) notes that this gives the PFI contractors the potential to earn significant additional money over a long period.

Indeed, although our trust became involved in a considerable amount of contractual change very soon after project implementation, these changes have not resulted in review of or amendment to the PSC. Changes broadly fall into one of two categories. First, additional new services, such as the new 12-bed facility, were not costed in the original PSC. Secondly, changes resulted from omissions in the service specification, which has proved inadequate, in some respects, despite its complexity:

There are some huge holes in it [the concession agreement] – *things that weren't covered – some are very silly, but the concessionaires work to the contract. So, you know, we forgot to put in marmalade, so patients don't get marmalade for breakfast, so we have to pay extra for that. Same with litter, we have to pay extra for litter, because nobody actually stated litter collection.*

Inadequacies, such as failure to specify marmalade and litter collection, represent errors that have arisen owing to a lack of experience in drawing up contracts. This is an interesting example of the procurer attempting to specify inputs (marmalade) rather than outputs (the nutritional requirements of breakfast). This interviewee believed that these types of problem may have been resolved in later contracts by using a template for a

basic contract. In a later section, under 'affordability', we discuss changes to service specification that became necessary after the contract was signed because the original specification omitted services that later proved essential. It has been put to the researchers that these omissions may have occured to ensure affordability, and to the extent that this is the case, a standard contract would not resolve the issue. Owing to staff turnover in both the public and private sectors, the distinction between error and omission is unclear, but the failures inherent in this contract have added to the cost and hence affect the actual VFM compared with the expected VFM.

Thus, the PSC has lost its value as a comparator across the total project. Also, the value of such a comparison is questioned since although it would consume resources, the knowledge gained from such a comparison would not necessarily lead to action: 'we wouldn't know what to do with the answer'. Nevertheless, the PSC may still be used to benchmark costs on individual elements of the project. For example, the project director indicated that the original contract documentation acted as a benchmark against which to assess the price of contract amendments in relation to a significant variation to the contract – to provide a new 12-bed facility. This interviewee indicated that such benchmarking was relatively easy, and that 'it gives you ammunition to make a case'. However, there appears to be much less certainty about the ability to use the PSC to benchmark soft services. In some cases interviewees indicated that benchmarking is not possible and in some of these instances public sector employees indicated their concern about whether amendments to contract had represented good VFM. At our trust, changes to the specified contract have to be agreed by a procedure that involves issuing a change notice. Then new payment rates are applied to the new specification and these must be approved by the trust. This can be a time-consuming process and since inception there have been more than 160 change notices. Consequently, change requires the goodwill of the contractors, who have been prepared to change the provision of some services before the approval process is complete. This goodwill, however, might also undermine the ability of the trust to negotiate on the cost of changes to services that they are actually receiving and perceive as essential.

Another way of measuring VFM is to benchmark services against the unit cost of similar services at other hospitals. At our case trust it was recognised that benchmarking could be done by using the costs at other PFI trusts, but it appears that there is no formal method for doing this. Trust interviewees have contacts with staff at other PFI trusts on an individual basis but indicated that the trust is not part of a formal benchmarking group and does not get involved in formal benchmarking comparisons. The reason given was lack of time and resources. An interviewee from the Estates-monitoring team argued that benchmarking is possible at a financial but not at an operational level. However, it is also the case that detailed cost comparisons are difficult. Although it is possible to identify the unit cost of providing some services, such as domestic, when the nature of the task is fairly routine, this is not possible for tasks such as portering. This is because in order to understand the costs of more complex services, the trust would need to track the time spent by porters on a multitude of different tasks, along the lines of a time-and-motion study, but there are no plans to do that. An interviewee from the financial area indicated that it would be helpful if the NHS provided data on a reasonable range of prices for common tasks. One example was the desire for standard rates per square foot to clean different types of accommodation space. In this context it is interesting to note that the NHS is currently devising a system that will enable comparison between hospitals. NHS Estates has developed the Estates Return Information Collection database (ERIC) (NHS Estates 2003a), which, together with the NHS Estates Data Collection Analysis System (NEDCAS) (NHS Estates 2003b), collects data from trusts and provides performance

benchmarking information to users in NHS trusts and PCTs on a real-time basis.

The OGC has devised the post-implementation review and the Gateway Process, which we discussed in Chapter 2, to help procurers introduce best practice and hence ensure good-quality project management. We also discussed the separate initiative relating to post-project evaluation introduced by the Department of Health in 1994 and updated in 2002. Although representatives from the finance area at the trust were not familiar with the detailed process of a Gateway Review they did recognise the concept and its importance, but indicated that no such evaluation had occurred. The project manager, who has responsibility for the new building, said that he had deliberately not conducted a post-implementation project evaluation because he believed that it was too soon after implementation and some issues still required time to settle. He indicated that no timescale had been set for any review. Also, there has been no formal review of the PFI's softer objectives. Nevertheless, informal reviews of activities do take place, and information about lessons learned is disseminated through a number of national forums. In addition, the trust has played host to international representatives from China, Canada and South Africa. An interviewee from the finance area said that the trust had a lot of experience of the financial issues surrounding PFI, especially relating to the monitoring and approval of payments, which nonetheless had not been passed onto other trusts.

The measurement problems highlighted above mean that it is difficult to assess in an objective fashion whether VFM has been achieved. Therefore, in the next sections we present some perceptions from interviewees about the effects of a lack of pre-implementation planning, complex organisational structures and the subsequent growth in bureaucratic structures and monitoring processes, and the potential for refinancing that are relevant to the assessment of VFM in this PFI.

PLANNING OF SERVICES MANAGEMENT PRIOR TO PFI IMPLEMENTATION

Our trust was a first-wave health sector PFI and consequently there was little expertise available either within the trust or in the sector about the ways in which the trust would need to plan for the implementation and future management of the PFI. In particular, the trust now recognises the lack of planning about how the relationship with service providers should be managed. One of the difficulties appears to have been that, at the time of signing the agreements, the priority was the new hospital building. Speaking about the service element of the contract, an interviewee at the trust said:

It was never planned properly . . . . You know we planned the concession, we spent two or three years writing it to come up with that nice legal document – really planned the building, but we never planned how the services would work, we didn't do it and neither did they (the private sector), so we're all at fault, and we should have put loads of time into it.

To resolve this control issue, interviewees from the trust indicated a need for better planning and especially the need to take a strategic position in order to manage the PFI in the future.

I suppose that's one thing which we need to take on board, which is the long-term strategy, you know, exactly what's going to happen later on in your PFI project . . . . There's so many variations as to how a PFI can deliver . . . . You never know what it is you're looking for them to achieve, whether it meets your needs.

Nationally, there are now forums at which project directors are able to share experiences, specifically in relation to planning: 'There's a lot of feedback in the industry. I would have thought there was a better awareness of the need to look at all aspects'. This

interviewee expressed the view that as an early PFI they were bound to make mistakes and, in relation to managing the delivery of the new building, he argued: 'Some of it you'll get right, some of it you'll get wrong, you'll learn and you can pass on the benefit of your mistakes and your achievements. So I think it is changing quite a lot now, there's more cross-fertilisation involved than there ever has been'.

A monitoring manager also acknowledged that mistakes had been made in relation to planning the transfer of services and the ways in which they would be monitored thereafter. Owing to the unexpected retention of some responsibilities and an unplanned retention of risk, which we discuss in more detail later in this chapter, monitoring was more complex than had been understood initially: 'My simplistic role was to monitor the PFI for estates, but it grew far more complex because of the risk element'.

The knock-on effect is that this monitor finds himself dealing with estate service provision issues, rather than simply monitoring the services provided by the private sector. Another monitoring manager explained that at the beginning of PFI his staff transferred to the private sector contracting company, and he was given a manual several inches thick and the title of monitor but no training. This manual contains some 20 performance indicators for which he has responsibility. The line manager for these monitors confirmed this lack of training, saying that the need for such training had not been recognised.

The staff were service heads up until the Friday, they came back in on the Monday and they're all monitors. It was a very awkward transition for the team and they took quite a while to settle down. I honestly believe they [the trust management] didn't feel there was a need for training, we've got [company X] responsible for the service providers because our contract is with [company X]. Their [company X's] contract is with [companies Y and Z] – ours isn't. I'm sure when the agreement was typed up it was – 'we've got all our bases covered'. You know we're one of the first-wave PFIs so I think it's probably down to naivety [of senior staff] rather than neglect.

Nevertheless, in the period since implementation of the PFI, the trust has moved to introduce structures and procedures aimed at managing the PFI, and in particular to try to manage the relationship with the various members of the private sector consortium. Ironically, given the perceptions that initial planning was lacking, some interviewees now perceive these procedures to be bureaucratic in nature. We examine these perceptions in the next section.

ORGANISATIONAL STRUCTURES

It is commonly believed that the public sector is inefficient because it creates bureaucratic structures which consume resources. It is also believed that the private sector does not do this. This case shows, however, that substantial bureaucratic structures also surround the implementation and operation of PFI. One member of the monitoring team argued:

Contracting something out, when someone else has the expertise, and can spend the capital, is not something I've fundamentally got a problem with. I do have a problem with the bureaucracy that's created by a concessionary agreement . . . . It needs to be less convoluted, less difficult, less need for interpretation all the time. We need to have the freedom to understand what needs doing here.

The nature of a PFI project, however, is that it is written as a formal legal contract and consequently there is a need for formalised structures to manage and control it, and these have increased over time. The formal structures associated with PFI are evident in both the private and public sectors, imposing costs on both. We consider each sector in turn.

Private sector

The ownership structures of the private sector contracting parties outlined earlier add to the bureaucracy of PFI. Typically, as in this trust, private sector ownership structures involve an SPV which signs the contract, and other entities that provide the various elements of the contract. This means that the legal contract is between the trust and company X, but the building and the services are the subject of further contracts between the SPV and its contractors, companies W, Y and Z. Therefore, there is an indirect relationship between the trust and its providers. A number of operational issues arise from this. First, after the building was complete the SPV appointed a general manager, with previous knowledge of the trust, which from the SPV's perspective was: 'Quite important in terms of understanding trust language and the NHS perspective, knowing what the issues are and helpful in terms of the dialogue'.

Secondly, meetings are required on a regular basis in a forum with representatives from the service providers, the SPV and the trust, and on an individual basis between managers from the trust and the individual service providers. There is also regular and informal contact, 'on an informal basis there is an almost continuous contact, it's almost daily'. Thirdly, although interviewees from both the private sector and the trust indicated that their working relationship was based on the principle of partnership, trust interviewees indicated that problems might arise and costs follow, because of the lack of direct relationship between the provider and the trust: 'There's a cost, and that cost is the bureaucracy required to make the PFI work – the fact that you're using service providers who aren't directly answerable to you'.

An interviewee from company X acknowledged this. 'The problem for the trust is that they don't have the level of control they would have had if they were delivering the service in-house. Whereas I think they feel they come through one organisation to go to another and that becomes more of a bureaucratic process'.

Fourthly, if problems are encountered in an area of overlap between the two service providers then there may be a lack of clarity about where responsibility lies: 'There's that many people involved in these sorts of agreements, nobody would take any responsibility for it, if they would pick up the cost'.

This lack of clarity may be exacerbated if a problem continues for some time. The trust normally deals directly with the service providers but if a problem persists then trust managers have begun to approach the SPV, since this is where the contractual relationship legally lies. From the perspective of the SPV, however, this circumvents the systems that are in place and may actually undermine the performance measurement system. The PFI has thus created more complexity than previously existed: 'We've created a bureaucracy; we've created a functionality that only exists because of the contractual agreement' (trust interviewee).

The contracting process, the bureaucracy that surrounds it and the working mentality of the private sector has represented a big cultural shock for trust staff, who perceive the private sector as expensive. Partly as a result of the loss of staff closely associated with the original negotiation of the contract and partly because of the legalistic nature of the contracts, trust staff quickly realised that they lacked an understanding of what the contract actually meant. There was some surprise and much concern about the need to have legal advice to interpret the contract, which they perceived as wasteful of a scarce resource. Here a cultural clash has been described by trust staff, surprised at the contractors' approach to contract outcomes, which they perceive to be oriented towards performances that are measured so as to ensure payment. Trust staff have developed negative impressions about the contractors and their lack of flexibility: 'They only do what they are contracted to do

and they're very cut and dried . . . and it's quite frustrating really' (trust interviewee).

From a service provider perspective, working to contract and providing agreed services have a positive value. A private sector interviewee pointed out that there is an agreed procedure, through contract changes, to obtain additional services, and that these can be provided within a partnership arrangement. Nevertheless, trust staff distinguish between this performance-for-payment orientation and their own approach, which they perceive as service oriented and focusing on patient and staff needs. Some trust interviewees perceive that this has led to a loss of team spirit, although in some cases they recognise that attempts are being made to revive that culture: 'The ownership and the teamwork don't exist because the staff work for [company X or Z]. . . . It was a different culture then [before PFI]. Different wards or departments will try and look to develop ownership and team working, but it isn't like that throughout the trust'.

Some interviewees also expressed surprise and concern about the profit motive that PFI has introduced to the health sector.

It's my belief that the companies, not necessarily the individual managers, but the service provider companies, are basically here to make money and therefore it's very much in their interest to make sure they meet the performance indicators. That is a focus that shifts attention away from other things that we want doing, and doing properly, and doing in a particular way, and that takes nothing away from the commitments and professionalism of the individual managers on the ground.

Trust interviewees believed that the contractors were more experienced at working to contract than they were, and consequently the trust was disadvantaged: 'We have to have surgeries, regular surgeries, wih our lawyers, asking for interpretations and opinions and to try and steer us through it, and we've been doing this now for four years and we still have to have these meetings to try and help us along'.

Public sector

Bureaucratic structures are also in evidence in the public sector. The nature of PFI is that it changes the public sector organisation from a providing to a procuring entity, and this introduces new tasks and new roles associated with those tasks. One important new task is monitoring the service providers' performance in order to approve the payment under the contract, and to discharge the trust's retained responsibilities in relation to some health and safety and legislative matters. Prior to PFI, there was no formal monitoring of services by the trust. Trust managers were responsible for ensuring that their services were performing within budget and for providing supervision. Problems or complaints from users were dealt with by direct contact between the user or manager and the appropriate supervisor. Under the PFI, problem solving involves a longer chain, through a help-line, to register a request for assistance with the service provider, who is then responsible for contacting the relevant supervisor. Consequently the 'concept of monitoring was never there', and 'so I suppose the trust didn't know what it wanted from monitoring . . . because we'd never sat down and thought about it'. The need for monitoring has resulted in substantial changes to employees' job descriptions. One interviewee, referring to facilities management, said 'it's one of those posts which have grown arms and legs'.

Both public and private sector interviewees agree that the methodology surrounding the implementation of the performance indicators has proved difficult to put into practice, and within the trust there is some concern about the content of the indicators. Consequently, this new task has proved complex and has been made more so because the trust retains some performance-related risk, especially associated with the statutory aspects of health and safety.

There was nothing definitive when we were drafted into these posts. I mean all we had were those performance indicators and it's up to you how you want to monitor it. How does the trust know that [company Y] *is performing on legionella, so I have to devise an audit process – we're not auditors – I'm a professional engineer.*

Prior to PFI, this same interviewee held responsibility for the trust's legionella programme, but now the task was not to control the programme, but to monitor the contractor's programme: 'We did have a regime in place prior to that [PFI] but it's a dynamic thing – it needs to be ongoing – the legislation's changing. So you need an audit process to be able to ask them the relevant questions – show me the information – have you got a current certificate?'

Unless the trust is able to use a 'light touch' approach to monitoring programmes such as this, effective monitoring requires the same detailed knowledge of the legislation and technical issues as was previously required to establish the programme. Here there is an issue of confidence and trust, especially because the trust carries the risk of failure and:

At the moment I don't have the confidence to be able to have a light touch, the way it stands at the moment it needs an in-depth look . . . . You need to dig and hassle them to make sure or to feel confident that they're doing what they should be doing. Once you gain the confidence then I suppose you could back off a little bit, and just spot check them, but now I am quite closely involved with them. I do talk to them on a daily basis.

Despite the length of time that the contract has been in place, gaining familiarity with these new tasks and roles continues to be a heavy burden for trust staff. Two issues are important. First, the transfer of many trust staff to the contractor affects the role of the monitors, who previously controlled them.

It's like I'm sort of a middle man. You end up trying to resolve people's problems, but you do get sucked in to the everyday environment, and they are – they were – my staff anyway. And it's funny really because I think a lot of them still have trust hats on. They still feel as though they are part of the trust.

The monitor now has no control over those who actually provide the services, since these staff are now employed by company Y or Z. Since the trust employees who use these services may not appreciate this distinction, the monitor becomes involved in service provision issues rather than acting as a monitor at a distance.

Secondly, monitors have struggled with information that is not always available in an accessible format.

We have struggled trying to audit [company Y]. We ask the questions, they don't always have the answers, or they can show you in some sort of difficult format. You could spend all day there with them trying to get what you're after out of them. I don't think there's anything that they are trying to hide, it's just that they don't have it in an easy-to-look-at format.

However, this interviewee indicated that there had been improvement over time on some aspects of information provision, for example, monitoring of hours worked and jobs attended as shown on labour dockets had become easier.

This presents another example of the procurer's interest in inputs as opposed to outputs, arguably because the input is easier to measure.

In summary, there has been a learning process about the nature of the PFI arrangements, which has changed the perceptions of public sector staff. Expectations that the whole responsibility for services could be handed over were soon dispelled and it was recognised that, as

their involvement was to be much greater than planned, new systems and processes for working together with the contractor would be needed. In Chapter 6 we saw how, over time, the Highways Agency had introduced more formalised monitoring systems. At the trust this process of achieving more formalised monitoring processes has been more complex and consequently it merits some detailed explanation.

MONITORING PROCESSES

Monitoring is an accountability procedure intended to ensure that the public sector agency discharges its responsibilities in relation to the procurement and availability of services and that payment is made properly in line with the contract. Payment is made for each service, for example domestic and estates, life cycle and finance costs and a management fee. Monitoring is intended to focus on service provision outcomes for which the public sector has responsibility, and not on inputs or methods of service provision, since these are intended to be the private sector contractor's domain. Thus, as we have noted in Chapter 3 above, although outputs need to be clearly specified in the contract if they are to be effectively monitored, the literature suggests that this has been problematic. The Audit Commission (2001), in its examination of the nature of contract specification, concluded that output specification should be a key feature of PFI schemes. Instead it found that input specification was a feature of the first wave of hospitals (paras 62–64), and indeed our trust contract has been described by interviewees as an unhelpful mixture of input and output specifications.

The payment tariff includes three elements: availability at two sites, performance over all services, and volume for catering and laundry. Each of these elements ought to be subject to monitoring. Nevertheless, although the trust currently pays a monthly sum of just under

£1 m in respect of an availability element for the new build units, there is no one in post to monitor whether or not it is correct to pay the full availability element: 'The process that's required in the concession – we're not able to go through . . . because of resource issues and so we're not able to check'. This interviewee indicated that following the very recent appointment of a new estates manager a decision was likely to be made about how to remedy this deficiency. In relation to volume payments, the trust is able to make reliability checks against patient numbers, and although some discussions have been held between the trust and the providers to clarify these numbers, this monitoring process is broadly deemed to operate effectively.

Although the tariff payment in relation to performance represents only about 10% of the total payment, it is in this area that monitoring has proved problematic. In part, this may be due to the nature of the service specification that mixes inputs and outputs, but more particularly to the difficulties in agreeing suitable methodologies for monitoring the performance indicators that assess the contractors' performance. In addition, the contract lacks detail. A monitor said: 'The concession agreement we've got is not that descriptive, and that can work to your advantage and then again it can work against you'.

According to the contractual arrangements, performance payments are made on the basis of a report from the SPV based on data provided by the contractors about their performance in relation to a series of performance indicators specified in the concession agreement. Table 8.1 sets out the numbers of performance indicators in each service area, and provides an example of each together with two percentage values, the standard expected and baseline minimum performances for that indicator. Some indicators, especially for the estates service, have multiple sub-indicators, but the percentage of standard and baseline performance applies across the main indicator. Each indicator has a weighting to prioritise its

Table 8.1: Performance indicators

Area of responsibility	Numbers of performance indicators	Example of a performance indicator	Standard/ baseline performance
Estates	20	Comply with planned maintenance schedule (including statutory maintenance)	100% / 95%
Portering	5	Porters meet timescale for very urgent routine and ad hoc tasks and responsibilities as set out in paragraph 3.15	98% / 87%
Domestic	6	Percentage of time during which the areas achieve the standard of cleanliness set out in paragraph 4.1	95% / 85%
Laundry and Linen	7	Maintenance of adequate stocks of clean linen at user points	95% / 90%
Switchboard	10	Compliance with the operator answering response times set out in paragraphs 3.1 (c) and 3.1 (o)	97% / 90%

contribution to the overall performance of that service, so that the service score is calculated as the score on each indicator multiplied by its weighting. Therefore, it is possible that over-performance on one indicator can compensate for under-performance on another. More detailed information is provided in the paragraphs of the output specification document, which also forms part of the concession agreement. So, for example, at paragraph 3.15, in relation to portering services, there is a requirement that very urgent tasks should have a maximum response time of five minutes. Six very urgent tasks are identified, for example, responding to violent visitors or patients. Payment is made on a rolling six-month average score for the service, and separate deductions may be made for failure in three consecutive months, or in four out of six months, to achieve the baseline for a specific performance indicator.

The performance reports are generated from a combination of data. For example, in relation to the domestic indicator in Table 8.1 (see page 189), performance measurement is based on monitoring samples of the cleaning service. For indicators that involve a response time element, a comparison is made between the time a request is made for assistance to the telephone help desks, recorded automatically on a computer system, and the time the service was provided, as recorded on dockets filled out by the contractors' staff. The result is either a pass or fail against the standard time for the relevant priority. Items such as planned preventative maintenance are also subject to report, but in these cases the comparison of actual work done is against a schedule of maintenance provided in the contract.

Monitoring by the trust involves checking this process, including auditing the relevant documentation. In relation to estates indicators, monitoring also requires an assessment of whether the time taken to perform the job matches expectations of a reasonable work rate, set out in standard times for common tasks: 'There's a

certain amount of scope and flexibility which could be detrimental to the trust, if they didn't play it with a straight bat . . . so we have to look at that closely and it's quite detailed really, but that's a big issue'.

To control this there is a labour time-management system, the Works Information Management System (WIMS), which is a series of databases described as being 'like a work study package'. This system allows sufficient flexibility to cope with unusual jobs for which a standard time is not readily available, but also permits control because at least 75% of labour time must be measured, thereby ensuring efficient working.

At the end of the month the contractor needs to achieve a pre-determined number of passes in order to qualify for the performance payment. If the percentages fall below the contract indicator, then there is provision for the trust to make deductions based on a formula. This has been a rare occurrence on estates but has happened on a number of occasions with the soft services. If a contractor fails to meet satisfactory performance targets, then the concession agreement requires the contractor to implement a service rectification plan. Such a plan has been required of one of the trust's contractors.

An important feature of the PFI, as intended when the concession agreement was signed, is that payments should be made on the basis that the private sector monitors its own work. Within our trust, this is referred to as 'lone monitoring'. The principle behind the trust's monitoring is simply to ensure that self-monitoring by the providers has integrity and in particular is based upon a large enough sample to reflect reality. However, experience has shown this process is unsatisfactory from the trust's perspective: 'Once we got into it [lone monitoring] it gave us some problems – it sounded brilliant on paper, we had the ability to monitor their monitoring but it was they [the providers] who had all the work in monitoring'. The trust became unhappy about the quality of some work, particularly in relation to cleaning services, and therefore became much more involved in checking than expected: 'They're [company Z] very good at putting things on paper, so we learnt a very valuable lesson. No matter what the paper says – where's the evidence – we need to see what is going on behind that'.

This led to an examination of the service provider's data collection process and a number of trust interviewees believed that in the earlier stages of the PFI the provider had not planned the data collection adequately. In essence, they argued that the sample size may not have been large enough to cover a wide diversity of tasks: 'We've probably got something like sixty four thousand tasks for domestics in any one week – is a thousand tasks being monitored reflective of reality? Because there isn't any detail about sample size or anything like that, that's been a real issue for us'.

Further difficulties arose from this dual independent checking by provider and trust because the results differed and therefore were disputed. Two important points need to be recognised here. First, since the hospital environment is a dynamic one, it is plausible that different results may be obtained with integrity at different times. Secondly, concern about the quality of cleanliness in hospitals is not restricted to PFI contracts, but may become more visible with PFI. Output specifications are difficult because:

A dynamic hospital is never going to be 100% clean 100% of the time. Output specifications should look at frequencies in terms of tasks and you need to have an agreement with the trust about what is acceptable and what is not acceptable. You need a line drawing about the level of expectation.

In this case, the disputed results caused discussions between the parties to become focused on very small details, which was time consuming for all parties, without resolving the overall issue. An example was provided:

If you come in this room and said, 'Is it clean?' – Well the floor's clean but the window sill's dirty – well, is it clean or is it dirty? So are you monitoring a room, or do you end up monitoring six things within a room? And if you get four out of six right, is it clean? You know, it sounds very easy, but it isn't. You get into 'the bath's clean but the taps are dirty' – it just creates a load of aggravation, that sort of argument.

These kinds of discussion continued for months and interviewees from both the public and private sectors indicated that an adversarial atmosphere had begun to prevail. A trust interviewee said: 'The trust was into, what can we sting them for this time, and Company Z were in defensive mode – getting as few bruises as possible this month'. This conflicts with the view held by both the public and private sector interviewees that the relationship ought to be one of partnership. A trust monitor argued:

If you've got a good relationship then you can steer through your problems . . . but it's when you don't agree that you then start to look for evidence to support your case . . . and this particular concession agreement is very light on detail in a number of areas, and it causes conflict because if they don't agree with what we want, then the next person you talk to is your lawyer and then you know it's expensive going to lawyers.

An interviewee from the SPV said: 'We are here to work in partnership in terms of services, to ensure we can deliver a service to the trust and ultimately to the patient.'

The disagreement became so heated that the trust sought legal advice about the possibility of going into formal dispute resolution. It became clear that this was not a practicable option since the service provider had significantly more performance-related data than the trust, and consequently more trust resources would have had to be dedicated to data collection. This was deemed inappropriate and an alternative was sought.

Eventually, these unhelpful discussions were halted by an initiative that came out of an 'awayday' meeting between the contracting parties. It was agreed that the trust would carry out no monitoring for six months. At the end of six months, a single joint monitoring activity would decide whether the performance payment was to be paid for the entire period. From the perspective of the trust, the intention of the monitoring moratorium was to 'step back from the contractual straitjacket' and allow the private sector contractor a period of time to focus on improving the underlying service rather than expending management time defending it. The trust would use the time to establish an improved monitoring process. From the perspective of the SPV, this moratorium offered the opportunity to get to 'the nub of the issues – issues around training or recruitment and vacancies and all of those kinds of things that make a difference to the service'.

With the benefit of hindsight, it became clear to an interviewee from the trust's finance area that what was needed was a precise method of monitoring, including a process that distinguished between items that are essential to the trust, such as cleanliness of wards, and those such as the cleanliness of office spaces, that are much less critical, so that a strategy for monitoring could be devised to allow a rolling programme of random monitoring based on priorities. Implementing such a strategy has not been easy however because: 'We're now trying to change the wheel on a vehicle that's moving as opposed to doing it before the vehicle started'. Nevertheless, progress is now evident and an interviewee indicated that the trust is: 'gradually developing joint monitoring and protocols of monitoring, which with hindsight should have all been done before we ever started'.

A different interviewee indicated that the need for producing an agreed service delivery plan and monitoring methodology had been recognised by the time the switchboard services were to be transferred and consequently that the trust and service provider Y had worked together to develop: 'a very rigorous monitoring protocol that we were happy with, and that complied with (company Y's) responsibilities within the concession, and that was a very good example, very close partnership, in getting something to work'.

Joint monitoring is intended 'to develop and promote the partnership ethos', and involves the trust's monitoring manager and a representative from company X, the SPV, conducting checks together. The intention is that the monitoring protocols will establish a 'robust way of monitoring' with a monitoring plan that involves prioritisation. An interviewee from company X indicated that joint monitoring places the company in a somewhat difficult position, because it is forced to act as a semi-independent arbitrator between its client (the trust) and the service provider with which it has a subcontracting arrangement.

Because there have been disputes around monitoring we have joined in – [company X] *has joined in, very much as an arbitrator. But my board was saying this is a very difficult position to put the SPV in, because one of the things that is important is that we retain independence, but relationships were such on either side that unless you had an arbitrator, who was seen as being independent, then the dispute would just continue.*

Nevertheless, this interviewee indicated that from company X's perspective, joint monitoring was achieving its aim. From the trust's perspective, joint monitoring should also involve random monitoring, because: 'Until the trust is allowed to random sample, that is, to ring [company Z] now and say we'd like to monitor in five minutes and we're going to the burns unit, we won't be confident.' The concession does not provide for this and company Z has not agreed. An interviewee from company X expressed sympathy for both parties:

My view is that it [random monitoring] *should be acceptable – from the relationship point of view, and* from the point of view of ensuring that the service is consistent. I think there is a reluctance from the service provider, which I can be sympathetic towards, that they are being asked to fulfil lots of different things and they need to pull back a bit – to focus on what is in the contract. The other thing I have to say is that the approach taken by the trust – because the relationship has broken down in a way – is extremely adversarial, so if they [company Z] commit to doing something outside the contract the service provider could be forgiven for thinking that is another stick to beat them with.

Therefore there is a monitoring schedule whereby six or seven areas are visited on a particular day. This has led to a perception among trust staff that the service providers operate to schedule:

There are issues with joint monitoring because our feeling is that it's following a specific schedule. On a weekly, bi-weekly, or bi-monthly basis the service provider knows when it's going to be monitored . . . I've got a domestic monitor, who's been a domestic services manager for over 20 years who gets extremely frustrated because she'll go onto the ward and the sister will say, 'Oh, I thought you were going to monitor, we've had an influx of [cleaning] staff'.

Now the focus has shifted from trying to penalise the provider to ensuring that the service is actually provided, a number of trust interviewees argued that : 'It isn't about penalties and money, because that doesn't stop patients getting infections or complaints coming in from the public'.

Consequently the concept of rectification has been introduced. From the trust's perspective, this is intended as a way of increasing the incentive for the private sector contractor to improve the service rather than defending it to ensure performance payments are made. Previously the trust believed that the contractor had an incentive to deny there was a problem, because

problems led automatically to the loss of income: 'I think they perceive there is a problem, but if they admit there's a problem they don't get a payment'. The concept of rectification now means that income can be safeguarded by the contractor:

If something's dirty, but they put it right in an hour then they can re-monitor and count the new score and that's good for them because they get a better score and it's good for us because we get the place cleaned. Having proved it's dirty with joint monitoring and rectification, they can get the points back and therefore their money back.

Although the most severe problems have been experienced in cleaning services, the concept of joint monitoring and established protocols is being used or being established for all services. Hence, although the performance element represents only a small proportion of the total payment, it has acted as a trigger to seek a remedy to agreed problems. This process is not straightforward, however, and there are a number of issues worthy of consideration. First, the quality of cleaning services is still the subject of concern and although the contractors were paid their performance money at the end of the monitoring moratorium, it was suggested that their performance was temporarily enhanced by increasing the numbers of cleaners immediately prior to the important monitoring date: 'The disappointing thing about it is that when we got to the month of total joint monitoring, [company Z] flooded this site with staff and management because their focus was on performance, not on service'. Another interviewee with the same perception said: 'Check the security passes. We issued a lot of new security passes to domestic staff in that period'.

One interviewee suggested that they had come full circle, having achieved little in the year that the service had been subject to intense negotiation. In contrast, the perspective of an interviewee from the SPV is that progress was made:

Because there was a dispute over the monitoring figures at the time, we had a period when [company X] joined in and I think both [company Z] and the trust have said that if we had not done that it would not have gone anywhere. So what we reached was a score that was between baseline and standard, which I think all agreed was where we were in terms of actuality.

Furthermore, this interviewee suggested that expectations about how much might be achieved in a six-month period may have been too high because of a need for cultural changes that take more time. Consequently the six-month period was helpful but: 'It has been difficult to sustain. Can we change something that has got systemic problems in six months? Organisationally, it is not a long period of time for somebody to change structure and be able to deliver in terms of sustained performance'.

In support of this perspective, the service provider subsequently took external consultancy advice and implemented a new scheme for improving domestic services. In addition, the SPV is currently commissioning an audit that is to focus on domestic services, and is intended to identify any barriers to partnership working in this area.

A second issue worthy of consideration is that although the trust knows what it is paying to each service provider, it does not know whether there has been a change in the application of resources to service provision following PFI, because control over inputs rests with the provider. Thirdly, there has been, at least in some parts of the trust, a change in the nature of expectations about the ability of PFI to deliver change:

[Company Z] had a history of CCT so they know about tendering, but this trust hasn't and we were possibly sold stories like, 'you can penalise them if they get it wrong', but of course it's the same staff, and the hospital was never, like, shiny bright before, so why did we suddenly expect it to be different when the staff work for someone else?

This same issue was raised by an interviewee from company X, who acknowledged that there had been some problems in relation to key supervisory staff: 'A lot of supervisors were people who transferred under TUPE so there are some historic problems, that have been transferred from the trust to [company Z], and it is very difficult for a company to take over problems and then turn them around'.

Finally, in relation to estates, there is concern within the trust that although the contractor is adequately measuring the performance indicators in the contract, the content of these performance indicators may not be what is actually required. An interviewee provided an illustration in relation to the monitoring sheets used for maintenance of a statutory nature, such as technical guidance surrounding the maintenance of hospital plant: 'We're four years on and I'm still arguing and negotiating with them about the content of the performance indicators.'

An SPV interviewee argued that there was a lack of understanding about what was behind the performance indicators because, owing to staff turnover at both the trust and the service providers, the people who actually agreed the indicators had moved on. The present position, from the perspective of the SPV, is that the performance indicators were agreed before the contract was signed and that issues surrounding the methodology for measuring these ought to be resolved before there are discussions about changing their content.

They [performance indicators] were agreed by everyone at the beginning of the contract . . . but we have had difficulties about how the data is produced and we are currently running through with our service providers the methodology surrounding the performance *indicators. There may be problems with them but we need to get to a situation where we've made them as effective as possible, before we look to change them, because if we change them, then that would affect the ways that the service providers look to provide the service. It affects their payment mechanism. If they provide a different service then they would deliver that – at an additional cost, I would say.*

REFINANCING

As indicated in Chapter 3, after the initial design and build phase, the risk of PFI projects has been perceived to decline, opening the way for a refinancing at lower capital costs. Early PFIs did not include any contractual arrangements for the public sector to recoup part of this benefit. Later PFI contracts have tended to share the benefits between the public and private sectors, and the contract at our trust provides for 10% of the benefit to go to the trust. Since June 2001, three quarters of PFI contracts have shared benefits on a 50/50 basis (NAO 2002e). The Refinancing Taskforce was established with responsibility for facilitating and implementing a Code of Practice for early PFI deals to try to ensure that the public sector receives a share of refinancing gains at least equal to 30% on most projects. Although this Code of Conduct is voluntary, since it seeks to change the terms of signed contracts, the CBI has welcomed it and is encouraging the private sector to honour it. Furthermore, the NAO has indicated that it expects public sector organisations to apply the Code and that it will review some refinancings. Consequently, following advice from the OGC (2002b), the trust may receive 30% of any gain from refinancing.

Refinancings can be very complex and difficult to identify unless the private sector partners reveal their intentions. Our trust knows that the SPV is seeking to refinance its loans and 'there is a dance around what information will be available to the trust'. Any benefit received above 10% would improve the VFM as

compared with the original business case. However, the various parties involved in a refinancing may have different interests and the overall impact was not clear-cut.

One interviewee believed that there might be an impact on the trust's ability to enforce standards. Refinancing will be possible only if the banks are satisfied that the contract is working adequately, and although this could, in principle, create pressure on providers to improve their service, the interviewee perceived that an alternative scenario was possible. He argued that because of the benefits achievable from re-financing, it was important for all members of the private syndicate to be perceived as performing and therefore less likely that the SPV, company X, would be prepared to terminate its contract with any one of the service providers. There is therefore a possibility that refinancing could reduce the risk to the trust, but may also complicate its relationship with the service providers. A second interviewee argued that some trust managers were concerned to press for better service in this context whereas others were more concerned to maximise the financial benefit. It is possible that the refinancing will involve an increase in the length of the repayment period as well as a reduction in interest costs. The profile of payments reflects the repayment of the finance and this change in repayment profile could benefit the trust, however, since the Government requires that any refinancing benefit be taken over the lifetime of the project, the annual effect is limited.

In these sections we have highlighted the difficulty in determining objectively whether the contract represents VFM, and the perceived need for pre-implementation planning, the establishment of new roles to fulfil the new tasks associated with PFI, and robust monitoring processes in order to control a PFI project. Thus the complexities of the contract and the subjectivity involved in assessing performance indicators have generated a formalised method of working, which consumes resources in terms of management time.

Given that our trust was an early PFI, it is perhaps not surprising that there is a perception of need for better planning and management to ensure VFM. What is perhaps a cause for concern is the length of time it has taken to work through the detail of the PFI contract and to establish the necessary role holders and systems. The fact that contract-related negotiations are still taking place so long after service transfer suggests that the related costs must have an impact on the VFM of this project and on the returns to the private sector. Consequently, it appears that the potential for obtaining VFM by increasing the efficiency of delivery is, at least in part, undermined by the costs associated with controlling and monitoring the performance of the contract. This is occurring for two reasons. First, the trust cannot, in common with many other public sector bodies, delegate all responsibility for the quality of the service. Secondly, because public money is involved, trust staff feel a responsibility to ensure the trust gets what it pays for. In the next section we examine the nature of risk transfer in more detail.

RISK TRANSFER

We have argued above, in Chapter 4, that risk transfer is critical to the financial justification of many PFI projects, since traditional procurement is less expensive before the costs of retaining risks are added to the PSC. Our review of the literature showed that risk transfer may be problematic in practice. In this section we explore some of the perceptions about risk transfer in this project.

Under the terms of the concession, the SPV carries responsibility for a number of clearly defined risks, especially those associated with the design and build of the new units. The SPV has responsibility for maintaining the two new build units and returning these to the trust at the end of the contract in good condition. Thus an SPV interviewee indicated that the SPV held a heavy burden in relation to 'life cycle' risk for these units.

We have got some heavy risks, without doubt, out there. The heaviest risk for us as an SPV is in terms of life cycle, because at the end of this contract we present back to the trust a building in the same condition, and there are a lot of things that can happen to a new building over that period of time. We have to ensure that there is an appropriate level of maintenance done by our service providers.

Two issues were raised in this connection. First, the nature of building use has life cycle costs that fall on the SPV, but the main user is the trust, and a trust interviewee indicated that they had not fully grasped the implications of this. For example, the trust changed its use of one area to create a new surgical assessment unit without notifying the SPV, even though company X needs to be informed because of the life cycle implications. Secondly, especially in connection with the provision of estates and the ancillary services, responsibility for life cycle costs is shared, and therefore it may be uncertain where the responsibility rests. An example was given by an interviewee from company X:

Doors come to be renewed, in, say, five years time but if the door needs to be replaced before that time, then we carry that risk, unless we can show that it is through lack of maintenance, or a latent defect, or it's through use, and the reason that is our highest risk is that, without a shadow of a doubt, that will get harder to prove.

Thus the SPV finds itself carrying risks associated with the use of the building but does not have direct control over the users of the building, including the employees of other syndicate members, trust staff, patients and the general public. One outcome of this is that when repairs are required, especially those associated with damage to the fabric of the building, there may be negotiations about where responsibility lies. One trust interviewee provided an example about damage to a wall:

There are examples of [company Y] retaining risk, but they don't just say 'Oh, it's our risk – fine'. They will fight and argue that somewhere along the line there's some culpability . . . . We get into all sorts of issues – if there's a damaged wall – who did it? Was it one of the other service providers in which case they'd be looking to bill [company Z]? Was it one of the trust employees? In which case they'd be looking to bill us.

An interviewee from the private sector indicated the need for these kinds of issue surrounding the duty of care when using facilities to be resolved through a partnership mechanism, in which there ought to be a sharing of responsibilities: 'There are issues we need to deal with, and the issue is one of partnership really. It is not always as clear-cut as users or design, but if there is a health and safety issue, I've very much put forward that it would be in all our interests to resolve this'.

The SPV interviewee argued that the trust employees did not always act as responsible tenants, thereby increasing the cost of maintenance to the SPV: 'There is a lack of responsibility out there about taking care of the building . . . . I think there has to be an acknowledgement by the trust of their responsibilities . . . and essentially there is a need to move on and to move forward with the partnership'.

One way in which company X has sought to move on is by establishing a reporting mechanism to capture information about damage to buildings, but that has not been fully implemented by the trust. Since this contract is only a few years old, relatively few life cycle issues have been raised, although company X has signalled its need to plan for these in the immediate future: 'It [life cycle] is something that we will need to concentrate on over the next years in terms of our strategy and business plan. It is a new build so the life cycle issues are not happening yet, but you can see that they will in the future. So we need to plan proactively'.

This planning will build upon regular life cycle reports, the first one of which, apart from the inaugural one, was due when the contract had run for five years.

The situation in relation to the provision of services in the pre-existing buildings is more complex. An early difficulty arose because the actual contract differed from the expectations of trust managers working in the finance and operational areas about the risks to be transferred under the PFI. In particular, they had expected that risk transfer in relation to services in pre-existing non-PFI buildings was to be the same for the new PFI units. After taking legal advice, however, it emerged that the contract had not transferred risk associated with the pre-existing building, and so: 'In terms of whether something is safe, whether something is adequate, whether something is doing what it should from a plant and estates point of view, all that risk stays with us [the trust].'

In particular it appears that this mismatch between perceptions and the contract was not restricted to those in middle-ranking managerial positions, but was evident at very senior levels, among executives who are no longer with the trust.

Now to give you a feel for just how much we didn't understand – the chief, not the present one, corresponded with me in such a way that led me to believe that they'd totally misunderstood. . . . And I didn't really get it at the time either. I took some advice and it suddenly dawned on me just exactly what we were dealing with, and in fact we've had practical examples of suffering from that risk. We have been set upon by the Health and Safety Executive with regard to a risk assessment.

The reason for this mismatch was put down to naivety by another interviewee: 'So I think in the trust's naivety they thought that they would have no further problems with all the services that transferred, but what transpired was that although the staff transferred and the service transferred, the risk didn't.'

Whether those who negotiated the contract on behalf of the trust shared this misunderstanding is not known, so it is not possible to determine whether there is a consequential impact on the actual, as opposed to the expected, VFM of the project. However, it appears that this mismatch between expectations and the contract did not exist in the private sector. For example, an interviewee from the SPV indicated that there had been no surprises in relation to risk transfer, which had occurred as expected.

From our perspective the risks that have transferred I would have expected, there is nothing we have taken that wasn't expected. However, I think there is a perception within the trust that all risk is put with us, and I think probably that wasn't as clearly defined at the beginning as it should have been. There are issues around, say, the services or even the building that the trust has some responsibility, but I think there may have been a level of expectation that it may have been totally undertaken. My view is that risk has been appropriately undertaken and that this is in accordance with the contract.

Therefore, the trust had to change its understanding about the ability to transfer service provision risks for both new and old buildings during the early period of PFI implementation. Several interviewees indicated that initially they had believed that they would lose all responsibility and hence all the workload associated with services, but that now it had become clear that: 'The trust had to have far more involvement in estates services and domestic services and all those things that they thought might have transferred but didn't'. Consequently: 'The PFI wasn't something you just sort of did and someone ran your services for you, there's an active management role monitoring them'. The most obvious manifestations of this realisation can be seen in the appointment of new role holders, increasing

quantities of monitoring activities, and a reliance on more formalised systems of monitoring, which we discussed in the previous section.

The trust has found that it retains risk for a range of activities that include: liability for accidents to staff and the public, many statutory obligations such as compliance with electrical, lift and pressure vessel testing legislation, programmes associated with issues such as legionella and asbestos control: 'We are the duty holder for the site and we're also the landlord for the properties, so it still falls to us to ensure a duty of care'.

In some cases, this risk is shared with the relevant service provider, but there is uncertainty about the proportions of risk sharing that apply:

How the proportionality would work out, that's in the heads of the HSE [Health and Safety Executive]. They would look at what have you done, what should you have done, what was deemed to be your part to play and what was the service provider's part to play, so the proportionality would change depending on what the topic was and how far we'd addressed the problem . . . . It's not a simplistic thing monitoring the PFI.

Trust interviewees acknowledged that risk had been transferred in relation to labour relations, especially in relation to labour disputes and 'the hassle of negotiations'. Nevertheless, the changes introduced by PFI have not been fully understood by all employees, especially those outside the administrative sphere, and neither have the changes been understood by members of the public. For example, service users did not always understand the transfer of responsibilities: 'If they feel as if things aren't working out for them, they're not getting what they expect, then they come to see the facilities manager'. The facilities manager is now a monitoring manager employed by the trust and the correct port of call is the service provider help desk.

Clearly such continued involvement, several years after the granting of the concession, implies a cost to the trust.

There may also be a problem for the SPV and the contractors. If service requirements are not directed through the help desks then they do not become part of the contractors' systems.

What happens is that the wards – rather than ringing through to the help desk and giving [company Y] *the opportunity to resolve the problem – they will ring the monitoring team. The monitoring team will go out . . . . It is escalated to the point where it is reported as a hospital incident – as a complaint – and it becomes very difficult to respond to. We are currently looking at a process of escalation that starts at the help desk because unless you have that it is not auditable.* (Interviewee from company X).

This interviewee indicated that there may be a lack of knowledge on the wards about the way that the performance indicator system works and the importance of the help desk in relation to measuring response times. Moreover, a trust interviewee suggested that some employees transferred to the subcontractors still believed that they worked for the trust: 'The porters are ninety per cent still the staff that used to work for us – some of them probably think they do work for us, or at least mentally have a culture of their working for the hospital'. This culture has persisted despite a re-launch by the relevant contractor, described by a trust interviewee as 'product branding' of the transferred staff.

In short, although it is clear that some risks have transferred from the public to the private sector in the expected manner, in essence it is too early to assess the impacts of actual risk transfer, as opposed to either the expected or even the contracted risk transfer, in relation to those activities about which there is shared responsibility. Indeed, it may be the case that the

extent of risk transfer can be known only in the event of problems that are so serious that the proportionality of risk sharing has to be negotiated between the parties or determined in court. Risk retention by the trust has had an impact on the monitoring processes and in the next section we will show that it overlaps with issues of affordability.

AFFORDABILITY

PFI ties the procurer into a long-term contract for the provision of specific services, of both a capital and a revenue nature, and the cost of the annual payments is a charge against its budget. Therefore, it is clearly essential that the procurer is able to afford these payments over the long term. The payment, as an aggregate payment that includes both capital and service elements, may have led to a number of trade-offs between immediate gain, in terms of obtaining a much-needed building, and the long-term provision of services. A number of interviewees provided examples of this kind of trade-off and we highlight three here: provision of facilities and services, transfer of risk and response times. These examples also illustrate differences in perceptions about the objectives of the PFI project, which we referred to earlier.

One interviewee believed that the need to ensure affordability had resulted in significant downsizing of the facilities available within one of the new build units, and that staff and clinical provision were suffering continuing problems as a result of this trade-off:

I think on the building side you could argue that the objective of the PFI has been achieved. We've got a building, and it's a reasonably good one, and it works fairly well, and yes, you know we got value for money. I think on another front, affordability, that very word was a disaster because in making it affordable, things were taken out, things were pared down and we, me, my boss, the people that work for me, are now suffering the consequences of that affordability. Out of 26 departments, pathology, pharmacy, sterile services – virtually all the therapies – only two were catered for – all the others had nothing out of the new build.

This perception was not, however, shared by two other more senior trust employees, one of whom is very closely involved with the PFI project. These interviewees have both indicated independently that the PFI plans never included these facilities and that downsizing did not therefore result. This difference in understanding appears to be linked to the very long period over which plans were discussed and the fact that many interested people were not closely involved with the discussions. This raises questions about whether the project was oversold. Under conditions where many of the original negotiators have left the trust, such perceptual variations are not easy to rectify.

Interviewees from both public and private sectors indicated that initially all parties tended to place a lot of emphasis on the new building as opposed to the arrangements for services and facilities management over the next 30 years. However, eventually the emphasis did shift to the services. A monitoring manager suggested that although the building is important to the clinical teams, the services now have a very important impact on the way in which clinical care is provided. One interviewee indicated that there was a lack of knowledge among clinical and medical staff about the nature of PFI. Speaking about service performance indicators, he said:

I remember a classic letter from a consultant, in fact he's very senior, very experienced, but the letter shows a total lack of understanding that the building he's working in is only there because we went into this arrangement. They don't get it. Most people in the trust don't understand what the PFI is about and what we've had to commit ourselves to, to get that building built without having to spend exchequer capital . . . . Affordability is a dirty word in this office.

Since the contract was signed, the trust has had to upgrade some service specifications and add others and the cost is consequently increasing. These changes may be undermining the affordability of the PFI.

When I'm doing change notices and we're agreeing to pay them more, I think we're probably near, if we haven't already reached, the level of financial cutbacks that I suspect needed to be made to get that [contract] signed. It was around affordability, and I'm sure we've probably gone over the threshold now, whatever it was that was needed for affordability, because the majority of the change notices that have been put in are because the service was required but wasn't in the concession.

One small, but quite costly, omission was the failure to specify litter collection. A more serious change notice arose: dedicated porters for the theatres in the new build proved essential, but were not in the original specification.

The trust couldn't possibly run without dedicated portering staff, but you know they weren't in [the concession agreement] – they were categorically not in . . . . That's what I mean we've either breached or are coming up to the threshold around what must have been affordability to actually get that contract signed off.

There is no evidence that negotiators deliberately reduced contract specification to an inappropriate level. As the project manager indicated, mistakes were likely to occur, especially at a first-wave hospital. Although, with the benefit of hindsight, the portering arrangements, as in the business case, were unworkable this is not necessarily related to PFI; many projects involve trade-offs between costs and specification. Nevertheless, this provides an interesting illustration of the very practice that PFI was supposed to end: that of the failure to specify properly in order to get a project through. In other words, PFI did not so much change a poor practice as make it more visible.

One disadvantage of these belated negotiations is that: 'We probably haven't got the economies of scale we could have had then'.

A second example of trade-off relates to the retention of risk. A monitor argued that the available money was insufficient to enable the transfer of risk in relation to the non-PFI buildings.

They are maintaining older buildings, that's why they won't accept the risk, they will not accept the risk on old buildings because of the implications of maintaining old buildings, and the fact that the money they were given, they felt, was not enough to take on board the risk. There are millions and millions of pounds in what we call backlog maintenance here, things that [company Y] have inherited, leaky roofs, poor infrastructure . . . if you don't give somebody enough money to maintain all of that and put it right, then you can't really expect them to take the risk.

As we have shown above, because the trust retains the risk there is a need to increase the monitoring of the provider. This creates additional bureaucracy and increases operating costs for both the trust and the contractor. The project director perceived the maintenance and affordability issues from a different perspective. He indicated that the need to resolve the trust's maintenance problems by obtaining a new building drove the trust into an agreement which had unnecessary elements: 'We had a backlog maintenance problem of about £20 million a year, and it was getting worse the whole time. All we needed to do was to get a new building to sort that out – we didn't really need to outsource all our other services, but we ended up having to do that to move forward'.

A third example was given in relation to the portering tasks and performance indicators. Portering services are measured on the basis of response times, which are categorised as: very urgent response in five minutes, urgent response in thirty minutes or routine response by

agreement and as soon as reasonably practicable. In the early phases of implementation of the PFI there was a misunderstanding about the meaning of these response times.

A response time is the time from when the call is made to [company Z] – please move this patient – to the porter starting the task, it is not the actual fulfilling of the task in totality, it's about responding. So you could have a call from theatres at two o'clock and in essence [company Z] have until two thirty to start that task.

This interviewee indicated that it took trust employees many months to understand this method of working, but went on to say:

I think the bandings are too great, between five and thirty minutes that's a big gap, but that was about affordability. So we've had to sit down and negotiate 'Well, can we include this?' and of course for most things there's a cost. So we have to negotiate, 'Can we fund this?' and 'Can we do something quite differently?' and again this is probably around affordability.

In addition to these examples, affordability problems may also have occurred in a number of other ways that have continuing effects. For example, it may have had an impact on the ability of the contractors to make a winning bid for some services, especially domestic services. Trust employees were transferred to the service providers under TUPE arrangements, which offer employee protection for existing pay and conditions of service, if these are better than market rates. Service providers had to take a view about expected rates of turnover of these protected employees and numbers of staff likely to be employed at market rates to create a winning bid. Market rates are low, however, and there is nationally some difficulty in recruiting sufficient staff. This is exacerbated by the location of our trust, which has a number of large competitors for these kinds of staff. Service providers have therefore experienced recruitment and retention problems.

An estates manager indicated his concern that over time the PFI may create a leakage of funds from the trust in relation to some kinds of estates work, raising potential affordability issues for the future. Prior to the PFI the estates department was able to earn additional cash over its annual budget by providing building services beyond the scope of the annual plan. This cash would then be used to bolster the estates budget: 'We would push that money back into repairing the estate, it was money that never left the trust, it was just reallocated. What's happening now is that it goes straight into [company Z's] pocket. So there's money leaving the trust, whereas in the past it was recycled.'

After financial close it has become necessary for the trust to add services to the original contract. In one instance, this was to provide more beds, which brings with it the possibility of more income. Other instances, such as the failure to specify marmalade for patients' breakfast, which added some £40,000 to the trust's costs, have probably resulted from misunderstandings. In other cases, the trust has been unable to operate with the original terms of the concession and has been forced to issue change notices, thus incurring additional costs. Therefore, the affordability of this contract would appear to have reduced since financial close.

DISCUSSION AND CONCLUSION

The relationship between risk, value for money and affordability is one of the most complex and controversial areas of the PFI. (Audit Commission 2001, para. 85)

The evidence from these interviews confirms this statement and provides detailed information about the nature of the complexities that arise. This case has highlighted a number of issues that have arisen

because it was in the first wave of hospital PFIs and therefore a pioneer in terms of both construction and managing the more problematical transfer of service provision. It is clearly the case that the experiences, both positive and negative, of the first wave of hospitals have been important in highlighting many areas where contract clarification, involving expensive legal consultations, is needed. In the case of service provision, some shortcomings in our trust's contract were not immediately apparent and are taking considerable management time to resolve.

Many other trusts may well be experiencing a similar level of problems as standard output specifications for 20 areas of non-clinical services were launched by the DoH only in December 2002. Indeed, when asked in an interview for PPP Forum if there have been any problems with the new facilities, Alan Perkins, chief executive of the Queen Elizabeth Hospital in Greenwich, commented: 'We outsource all of the non-clinical support services. It is not working as well as we would like yet, but it is consistently improving. Like any new hospital it is mostly teething troubles' (PPP Forum 2003a). He also went on to comment in relation to staff transfer that: 'Although the concept was right it was thought that the concessionaire could have resourced training more adequately. Catering and portering have had teething troubles, which were felt by the staff' (PPP Forum 2003a).

An interviewee at our trust suggested that this may underestimate the difficulties at Greenwich. Nevertheless, since our trust is a first-wave hospital PFI, it could be argued that its difficulties may have formed the basis of a learning curve for other hospital PFIs. In some respects this is undoubtedly the case. A number of interviewees indicated that they have been visited by representatives from other trusts, which have been able to benefit from their experience. Although the DoH has put considerable effort into the standardisation of contracts since the first wave of PFI hospitals, legal costs are still extremely high. There is also some dissent as to whether standardisation of contracts is the best way forward: 'I do not believe standardising contracts is the right way forward. It should only be a part of the process. More weight has to be given to innovation, change and flexibility. We have got to get more innovative in contract structures and how we do the core business.' (Malcolm Stamp, chief executive of Norfolk and Norwich University Hospital, quoted in PPP Forum, 2003b)

The interview material that we have provided above shows that implementing this PFI involved and continues to involve an enormous workload for the trust and their service providers in terms of very detailed discussions about elements of the contract, performance assessment and monitoring. Given the level of detail that is involved, it is unlikely that other trusts can learn these lessons and/or implement the solutions very easily. The information we have been given suggests a piecemeal approach to contacts between trusts and the use of benchmarking data, so that it is not certain that all the lessons or available information is moving around the health sector. Furthermore, this first-wave hospital has not yet conducted a post-implementation review, and nor is there a timetable for doing so. Given the length of time that the PFI has been in action at our trust, it is simplistic and inappropriate to write off the issues we have raised about contract specification, performance indicators, monitoring and benchmarking, as 'teething problems' that need not arise elsewhere.

Although our trust interviewees were pleased with the hospital's design and construction, it was much smaller than the facilities that it replaced. The planned reduction in caseload had not occurred, causing capacity problems. Although the project aimed to reduce the duplication of working on two sites, there was still some fragmentation and duplication. Furthermore, the expected cost savings had not been achieved because of the failure to reduce length of stay and shed the anticipated caseload to other trusts in the

area. Combined with the evidence from the commercial press cited in the previous chapter and our financial analysis, this suggests that PFI has the potential to destabilise the trusts' financial position if capacity is insufficient to generate the necessary income to cover the full costs. Although this problem exists irrespective of the financing method, the effects become more acute with the additional costs of PFI and the reduced flexibility it imposes on the budget.

A number of interviewees provided examples that suggest that costs of managing the PFI have been far greater than expected, thereby reducing the actual VFM compared with that expected in the business case. In part, this is inherent in the nature of contracting, particularly in human services that unlike roads are so difficult to define and operationalise, eg cleanliness. In part, it is the result of trust inexperience with contracting. Whereas trust personnel may have expected that some performance monitoring would be needed, there was little appreciation of both the extent and the active nature of the monitoring required, as opposed to merely checking the performance measurement systems.

Furthermore, the nature of the changes that have been made to the contract raise questions about whether the original comparison between the PFI bids and the PSC was an equal comparison. Some examples illustrate the point. If the PSC costing assumed patients would receive marmalade for breakfast and litter would be collected, as was the case at the time it was created, and the PFI bid did not include these costs, then the FBC did not compare like with like. Similarly, if the trust obtains more than 10% of any refinancing benefit, this was not included in the PSC. A 12-bed unit, additional to the original design, was not costed in the PSC. In addition, a current member of the trust has argued that the PSC may have lacked rigour because 'it was an option you were never going to do', throwing doubt on the methodology of PFI decision-making processes.

It has become clear that a number of important issues still need to be resolved in relation to this PFI. These include: the need for better planning; completion of monitoring protocols; more streamlined procedures for negotiating changes to contracts; and the conduct of a post-project evaluation. The additional costs to the trust relating to changes in the design, contract changes, and the cost of double monitoring indicate a need for careful monitoring of the affordability of this project, since the payments will have to be made for the duration of the contract, whatever the impact on the rest of the trust's budget.

In addition, there are issues that need to be resolved over the long term, and an important one is the question of handover at the end of the contract when the new build PFI reverts to the trust: 'Life cycle investment is identified so that everything is replaced right up to the last year, so that when we get it, it will be good as new, and in theory the building is almost guaranteed not for one year but for 35 years'. This interviewee nonetheless accepted that within the concession terms 'there's room for interpretation and debate'. Life cycle replacement also covers important pieces of equipment throughout the life of the PFI, but as yet it is too early in our case study for any experience about equipment replacement to have been gained.

In this chapter we have sought to present evidence drawn from interviewees about the practicalities of implementing a first-wave hospital PFI. Interviewees do not always share the same experiences about such a large project. Nevertheless, this case raises important issues about the complex organisational structures surrounding PFI in health, especially in relation to the accountability processes of monitoring performance indicators. Government advice about the need for contracts to focus on output specifications has been shown to be difficult to put into practice, especially in complex practical situations such as cleanliness in a dynamic environment.

9. Discussion and conclusions

Our analysis shows that PFI is a very expensive way of financing and delivering public services that must, where public expenditure is constrained, lead to cuts in public services and/or tax rises, that is, a cut in the social wage.

Discussion and conclusions

Our study has focused on three interrelated issues: the VFM of implemented projects, the procedures for managing risk transfer, and the reporting of and accountability for PFI projects. In this chapter, we draw together important issues raised in our literature review, and from our findings from the financial analysis of the roads and health sectors and the two case studies, in order to discuss them and present our conclusions. Although we consider each in turn, there is in fact a considerable degree of overlap.

PFI is a keystone of the Government's reform of the public services and the scale of these projects is significant. The DBFO projects signed in 1996 represented about 35% of all new construction in the roads sector between 1996 and 2001, and about 25% of the £21 billion allocated in the Government's ten-year national plan to the strategic highway network will involve private finance. However, since the eight first-tranche projects were signed new projects have been less frequent. In the health sector there has been a continuous expansion of private finance since the first health contract was signed in 1997, and by March 2003 there were 148 approved health schemes in England with a value of some £4.5 billion. Since 1997, about 85% of the funds for major NHS capital investment projects have been provided by private finance. Given the size of the commitment in these two sectors alone it is not surprising that the Government should seek to control the Private Finance Initiative. The development of organisational systems to manage, support and control the PFI procurement process has resulted in a complex structure of interrelated organisations with different roles in relation to advising and supporting both the relevant public sector and private sector organisations that form the partnerships.

Owing to a lack of management data, and because projects are still in the very early years of long-term contracts, it has not been possible to reach definitive conclusions about whether VFM has been or is likely to be achieved. Rather, we have been able to investigate

and evaluate issues that are indicative of the VFM outcome, using a framework provided by the NAO. The NAO (1999c) stressed the importance of assessing whether the contract had adequate incentives, remedies and safeguards to ensure that the service that was the subject of VFM appraisal would be delivered to a satisfactory standard throughout the contract period. In effect this would be underpinned by:

- adequate arrangements to manage the contract

- suitable bonuses and other incentives for good performance backed up by contractual sanctions to deter poor performance from the provider

- arrangements for compensation for poor performance

- satisfactory termination or handover arrangements

- suitable arrangements for dealing with changing requirements.

The NAO has recommended that when assessing VFM it is important to examine the mechanisms and procedures for monitoring the contract, to identify and analyse the risks to be transferred and to examine contingency planning. This has formed the basis of our case study investigations. In addition, in order to assess the effects of the policy initiative we have sought, by way of a financial analysis of the sectors, to reach some conclusions about the wider reporting and accountability issues.

In this chapter we begin by presenting our conclusions about the nature of the partnership model and the management of the contract as it is evidenced in our two cases. We then consider the available evidence in relation to VFM and risk transfer associated specifically with our two case studies. This is followed by a broader assessment of our conclusions in relation to the general financial reporting and accountability issues associated with PFI. After indicating some issues for future research, we draw some general conclusions about PFI and accountability.

THE PARTNERSHIP MODEL AND MANAGING THE CONTRACT

In Chapter 1 we highlighted four potential models of partnership that PFIs might follow: collaborative, operational, contributory and consultative. In practice, our literature review shows that the PAC (1999a) has identified a failure to work in partnership, especially on early projects, because of the use of a narrow definition of responsibilities. In addition, we noted that the Transport Select Committee (2003) had shown an inherent conflict within the partnership model because attempts to build positive partnerships were undermining the use of appropriate contractual sanctions to enforce maintenance standards. The NAO (2003e) has stressed that the relationship should not be that of customer/supplier but rather should be built upon a whole-business approach with both sectors interacting through good governance procedures. Essentially the NAO has indicated that good contract management can achieve this.

Our cases suggest that the nature of the relationships between the public and private sector are not collaborative partnerships, in which there is a pooling of equal resources and a relinquishing of autonomy in pursuit of shared goals. It is probably the case that both sectors are seeking to achieve operational partnership in which there is a sharing of work but not of decision-making authority. There appears to be a consensus that although partnership is an ideal, it is not a position that has yet been reached, and interviewees from both sectors have discussed the need for changing methods of working in order to achieve partnership. Essentially the cases provide evidence about how the partnerships operate in practice, and they raise several important issues: the legalistic nature

of the concessions, the kind of monitoring systems chosen to measure performance and the nature of procedures used to ensure that risk is transferred in the way that the public sector anticipated.

Legalistic contracts
The intention is that procurers should specify required outcomes, which form the basis of the contractual relationship between the partners. Our literature review indicated that there were concerns about the ability of contracting parties to write a contract with adequate outcome specifications and that consequently contract monitoring and assessment of VFM would prove problematic.

When the expected outcomes from a contract can be clearly written, for example the specifications for a brand new construction, then the private sector has shown itself capable of delivering on time and to budget, within the context of PFI. Nevertheless, it should be noted that the same contracting companies did not achieve this level of performance under traditional procurement methods. This success should be viewed in the context of the pre-negotiating phase, which typically takes longer under PFI. Nevertheless, in terms of constructing new assets such as roads or hospitals, PFI has operationalised an incentive system and payment mechanism that enables the public sector to use penalties to control the delivery of new build projects that it was previously less able to control.

There is no particular evidence that this is due to the integration provided by PFI of the design, build, operate and finance elements that make up a large-scale project. Rather it is due to the writing of a contract that heavily penalises late delivery and insists that the quoted price and the final price should match. Such conditions could equally be applied to projects financed in the conventional manner, begging the question of why such conditions were not previously made. The PFI contract model raises a number of issues.

First, late delivery penalties are likely to lead to more cautious time estimates and to contingency reserves being included within bids, so there may be a trade-off between cost and prompt delivery. This is a trade-off that has been recognised by both the NAO and the PAC. The NAO (2001d) has noted that arrangements that give incentives to the contractor to complete on time and minimise the risk of cost variations to the department may be an important consideration in the choice of procurement. In addition, the Department of Health has acknowledged that certainty on price and timing of delivery formed part of the decision that the PFI contract for the redevelopment of the West Middlesex University Hospital represented VFM (PAC 2003a, para. 6).

Secondly, to the extent that price fluctuations between the original contract and finished cost previously represented genuine unforeseen circumstances, such as unexpectedly adverse ground conditions, then price rises reflect the holding of risk by the public sector. Whether the private or the public sector is best able to carry that risk is a matter for future research. Thirdly, to the extent that price fluctuations previously represented the private sector's recouping of a contract price that was deliberately underpriced or simply incompetently priced, tougher contractual terms under either PFI or conventional procurement may be beneficial in a competitive environment.

By way of contrast, we found that specifying outcomes for the service element of the contract is far from straightforward, particularly in hospitals that rely on team working and human services that are difficult to define precisely. Furthermore, the legalistic nature of the arrangements may place stress on the notion of a partnership.

- The trust, which had no previous experience of CCT, had a lack of expertise, which was not evident at the Highways Agency, in writing the very fine detail of its requirements for services.

- Since the nature of the contract is that quality assessment is a matter of judgement, sometimes it was disputed. In addition, the nature of some services at the trust is less amenable to specification and measurement than the engineering type services relevant to the Highways Agency.

- The trust requires a variety of services that are provided by different subcontractors that may have conflicting interests under conditions where the nature of healthcare requires staff to interact and work as a team, a task rendered more difficult when staff are managed by different employers.

- The complex chain of subcontracting through which the private sector operates means that the partnership relationship is far from simple and governed by multiple contracts within the private sector.

- Amendments to contracts are simple to achieve in terms of obtaining new services, but negotiations surrounding appropriate payment mechanisms tend to be complex, detailed and consequently resource-consuming for all the contracting parties.

Consequently, the public sector is forming secondary, consultative relationships to seek legal advice about the contractual terms that govern the primary relationship. Our cases show that when it is difficult to write contractual terms clearly, for example because the evaluation of outcomes is a matter of opinion or where responsibility and risk is shared, then the very legalistic nature of PFI results in time-consuming assessments and conflicts about the quality of performance. It leads the public sector to seek expensive legal advice. The evidence from our cases is that these problems occur in the operations and maintenance phase of projects rather than the construction phase.

Monitoring systems

Fundamentally, the following factors put the notion of partnership under strain.

- In both public sector organisations there was a lack of planning about the types of information systems that would be needed for monitoring, and consequently both the Highways Agency and the trust strengthened and formalised these in the post-implementation period.

- Although the principle of PFI is that private sector contractors should be self-monitoring and subject only to limited checking by the procurer, in practice, data collection and its monitoring have proved more problematic than expected.

- The procurer has not always been content with the quality of information provided by the private sector and changes have been requested but not always implemented.

- Active monitoring has been required and therefore monitoring has been a more onerous task than expected.

- Additional and significant monitoring costs have been incurred but the organisations are not able to put a price on them.

Despite the similarities in the ways in which the management procedures operated in the two case organisations, we did identify an important difference in the nature of the partnerships due to the difference in the level of previous contracting expertise.

- Previous experience in dealing with private sector contractors and the pre-existence of written quality standards in relation to road maintenance appear to have eased the path of the Highways Agency into PFI. Such experience was not a feature of our case hospital trust, although some trusts have had experience of CCT. Consequently, the establishment of partnership, and monitoring procedures to oversee it, has been more complex in healthcare and there is more conflict between the contracting parties.

- Where the operational aspects of the contracts are concerned, the hospital trust's lack of previous experience means that the balance of power rests largely with the private sector, whereas this is not the case with the Highways Agency contract. Previously the NHS had accumulated a central body of knowledge about the procurement of new hospital builds, but under PFI procurement responsibility is at unit level, that is, with the individual hospital trust.

We argued in Chapter 2 that official advice from government sources tends to be difficult to put into practice. The case studies show that this is especially so when employees lack experience, when outcomes are difficult to assess objectively, and when contract terms do not transfer readily into measurable performance indicators. Sector-specific help on contract writing has been forthcoming but it does not resolve the difficulties of writing specifications for complex practical situations in a dynamic environment. Although the OGC has recognised the importance of continuity of key personnel to good-quality management of projects, the length of contracts means that key role holders will change. Hence continuity needs to be very carefully managed and cannot be assumed.

Procedures to ensure risk transfer

Although procedures for ensuring the transfer of risk in the construction stage seem to have worked in our cases, at least to the extent that the assets were constructed on time and to budget, the procedures for ensuring risk transfer during the operational phase are more problematic. In part, this was because, as one trust interviewee explained, their attention was focused on the asset not the service element of the contract. In part, this was because the contract may not have adequately reflected the expectations of the trust. There were instances where the trust believed that the private partner held the risk in that it was responsible for certain tasks, but the contract did not in fact transfer the risk to the private sector partner.

- The difficulty in specifying performance standards and thus in monitoring and enforcing them also means that it is difficult to ensure that the payments deliver the expected level of services. Or put another way: it is difficult to ensure that costs are transferred in the way that was anticipated.

- Although it is possible to identify the circumstances in which risk is probably shared between the private and public sectors, there is sometimes a lack of clarity about the proportion of risk that each sector holds. This means that the division of risk may be resolved only in the event of service failure, that is, once it is too late to manage the risk, thereby creating the potential for additional costs (risks).

- It was noticeable that neither of our case projects had developed contingency plans for exit strategies in the event of total failure of the private sector. This was because there is no concept that such an event is possible.

In summary, the case studies show that although the Highways Agency and the hospital trust operate within a common policy framework for PFI, there are important sectoral differences as to how management of the contracts operates, indicating that these PFI experiences may be present in some but not all sectors. Broadly the differences relate to variations in previous experience of contractual relationships, to the greater technical nature of road building, operation and maintenance, to the importance of team working in health, and to the perceived success of the service provision. The two cases also provide a number of instances where similar operational issues have arisen across these two sectors, indicating that such issues may be found also in other sectors. These relate to

inadequacies associated with: planning; data collection and monitoring systems; assessment of soft project objectives; uncertainties about where risk is shared; performance measurement; and the measurement of VFM. PFI has made visible poor performance on delivery in terms of both time and cost (a problem which afflicted public sector projects), because PFI should ensure good delivery performance. It is the contractual penalties that create this good performance, however, and these are a separate element of PFI.

The result is that although partnership is a relationship to be aspired to, it has not been achieved in practice. This is means that it is unclear that the procedures for managing contracts are capable of delivering the appropriate levels of service provision, given that it is almost impossible to specify some services adequately. But without obtaining this level of service, the public agency cannot be assured of the balance between cost and quality that is implicit in VFM.

MANAGING THE CONTRACT TO ENSURE VFM

VFM on individual projects may be achieved in a number of different ways. Our literature review showed that competitive forces might not operate to create VFM because of a lack of bidders, market concentration, uneven power relationships between the partners, and the locking-in to an existing provider that has become associated with PFI. Alternatively, the literature suggests that reduced costs may be achieved by reductions in labour costs, but that these savings may fall elsewhere on the public sector budget. Lack of competition at the bidding stage has not been a feature of our cases but there is evidence that additional work not originally contracted for is locked in. In the trust case, labour costs are an issue of some concern, because one of the contractors is finding it difficult to recruit and retain staff. The implication is that too much labour cost has been stripped from the supplier's bid and that this could adversely affect the quality of service provision.

Much previous evaluation of PFI contracts has focused on the delivery of the construction phase and in this respect success has been identified generally, but not uniformly. There seems to be much less information about the operational phase of contracts. In general terms, although both our case contracts have delivered new construction on time, to budget, and much as was anticipated, there is some diversity of perception about the performance of contractors in relation to services. At the Highways Agency there is broad satisfaction that the road is well maintained. PFI contracts ensure that maintenance is carried out and to a prescribed standard, whereas under the *ancien régime*, maintenance suffered when budgets were tight. In contrast, at the trust there is some concern about the quality of services, especially the cleaning service. The literature suggests that our trust is not unique. It is interesting to note that those responsible for monitoring the contracts take a different perspective on costs. Whereas the trust monitors were very conscious of the costs associated with the service that is perceived as under-performing, the Highways Agency representatives with close operational association tended to focus on performance that is deemed to be successful, without regard to the associated costs.

From the case studies it is possible to draw a number of conclusions about the arrangements that exist in relation to managing the contract so that VFM is likely to occur.

- At the appraisal stage, projects' VFM is assessed against the PSCs, but even in the early days of implementation the PSCs are not fair comparators for actual performance because they are not updated for contract amendments.

- Some contract amendments have been required owing to the failure to specify the required level of service accurately enough. This raises questions as to whether in fact the PSC and PFI options were comparing like with like.

- In order to measure actual VFM it would be necessary to make a comparison of the PFI's whole-life costs against a fair comparator. However, because the project lifetimes are so long and so many changes are made to the initial project specification there is unlikely to be any meaningful comparator against which to judge VFM in any holistic sense. Benchmarking of elements of projects is possible but at present this is not and cannot be done in any systematic way.

- At the hospital trust there is a lack of evidence about quality standards before PFI was introduced so that current performance cannot be measured against these in any objective manner. This is a common problem in human services, as the NAO's report into the operational performance of PFI prisons acknowledged (NAO 2003g).

- Projects may have multiple objectives including 'softer' objectives and there is little information available to enable a formal assessment of whether these objectives have been achieved. For example, service user feedback is not systematically evaluated, but depends upon a complaints-based system at both the hospital trust and the Highways Agency.

- The focus of contract incentives is response time rather than performance per se. The implication is that contractors are not necessarily penalised for poor performance, but only for failure to respond to a problem within a reasonable time once it has been detected. In the context of the team working required in hospitals, any failure to deliver the required level of service and respond in time may have an adverse impact on the hospital's performance and its performance ratings. In the context of patient choice and financial flows where money follows patients, poor quality of service may affect future income.

- The additional and unexpected costs of managing the PFI contracts suggest that VFM is unlikely to be as high as anticipated.

- The complex web of companies through which the private sector partner operates imposes extra monitoring costs and supervision difficulties for the public sector, particularly in healthcare.

- Payments are made on the strength of data that have not been subject to monitoring at the trust, and estimated data for which actual details will never be available at the Highways Agency.

- Although the residual life of assets after the PFI contract is complete will affect the eventual VFM, systems to ensure that residual lifetimes are as anticipated are not yet in evidence. However, contract periods on some hospitals have been extended since financial close to 60 years or more, begging the question as to whether in fact there is any intention that the assets should revert to the public sector.

Advice from official sources recognises the need for evaluation of projects and the dissemination of results. Our cases indicate that PSCs, often suggested as a base for this assessment, quickly become out of date and are not an appropriate benchmark against which to measure VFM. Alternative benchmarks need to become the norm but there is a lack of familiarity in some quarters about government initiatives to create comparative databases for this purpose. Although there is informal person-to-person transfer of PFI-related knowledge, experience and networking through national contacts, benchmarking is unsystematic, post-implementation evaluation of projects is slow and the dissemination of outcomes is restricted or unsystematic. Taken together, this means that there are as yet inadequate arrangements to monitor the contracts in ways that will ensure they will deliver VFM.

RISK TRANSFER OR RISK CREATION?

Our literature review shows that risk transfer is a critical feature of many PFI projects, because without the inclusion of the cost of risk transfer in the VFM analysis the PSC has a lower net present cost. However, the methodology that surrounds the valuation of risk is problematic. The assessed value of risk transferred is based on probabilities, but there is an acknowledged shortage of risk management skill within the public sector so that the establishment of appropriate probabilities may be difficult. In addition, the decision-making methodology uses discounted cash flows so that the rate of discount applied is critical to the outcome.

There is a concern also that too much risk may be transferred to the private sector because of the technical accounting regulations. If a PFI scheme is to remain off balance sheet in the public sector – something that the Treasury is anxious to achieve – it is necessary to show that risk transfer has taken place. This is because a strict interpretation of FRS 5 *Reporting the Substance of Transactions*, the relevant reporting regulation, would have seen many PFIs remain on balance sheet, contrary to the wishes of the Government, since the public sector holds the main risks, demand and residual risks. At present, 57% of PFI projects are on the public sector's balance sheet (HM Treasury 2003d), rather less than the Treasury had expected originally. This accounting regulation may have increased pressure to transfer risk into the private sector. Some evidence that this is so is provided by the credit ratings agency, Standard and Poor's (2002), which notes that the private sector has been asked to take on more risk in more recent schemes and implies that the Government has been willing to support the extra cost. This conflicts with the fundamental premise of PFI that the contracting party best able to manage it ought to hold risk.

A number of other risk-related issues have been identified from our study. First, the assumption that the private sector is willing and able to carry risk may not always be well founded, and risk transfer may be difficult to operationalise in practice. Specifically in relation to roads, the private sector may be reluctant to carry risks associated with projects that do not have statutory approval.

Secondly, although it is argued that demand risk has transferred in relation to the road projects, the Highways Agency may still retain the risk. Should demand change in ways that make it impossible for the private sector to generate the revenue to spend on maintenance, then it may not be able to maintain the road. In such circumstances, given the essential (or in other cases statutory) nature of the service and the fact that the public sector retains responsibility for service provision, then, as our literature review shows, the public sector must shoulder a cost for a risk which it thought it had transferred and for which it had already paid. This means that the public sector retains responsibility without control.

Thirdly, although it is a fundamental premise of PFI that risk should be transferred to the party best able to manage it, which usually means that the public sector should carry the demand risk, in the case of roads the private sector is very interested in deals that have some element of demand risk.

Fourthly, our hospital case study has shown that there is some confusion as to whether the contract has transferred risk and responsibility in the way that was intended or expected by the public sector. In any event, since there is no information in the public domain about the level of penalties imposed for poor performance and little indication from our case studies that many penalties have been imposed, it is impossible to assess the degree to which risk transfer has taken place in practice.

Fifthly, our financial analysis shows that there is a high premium in respect of the expected risk transfer. At the 6% discount rate, risk transfer varied between 31% and 85% of road construction costs, with similar and wide variations for hospitals. It seems unlikely that the degree of risk warrants such a high cost since, first, Fitch Ratings (2003) argues that the PPP sector will remain investment grade and will offer a comparatively safe haven in times of economic downturn. Secondly, the companies have been able to refinance their loans at lower rates of interest and generate an additional source of profit after the construction phase was completed.

The National Audit Office (1999a) argued that the companies' cost of capital above that of public sector debt costs reflected project risk. Our financial analysis showed that the risk premium was about six and five percentage points above the cost of Treasury gilts for roads and hospitals respectively. Although the Highways Agency reports its PFI assets as on balance sheet, most of the trusts do not, implying that the Highways Agency has transferred less risk than the trusts. Despite this, our analysis shows that both projects very quickly earned high post-tax returns on shareholders' funds. The actual risk is very limited and hardly commensurate with their abnormally high returns. Taken together, our evidence shows that risk transfer, the fundamental component of VFM, has proved very expensive.

As well as the problems and cost of risk transfer, PFI may create additional risks. First, the PAC considered risk creation to be an outcome of the demand risk transfer in roads. It made the following recommendation with regard to the first four design, build, finance and operate roads contracts (PAC 1998d, Recommendation 3):

Departments should consider carefully the implication of basing payments to operators on volumes of activity over which neither the public sector nor the operators have any effective control. In the case of these four contracts, payments to operators are based primarily on traffic volumes which are, however, notoriously difficult to forecast. In other words, the Agency have created a risk which is borne by the operators and which can be expected to increase their costs. PFI can deliver better value than traditional methods of procurement if risks are transferred to the parties best able to handle them. But it is a mistake to confuse risk transfer with risk creation, which is simply likely to increase costs to the taxpayer.

Secondly, the corporate form (the SPV), typically a shell company with no employees, and the complex web of subcontracting through which the private sector operates serve to minimise the SPV's risk. Because each contract is held by a separate SPV, whose only activity is the PFI project, there is no cross subsidy between projects. Although this serves to isolate the private sector's risk, it also generates extra costs and creates additional risk for the public sector. Extra costs are created by the monitoring required to ensure service delivery across a range of subcontractors. Additional risk is created because should the SPV fail financially, for whatever reason, it has no recourse to its parent companies. Thus the SPV can walk away from a PFI contract without jeopardising the position of the parent companies. Given that the SPV's debts are underwritten by the government, either de jure or de facto, the parent companies that have provided the loan finance are protected. This places the SPV in a very powerful position in relation to the public sector purchaser.

Thus, to conclude, it is unclear that risk is transferred in the way anticipated at financial close. Some risks have been transferred to parties that are not best placed to manage them. Even more importantly, PFI has generated additional risks to the purchaser, the public sector as a whole, and service users that were not predicted and/or quantified when the VFM comparison was undertaken. This means first, that the

VFM comparisons did not compare like with like and, secondly, the projects are unlikely to achieve the risk transfer that provided the original justification for both the project and the policy.

REPORTING AND ACCOUNTABILITY

In this section we present our conclusions relating to the publicly available information for these two sectors. Before so doing it is worth making the general point that information is not easy to obtain, even in some cases where it is intended to be in the public domain. Much remains hidden behind the cloak of 'commercial confidentiality'. Although the NHS has released more financial information than the Highways Agency, it is by no means adequate. This lack of transparency exists at Treasury, departmental, purchaser and contractor level.

Considering first the reporting of PFI at government level. First, even the most basic data showing the number, size and cost of PFI projects are difficult to collect. For example, numerous government sources produce information in ways that do not reconcile. Secondly, it was impossible to produce a table showing the amount of PFI and non-PFI expenditure on a departmental basis for each year since the policy was introduced. Thirdly, it is almost impossible to ascertain PFI expenditure as a proportion of total public capital expenditure. This is because although the Treasury produces a list of all signed deals, dates and their capital values on a departmental basis, we could not find a comparable list of non-PFI or even total capital expenditure reported on a departmental basis. In addition, it is not clear that the government records all IT PFI projects as PFI capital expenditure, since it maintains it is purchasing services not assets. Certainly, the Treasury list was not complete, eg the Home Office did not show the problematic Criminal Records Bureau project. Furthermore, PFI will not be scored as government expenditure if the underlying asset is off the government's balance sheet. Since the statistics do not identify whether the asset is on or off the government's balance sheet, the ratio of public to non-public capital expenditure is impossible to calculate. Fifthly, it is impossible to find out, in a systematic way, the public sector's expected annual payments on a project basis (since the full business cases setting out the financial costs are not in the public domain for reasons of 'commercial confidentiality') or even on a departmental basis. However, the Treasury does produce aggregated data that suggests that future commitments now constitute about 3% of departmental expenditure (excluding welfare payments). Finally, despite the fact that central government is known to guarantee the Highways Agency's payments to the private sector and presumably its other contracts, and implicitly to do so in healthcare, the departmental accounts make no mention of such future commitments.

Although the use of parliamentary questions has elucidated some information (Health Select Committee Memorandum 2000), this is a cumbersome route that provides data on an ad hoc basis only and has limited visibility. Thus it only serves to highlight not resolve the problem.

At purchaser level, despite a considerable amount of information about DBFO in general, the Highways Agency's reporting of its DBFO payments was missing for three years and was then very limited. Although the trusts put their summary accounts on their websites, these do not contain any financial information relating to PFI. Some trusts required frequent reminders to send financial statements. In the context of stakeholder reporting, the research team, all of whom are UK tax payers, was also surprised to be charged for a hard copy of the accounts of one hospital trust. In addition the financial information in both sectors lacks clarity, the message from annual reports is opaque and consequently public accountability is reduced. Information that was promised by other public bodies was not always forthcoming. Although none of this was necessarily a deliberate attempt to reduce public

accountability, it does mean that only the persistent are successful. There is no information in the notes to the accounts explaining the performance levels, payments, any deductions for poor performance, or why payments were higher than expected at financial close or even the previous year, or any contract renegotiations. Neither is there an explanation for the accounting treatment of the PFI assets and liabilities and any changes that have occurred. A further point relates to the reporting of the operation of the contracts. Neither sector provides any financial or other reporting on how satisfactorily or otherwise the contract is operating. Yet this information is crucial for assessing the degree to which the contracts provide incentives for the private sector partners to deliver the appropriate level of service and thus achieve risk transfer.

The reporting of PFI transactions by companies wholly dependent upon public funding is opaque in the extreme. The ability to hide behind the 'corporate veil' means that related party transactions and the full extent of the financial gains made out of PFI are not disclosed. This is not a small matter since our evidence shows that, at least in the roads sector, a significant proportion of the payments made by the Highways Agency constitute additional costs that would not be borne under conventional procurement. There is a lack of open book accounting that would enable the purchasing agency to trace the contractors' costs and profits. In both sectors, the purchasing agencies were unaware of the extent of the financial gains made by the private sector out of their PFI contracts, particularly by the related parties.

In short, there is a lack of consistent and useful data about the extent of private finance in public services at project, programme or policy level, making it difficult to analyse the efficacy of private finance and its wider implications. The reporting of PFI is not simply a question of the annual revenue cost, although this is not insignificant. More importantly, it is about the present Government's implicit debt levels and future commitments under long-term contracts that have the effect of binding future government administrations and of creating ring-fenced resources within departmental budgets. Such commitments have the potential to destabilise the financial viability of purchasing agencies and squeeze out other public sector activities. In addition, there are sector-specific issues that reflect the same lack of accountability in relation to private sector profits and the scale of the Government's financial dealings, as our literature review found to be the case in Australia.

The roads sector

PFIs have been used to improve, widen and build new road length and structures so that, unlike the health sector, PFIs have inserted new capacity into the system. Compared with the health sector, where according to the IPPR (2004), the NHS has a better framework than central or local government for releasing information to the public, there is less information about DBFOs in the public domain. For example, the full business cases are not available in roads and there is less public information about contract values and payments. It is important to recognise that this is government-imposed secrecy. As a consequence, there has been less empirical evaluative research. No one at the Treasury, the DoT, the Highways Agency or the National Audit Office has carried out a post-implementation evaluation of the VFM obtained under DBFO.

Financial reporting within the private sector is opaque, from a public accountability perspective, because of the complexity of the web of companies that make up the SPV and the contracting organisations. The SPV normally lets the operational contracts to the companies that own it, and so transactions and transfer prices need not be at arm's length. Consequently it is difficult to measure the total returns on capital and to assess the cost to the public of paying for that return. Moreover, as we noted earlier in the literature review, the PAC has called for a review of contractors' returns

earned on PFI projects (PAC 2003d). To do this, however, it would be necessary for the NAO as the external auditor to exercise its 'right to roam' through these organisational structures.

The analysis in Chapter 5 shows a high cost of capital in the SPV, which is likely to be an underestimate because of transfer pricing between the SPV and its contractors, and indeed our analysis suggests that the contractors have higher profits on PFIs than on other contracts. The private sector parent organisations may profit from the DBFO in different ways, including an equity stake in both the SPV and subsidiary organisations that carry out work and from interest on any loans to the SPV. We have made the following estimates.

- The Highways Agency pays about £210 m a year based largely on the amount of (rising) traffic flows.

- For the first three years, the Highways Agency did not report its DBFO payments and could not make such information available to the research team.

- In the subsequent three-year period, the Highways Agency has paid more than the initial capital cost of £590 m on the first eight projects, so that in effect the remaining payments on the 30-year contract worth about £6 billion in total are for risk transfer, the cost of finance, operation and maintenance.

- Finance costs are in the order of three times the initial construction cost and one third of the total £6 billion cash cost of the projects.

- 68% of the DBFO companies' receipts from the Highways Agency is operating profit, in effect the public sector's effective cost of using private finance. And even this is an underestimate since this figure relates to operating profits after deductions of payments to their subcontractors, usually sister companies.

- About 35% of the payments made by the Highways Agency actually go towards the operation and maintenance of roads.

- In so far as the Highways Agency is pleased with the operation and maintenance of the roads under DBFO, this appears to be because there has been adequate financial provision within the contract for this.

- The Highways Agency is paying a premium of some 25% of construction cost to ensure the project is built on time and to budget.

- Although the Highways Agency's payments of about £210 m per year are set to rise because of the payment profile and rising traffic volumes, future payments are not disclosed in ways that identify these factors.

In addition, the payments profile raises some cause for concern. Although the payment mechanism may include a higher payment in years in which significant repairs are expected, the volume-based nature of the toll means that payments are also front loaded and consequently money that should be applied to maintenance is held in the private sector. There is no ring-fencing of that resource within the private sector (so for example one company made an interest-free loan for an indefinite period to its parent company), nor is there a requirement that the monies be set aside in, say, an escrow account for future maintenance. This creates risk for the taxpayer, who may be faced with paying a second time for maintenance, if for any reason the private sector is unable to pay.

Several other reporting issues have been identified.

- There is no reporting of any deductions for poor performance.

- In the 1999/2000 Highways Agency accounts, seven of the eight first-tranche projects were off balance sheet, although intangible assets representing the reversionary interests were recognised. Subsequently, the Agency has had to change its accounting policy and in 2000/1 all eight projects were on balance sheet for construction costs together with associated long-term and short-term creditors. The Agency has indicated that it will continue to look for risk transfer to ensure that future DBFO contract liabilities are off balance sheet, and that it has developed a strategy for taking a view on the accounting treatment before contract award (Highways Agency 2003). Although the Agency accepts that the accounting treatment should not be an aim in itself, this suggests that there is pressure to transfer risk for accounting purposes without considering which party is best able to carry the risk.

- Although the Highways Agency's payments to the SPVs are guaranteed by the government there is little transparency about future payments, obligations and the implications for public expenditure.

- There is no reporting of how much DBFO is costing the public sector as a whole. For example, under DBFO, the complex reporting web of SPVs and related companies makes it impossible to tell what the true rate of tax is.

In conclusion, the road projects appear to be costing more than expected as reflected in net present costs that are higher than those identified by the Highways Agency (Haynes and Roden 1999), owing to rising traffic and contract changes. It is, however, impossible to know now whether or not VFM has been or is likely to be achieved, because the expensive element of the service contract relates generally to maintenance that will not be required for many years.

The health sector

The PFI has been used to build new hospitals and refurbish existing ones and to operate and maintain the estate. Compared with the roads sector, there is more information in the public domain, particularly in relation to the business cases used to support the case for PFI. However, health sector PFIs are also more complex to understand because:

- PFI contracts are at various different stages of completion

- data are available at unit level as opposed to agency level

- there is considerable and continuing restructuring within the sector and the PFI hospitals, which creates organisational change

- the sector is more politically charged and highly visible and the environment is confused by issues such as waiting lists and patient flows and

- the issues around performance and its measurement are more subjective.

The financial statements of our trust case were not easy to interpret over the relevant period because a number of related and significant transactions were booked to fixed asset, debtor, creditor and income accounts. Given that these transactions crossed more than one year and were linked to transactions with the relevant primary care trusts (PCT) and the Department of Health, they act to disguise the effects of PFI from all but the trained reader, who will probably also need additional information from the trust. We experienced the same difficulties with the complex SPV accounts as were evident in the roads sector, but nevertheless the following issues have been identified.

- The annual cost of about £205 m for our trusts is likely to rise because of the contractual arrangements. These include increases for inflation, volume increases and contract amendments and additions.

- Because the effects of PFI are not separated from other means of procurement, it is impossible to identify, from information in the public domain, the current or long-term service and finance commitments being made under PFI.

- New additions to contract may not be subject to benchmarking, raising questions about the power of the contractors to charge higher than normal prices.

- Returns to contractors are higher than typically available under their conventional business contracts.

- The contracting companies also benefit from user charges for parking, patients' televisions and telephones, retail concessions and catering in ways that are not transparent. This underestimates the revenues to the SPVs' subcontractors, lost revenues to the trusts and/or the additional costs to staff and patients.

- Although the Government does not guarantee the payments, as it does for the roads projects, it did issue a letter of support to investors in the case of the Meridian hospital, which the credit ratings agency believes to be almost as good as a formal government guarantee.

Two technical accounting issues have been identified which have practical implications for the management of trusts in the future. First, revenue expenditure associated with PFI is allocated between different budget lines of the standard operating expenses. Although traditional costing patterns are likely to be used where possible, any PFI revenue cost that cannot be readily allocated will be recorded in the category 'other expenditure'. Consequently, although each trust is likely to maintain comparability across time, cross-sectional analysis between trusts may be distorted if trusts account for PFI on different lines.

This distortion has the potential to invalidate the system of National Reference Costs, which is to be used as the basis for paying the trusts on a fee per service basis whereby money will follow patients after 2007. This is an important issue in relation to future funding because any hospital that has costs running above the National Reference Cost benchmark could lose income. Since the trusts are committed to paying the SPVs for the duration of the contract, they must seek to increase their income either from the local PCTs, which must therefore divert income and patients to the PFI hospitals (although how this will be possible under 'patient choice' is unclear), and/or cut other services.

Secondly, our analysis of 13 schemes that are operational shows that nine are off balance sheet and four are on balance sheet, but that in at least one case, Bromley, there has been a change in accounting policy, because a scheme that was intended to be off balance sheet was eventually included in the balance sheet. It is important to recognise that the off balance sheet treatment may have consequences for managing the trust's budget. In our case trust, the PFI element for the new build is an operating lease in its accounts, and an annual transfer into tangible fixed assets is made which cumulatively builds up to the expected valuation of a hospital, taking into account its expected residual life at the end of the contract. This asset, like other trust assets, is revalued using a national indexation formula, which is fine-tuned for local conditions by the District Valuer on a five-year cycle. The timing of these revaluations can be critical to the trust, especially if they fall late in the financial year, because a sudden upward movement reduces the trust's ability to meet its financial target. In cases like this the implication of the PFI transfers to fixed asset accounts is that they increase budgetary uncertainty.

Our literature review indicated that there is little attention paid in evaluation studies to the question of project affordability in the long term at either trust or NHS level. Our analysis suggests the following important issues.

- In some cases PFI charges are higher than expected at the decision-making stage only a few years earlier (Health Select Committee 2000). Although a feature of PFI contracts was supposed to be that costs would be fixed and determined by the contract, the contract provides numerous ways of increasing costs to the trusts. This undermines the reliability and validity of the VFM case, which in any event showed that the financial advantage of PFI was very marginal.

- It is likely that our trust was dissatisfied with some aspects of the operational phase of the contract because it is simply not possible to provide the level of service required at the contract price. Any further efficiencies would have to be made over and above the hospitals' repeated 'efficiency savings' over the last 20 years as others have acknowledged (Arthur Andersen/LSE 2000).

- The cost of capital for trusts rises with PFI. When the cost of capital rises, then labour, the main cost, must be cut. Any labour cuts could threaten the ability of the trusts to process the necessary throughput either to meet the Government's waiting list targets or to generate sufficient income, thereby threatening the trusts' financial viability.

- Six out of the 13 trusts we analysed are in deficit. Four of the nine trusts with off balance sheet PFI projects and two of the four trusts with on balance sheet PFI projects had significant net deficits after paying for the cost of capital.

- Assuming that the financial performance of trusts is a proxy for affordability, then it is disconcerting that hospitals with PFI contracts are more likely to be in deficit in 2002/3.

- We estimate that the additional capital costs of the new hospitals, which are smaller than the ones they replace, took about one quarter of the increase in the trusts' income between 2000 and 2003. In other words, a significant proportion of the new money is not going to front-line services.

- The total cost of PFI to the public sector is unclear. It includes the 'leakage' of the capital charge element contained in the trusts' budgets – at least £125 m a year – that would normally be recycled within the healthcare economy, and the capital allowances that reduce the SPVs' tax.

Although the Government maintains that costs under PFI are fixed and contractually determined in ways that reduces uncertainty, this is misleading. There has been contract cost 'drift'. PFI charges have risen more than expected in five trusts and are expected to increase for at least three more. This indicates that within a very short time these projects have turned out to be less economical than those who prepared the supporting business cases expected.

Taken together, this financial analysis shows that some of the contracts have turned out to be more expensive than expected at financial close. Furthermore, since these are all long-term projects, it is impossible to know how the contracts will perform over the entire life cycle. In so far as they are costing more than expected, this has an impact on the individual trusts and the wider NHS budget that must affect both staff and patients.

SUMMARY

Our findings may be summarised under three headings: financial performance and accountability; partnership and managing the contract; and value for money and risk transfer.

Financial performance and accountability

- Financial information about PFI is opaque, partly because of government-imposed confidentiality, which especially restricts access to business cases in the roads sector.

- Private sector organisations use complex structures that involve close company status and related party transactions that are thus not disclosed, the result being that returns on PFI projects are disseminated between various entities and are thus disguised.

- In both sectors some PFI projects are accounted for on balance sheet but others are off balance sheet and there has been a change in accounting policy in some projects. In addition, accounting across the private and public sectors may not be symmetrical, for example, the Worcester Hospital scheme is off the balance sheet of both the public and private sectors.

- The relationship may not be causal but the propensity for trusts with PFIs to be in deficit is greater than the current national average.

Partnership and managing the contract

- Partnership is an aspiration rather than a description of the actual working relationship between public and private contracting parties.

- Planning of the performance monitoring systems has been poor and has led to an increased workload once the projects have been implemented.

- Self-monitoring systems require high levels of trust that are not always present, and public sector partners are conducting more monitoring activities than was expected.

- Outcomes that are subjective in nature are difficult to write in contractually effective ways, and cause monitoring difficulties.

- Contingency plans should be identified at least in principle for all large-scale PFIs against the possibility of default by the private sector.

Value for money and risk transfer

- Measuring VFM against the PSC is inappropriate because it quickly becomes out of date.

- Soft project objectives may not be evaluated and user opinions about service are not always sought.

- Additional monitoring costs have reduced VFM compared with the original expectations.

- Transactions and monitoring costs have a fixed element and, consequently, small projects may be unsuitable for PFI. Indeed, more recent health schemes have tended to be larger than those in the first wave.

- Where risk is shared between partners its allocation may be unknown and therefore its transfer is uncertain.

- In roads, demand risk is held by the private sector but this may create a new source of risk because the private sector cannot control demand.

- In practice, the government appears to retain ultimate responsibility for the SPVs' debt, which is higher than the cost of the assets and carries the burden of higher interest rates, since payments are guaranteed either explicitly or implicitly.

- There is a lack of ring-fencing of profiled annual payments so that in the event of a private sector failure, money intended for future maintenance may be lost.

In the study we have followed recommendations by the NAO (1999c) for examining the procedures put in place by the agencies to monitor the contract, risk transfer and contingency planning. We have identified areas in which change has been needed and implemented within the sectors, but also areas where problems remain. Monitoring of performance where its assessment is subjective is problematic. Risk transfer is not always certain especially when it is shared and there is a lack of detailed contingency planning for ultimate failure.

The net result of all this is that although risk transfer is the central element in justifying VFM and thus PFI, our analysis shows that risk does not appear to have been transferred to the party best able to manage it. Furthermore, rather than transferring risk to the private sector, PFI has, first, created additional risks to the public agency and the public sector as a whole that must increase costs to the taxpayer and/or reduce service provision, a travesty of risk transfer. Secondly, PFI has generated extra costs to hospital users, both staff and patients, and to the Treasury, through tax concessions and the leakage of the capital charge element in the NHS budget, in ways that are neither transparent nor quantifiable. Thus, inadequate financial reporting means that it is impossible to demonstrate whether or not VFM has or indeed can be achieved in these or any other projects.

Although the Government's case rested upon value for money, including the transfer of risk, PFI is likely to lead to a loss of benefits in kind and a redistribution of income, from the public at large to the corporate sector. It has boosted the construction industry, whose PFI subsidiaries are now the most profitable parts of their enterprises, and led to a major expansion of the facilities management sector. The principle beneficiaries, however, are likely to be the financial institutions whose loans are effectively underwritten by the taxpayers, as evidenced by the renegotiation of the Royal Armouries PFI (NAO 2001a).

Finally, two points should be made. First, the Government, by focusing on the need for private finance to modernise Britain's ageing infrastructure and on concepts as ambiguous as value for money and risk transfer, made the distribution issue invisible in order to justify a deeply unpopular policy. Secondly, the inadequate financial reporting of and lack of accountability for PFI serves to obscure what the Government does not wish to reveal.

ISSUES FOR FUTURE RESEARCH

From the sectoral analysis and the two case studies we have explored in this work, it is possible to identify a number of future research projects. These include the following.

- Given that the contracts are written for very long periods of time, it would be useful to carry out another financial analysis of the two sectors, particularly in health, when the schemes have settled down. Furthermore, longitudinal case studies that track changing relationships between the contracting parties are necessary because sectoral and contract-specific issues change over time.

- Risk transfer, the main component of VFM, is critical if the public sector is to approve a PFI/DBFO contract. But less risk transfer implies a lower rate of return to the private sector, and that the project will be on balance sheet in the public sector. An extended financial analysis as projects mature should make a comparison of the rates of return between on and off balance sheet schemes. Although we have indicated that measuring the VFM of projects is problematic, it would be interesting to

compare the financial performance with any available evidence about VFM or the procurers' perceptions about the success or failure of projects.

- Demand risk is carried by the private sector in roads, but owing to increasing traffic volumes nationally it is possible that there is little real downside risk. An analysis of forecast against actual volumes across all roads PFIs would be interesting.

- There are a number of issues in relation to asset values worthy of future research. For example, our hospital trust is concerned about the proposed changes to the way in which assets are to be accounted for, since it estimates that under the new rules, whereby control will create an asset, it is likely to see a significant rise in its asset base. The concern is that this will create problems in relation to its external financing limit and its ability to meet its financial target. A sectoral assessment of the effects of this change in accounting regulation might influence policy. In addition, the SPV for our roads project indicated that it had some concerns about the valuation and depreciation of the roads asset. A further issue relates to the basis of valuation and the reporting of construction values in both the purchasing agency and the Government's accounts. Finally, although symmetry between the accounting for the assets provided by PFI across the private and public sectors is not currently required, empirical evidence about the nature of the differences would be of interest to regulators.

- We have no evidence of a causal relationship but our analysis shows that 6 out of 13 hospital trusts with PFIs are in deficit for the current financial year, and that this is a higher proportion than the national average, measured using the most recent available statistics. Further investigations of any association between PFI projects and trust deficits tracked over time are needed. Similarly, the implications of such deficits on the local healthcare economy (the primary care trusts and acute hospital trusts) need to be examined.

- Although it is possible to draw very general conclusions about the distributive implications of the policy, more detailed research is needed to quantify the impact on public expenditure, the financial stability of the public agencies that are using PFI, the performance and outputs of such agencies, the SPVs and their financial backers.

- Given that PFI/PPP is new way of delivering public services that blurs the lines between the public and private sector, further research is needed to examine the degree to which the current forms of financial reporting, corporate governance and ownership structures, particularly in the context of internationalisation, provide accountability to the tax payers and service users. The implications for national accounting also need to be considered since PFI, like pensions commitment, climate change, etc, creates implicit debt for governments.

CONCLUSION

As we stated earlier, our concept of accountability in the context of public expenditure on essential public services implies that, first, citizens or at least their political representatives, the media, trade unions, academics, etc can see how society's resources are being used, and secondly, that no members of that society are seen to have an explicitly sanctioned unfair advantage over others in relation to how those resources are used. These two axioms are of course intimately related. With respect to the first point, the difficulties experienced by the research team in obtaining and interpreting the financial statements of the relevant parties do not generate much hope that patients, road users, tax payers and other citizens can see how society's resources are being used. It is significant that more information is made available by both the companies and the Government to the capital

markets than to the public at large. Within the financial statements there is little information about the impact of PFI contracts on the performance of the procurer, and there is a build-up of commitments and implicit guarantees within very long-term contracts about which there is little transparency. With respect to the second point, our analysis shows that PFI is a very expensive way of financing and delivering public services that must, where public expenditure is constrained, lead to cuts in public services and/or tax rises, that is, a cut in the social wage. In contrast, the chief beneficiaries are the providers of finance and some of, though not necessarily all, the private sector service providers, leading to a redistribution not from the rich to the poor but from the mass of the population to the financial elite. In short, PFI does not pass the accountability test.

References

Abadie, R. and Larocca, D. (2003), 'Streets Ahead – PPP Road Schemes Lead the Way', *Project Finance Yearbook 2002/03* (Euromoney Publications).

Accounts Commission (2002), *Taking the Initiative: Using PFI Contracts to Renew Council Schools* (Edinburgh: Audit Scotland).

Accounting Standards Board (1994), *FRS5: Reporting the Substance of Transactions*, Accounting Standards Board (London).

ASB (Accounting Standards Board) (1998), *Amendment to FRS 5: Reporting the Substance of Transactions – The Private Finance Initiative and Similar Contracts* (London).

Accounting Standards Committee (1984), *Statement of Standard Accounting Practice No. 21 Accounting for Leases and Hire Purchase* (London).

Akintoye, A., Taylor, C. and Fitzgerald, E. (1998), 'Risk Analysis and Management of Private Finance Initiative Projects', *Engineering Construction & Architectural Management*, Vol. 5, No. 1, pp. 9–21.

Appleby, J. and Coote, A. (2002), *Five-Year Health Check: A Review of Health Policy 1997–2002* (London: King's Fund).

Arruñada, B. (2000), 'Audit Quality: Attributes, Private Safeguards and the Role of Regulation', *The European Accounting Review 2000*, Vol. 9, No. 2, pp. 205–24.

Arthur Andersen and Enterprise LSE (2000), *Value for Money Drivers in the Private Finance Initiative*, (London: Treasury Taskforce). [online report] <www.treasury-projects.gov.uk/series_1/Andersen>, accessed 02 August 2000.

Audit Commission (2000a), *Aiming to Improve the Principles of Performance Measurement* (London).

—— (2000b), *On Target: The Practice of Performance Indicators* (London).

—— (2001), *Building for the Future* (London).

—— (2003), *PFI in Schools: The Quality and Cost of Buildings and Services Provided by Early PFI Private Finance Initiative Schemes* (London).

Auditor General Western Australia (1997), *Private Care for Public Patients: The Joondalup Health Campus*, Report No. 9 (Perth).

Ball, R., Heafey, M. and King, D. (2003a), 'Risk Transfer and Value for Money', *Public Management Review*, Vol. 5, No. 2, pp. 270–90.

—— (2003b), 'Some Lessons from Using PFI for School Building Projects', *Local Government Study*, Vol. 29, No. 2, summer, pp. 89–106.

Barclays Capital (1998), *Meridian Hospital Company Plc*, Initial Public Offering Circular (London).

Bates, M. (1997), *Review of the PFI (Private/Public Partnership) Process* (London: HM Treasury).

Boase, J.P. (2000), 'Beyond Government? The Appeal of Public-Private Partnerships', *Canadian Public Administration*, Vol. 43, No. 1, p. 88.

Boyne, G., Gould-Williams, J., Law. J. and Walker, R. (2002), 'Plans, Performance Information and Accountability: The Case of Best Value', *Public Administration*, Vol. 80, No. 4, pp. 691–710.

Broadbent, J. and Laughlin, R. (2002), 'Accounting Choices: Technical and Political Trade-Offs and the UK's Private Finance Initiative', *Accounting, Auditing and Accountability Journal*, Vol. 15, No. 5, pp. 622–54.

—— Gill, J. and Laughlin, R. (2003), *The Private Finance Initiative in the National Health Service: Nature, Emergence and the Role of Management Accounting in Decision Making and Post-Project Evaluation* (London: Chartered Institute of Management Accountants).

Catalyst Healthcare (Worcester) Holdings Ltd (2002), *Annual Report and Accounts 2001* (Worcester).

Cabinet Office (2000), *Successful IT: Modernising Government in Action* (London).

Centre for Public Services (2002), *Privatising Justice: The Impact of the Private Finance Initiative in the Criminal Justice System* (Sheffield).

Collyer, F. (2001), 'Port Macquarie Base Hospital' in Collyer, F., McMaster, J. and Wettenhall, R. (eds.), *Public Enterprise Divestment: Australian Case Studies* (Suva: The University of the South Pacific).

Cutler, T. and Waine, B. (1997), *Managing the Welfare State* (Oxford and New York: Berg).

Deakin, N. and Walsh, K. (1996), 'The Enabling State: The Role of Markets and Contracts', *Public Administration*, Vol. 74, Spring, pp. 33–48.

Debande, O. (2002), 'Private Financing of Transport Infrastructure: An Assessment of the UK experience', *Journal of Transport Economics and Policy*, Vol. 36, Part 3, September, pp. 355–87.

Deloitte and Touche Corporate Finance (2001), *London Underground Public-Private Partnership – Emerging Findings* (London: Transport for London).

DoH (Department of Health) (2000), *Sold on Health* (London).

—— (2002a), *Good Practice Guide: Learning Lessons from Post-Project Evaluation* (London).

—— (2002b), *Improving PFI Procurement* (London).

—— (2004), *Progress of New Hospital Schemes approved to go ahead* [online spreadsheet] <http://www.dh.gov.uk/assetRoot/04/09/03/37/04090337.xls>, (accessed 8/12/03).

DoE (Department of the Environment) (1995), *Digest of Data for the Construction Industry*, 2nd edition (London).

—— (1996), *Digest of Data for the Construction Industry*, 3rd edition (London).

—— (1997), *Digest of Data for the Construction Industry*, 4th edition (London).

DoT (Department of Transport) (2003), *Transport Statistics Great Britain: 2002* (London).

DETR (Department of the Environment, Transport and the Regions) (1998), *Digest of Data for the Construction Industry*, 5th edition (London).

—— (1999), *Digest of Data for the Construction Industry*, 6th edition (London).

—— (2000a), *Construction Statistics Annual – 2000* (London).

—— (2000b), *Transport 2010: The 10-Year Plan* (London).

DTI (Department of Trade and Industry) (1993), *Paying for Better Motorways* (London).

—— (1994), *Design Build Finance Operate Concessions for Trunk Roads and Motorways* (London).

—— (2001), *Construction Statistics Annual – 2001* (London).

—— (2002), *Construction Statistics Annual – 2002* (London).

—— (2003), *Transport Statistics Great Britain: 2002* (London: The Stationery Office).

Edwards, P. and Shaoul, J. (2003), 'Partnerships: For Better, for Worse?', *Accounting, Auditing and Accountability Journal*, Vol.1 6, No. 3, pp. 397–421.

Egan, J. (1998), *Rethinking Construction* (London: Office of the Deputy Prime Minister).

Estache, A., Romero, M. and Strong, J. (2000), 'Toll Roads', *World Bank Policy Research Working Paper*, No. 2387 (Washington DC: World Bank).

Fitch Ratings (2003), *PPP-PFI: UK Market Trends and Fitch Rating Criteria for European PPP Transactions* (London).

Flyvjberg, B., Bruzelius, N. and Rothengatter, W. (2003), *Megaprojects and Risks: An anatomy of ambition* (Cambridge: Cambridge University Press).

Freeman, P. (2004), *Evaluating Project Performance in Transport Projects in Developing Countries: Presentation to Transport Research Congress, Istanbul*, July (Washington, DC: World Bank).

Freedland, M. (1998), 'Public Law and Private Finance – Placing the Private Finance Initiative in a Public Law Framework', *Public Law*, summer, pp. 288–307.

Froud, J. and Shaoul, J. (2001), 'Appraising and Evaluating PFI for NHS Hospitals', *Financial Accountability and Management*, Vol. 17, No. 3, August, pp. 247–70.

Gaffney, D. and Pollock, A. (1997), *Can the NHS afford the Private Finance Initiative?* (London: British Medical Association, Health Policy and Economic Research Unit).

—— —— (1999a), *Downsizing for the 21st Century*, a report to Unison Northern Region on the North Durham Acute Hospitals PFI scheme (London: University College London, School of Public Policy).

—— —— (1999b), 'Pump Priming the PFI: Why are Privately Financed Hospital Schemes being Subsidised?' *Public Money & Management*, Vol. 17, No. 3, pp. 11–16.

—— —— Price, D. and Shaoul, J. (1999a), 'NHS Capital Expenditure and the Private Finance Initiative – Expansion or Contraction?' *British Medical Journal*, Vol. 319, pp. 48–51.

—— —— —— —— (1999b), 'PFI in the NHS – Is There an Economic Case?' *British Medical Journal*, Vol. 319, pp. 116–19.

—— —— —— —— (1999c), 'The Politics of the Private Finance Initiative and the New NHS', *British Medical Journal*, Vol. 319, pp. 249–53.

Gershon, P. (1999), *Review of Civil Procurement in Central Government* (London: HM Treasury).

Glaister, S. (1999), 'Past Abuses and Future Uses of Private Finance and Public Private Partnerships in Transport', *Public Money and Management*, Vol. 19, No. 3, pp. 29–36.

Grimsey, D. and Lewis, M. (2002), 'Evaluating the Risks of Public Private Partnerships for Infrastructure Projects', *International Journal of Project Management*, Vol. 20, pp. 107–18.

Grimshaw, D., Vincent, S. and Willmott, H. (2002), 'Going Privately: Partnership and Outsourcing in UK Public Services', *Public Administration*, Vol. 80, No. 3, pp. 475–502.

Hastings, A. (1999), 'Analysing Power Relationships in Partnerships: Is There a Role for Discourse Analysis?' *Urban Studies*, Vol. 36, No. 1, February, pp. 91–106.

Haynes, L. and Roden, N. (1999), 'Commercialising the Management and Maintenance of Trunk Roads in the United Kingdom', *Transportation*, Vol. 26, No. 1, pp. 31–54.

Heald, D. (1997), *Privately Financed Capital in Public Services* (Manchester: The Manchester School of Economic and Social Services).

Health Select Committee (2000), *Public Expenditure on Health and Personal Social Services 2000: Memorandum received from the Department of Health containing replies to a written questionnaire from the Committee*, HC 882, Session 1999–2000 (London: The Stationery Office).

Health Committee (2002), *The Role of the Private Sector in the NHS*, HC 308, Session 2001–02 (London: The Stationery Office).

Hewitt, C. (1997), 'Complexity and Cost in PFI Schemes', *Public Money and Management*, Vol. 17, No. 3, pp. 7–9.

Highways Agency (1997), *Value in Roads – a DBFO Case Study* (London).

—— (1999a), *Framework Document* (London).

—— (1999b), *Paving the Way* (London).

—— (2002), *Improving DBFOs – A Consultation Document* (London).

—— (2003), *Design, Build, Finance & Operate*, [online text] <http://www.highways.gov.uk/roads/dbfo/dbfo_intro.htm>, accessed 26 August 2003.

Hodges, R. and Mellett, H. (1999), 'Accounting for the Private Finance Initiative in the United Kingdom National Health Service', *Financial Accountability and Management*, Vol. 15, Nos. 3 and 4, pp. 275–90.

—— —— (2002), 'Investigating Standard Setting: Accounting for the United Kingdom's Private Finance Initiative', *Accounting Forum*, Vol. 26, No. 2, pp. 126–51.

Hood, J. and McGarvey, N. (2002), 'Managing the Risks of Public-Private Partnerships in Scottish Local Government', *Policy Studies*, Vol. 23, No. 1, March, pp. 21–35.

House of Commons Official Report (Hansard) (1997), *Untitled document deposited in House of Commons Library in response to question 6555*, July 16, p. 298, col. 534, No. 43.

Howard, M. (2002), 'Losing the Initiative', *Financial Management*, November, pp. 26–7 (London: Chartered Institute of Management Accountants).

Inland Revenue (2004), *CT6001 – Close companies: broad definition*, [online text] <http://www.inlandrevenue.gov.uk/manuals/ct123manual/ct6001.htm>, accessed 16 September 2004.

Institute of Fiscal Studies (2002), *The Green Budget* (London).

Institute for Public Policy Research (2001), *Building Better Partnerships: The Final Report of the Commission on Public Private Partnerships* (London).

—— (2004), *Openness Survey* (London).

Kernaghan, K. (1993), 'Partnership and Public Administration: Conceptual and Practical Considerations', *Canadian Public Administration*, Vol. 36, No. 1, Spring, pp. 60–5.

Kirkpatrick, I. and Lucio, M.M. (1996), 'Introduction: The Contract State and the Future of Public Management', *Public Administration*, Vol. 74, Spring, pp. 1–8.

Levy, S.M. (1996), *Build Operate and Transfer: Paving the way for Tomorrow's Infrastructure* (Stamford: Frank Mercede & Sons, Inc.).

Lister, J. (2003), *The PFI Experience: Voices from the Frontline* (London: Unison).

Mackie, P. and Preston, J. (1998), 'Twenty-one Sources of Error and Bias in Transport Project Appraisal', *Transport Policy*, Vol. 5, No. 1, pp. 1–7.

McKendrick, J. and McCabe, B. (1997), 'An Observer's Tale: Stonehaven Community Hospital', *Public Money & Management*, Vol. 17, No. 3, pp. 17–20.

McWilliam, J. (1997), 'A Commissioner's Tale: Avery Hill Student Village, University of Greenwich', *Public Money & Management*, Vol. 17, No. 3, pp. 21–4.

Meara, R. (1991), *Unfreezing the Assets: NHS Estate Management in the 1980s*, King's Fund Institute Research Report 11 (London: King's Fund).

—— (1997), *A Capital Conundrum: The Effect of the Private Finance Initiative on Strategic Change in London's Health Care* (London: King's Fund).

Methven, A. (2004), 'East Lothian Rescue: Global Infrastructure Review, Rescuing a PFI Deal', *Project Finance International*, May, pp. 42–5.

Mills, G. (1991), 'Commercial Funding of Transport Infrastructure: Lessons from Some Australian Cases', *Journal of Transport Economics and Policy*, September, pp. 279–98.

Miquel, S. and Condron, J. (1991), *Assessment of Road Maintenance by Contract*, Infrastructure and Urban Development Report INU 91 (Washington DC: World Bank).

Mulgan, R. (2000), 'Accountability: An Ever-expanding Concept?' *Public Administration*, Vol. 78, No. 3, Autumn, p. 555.

Nathan, S. and Whitfield, D. (2000), 'The PFI and Europe's Most Privatised Criminal Justice System', *The PFI Report*, February, No. 39 (London: Centaur).

NAO (National Audit Office) (1988), *Department of Transport, Scottish Department and Welsh Office: Road Planning*, Report of Comptroller and Auditor General, HC 688, Session 1987–88 (London: The Stationery Office).

—— (1997), *The Skye Bridge*, Report of Comptroller and Auditor General, HC 5, Session 1997–98 (London: The Stationery Office).

—— (1998a), *The Private Finance Initiative: The First Four Design, Build, Finance and Operate Roads Contracts*, Report of Comptroller and Auditor General, HC 476, Session 1997–98 (London: The Stationery Office).

—— (1998b), *Cost overuns, Funding Problems and Delays on Guy's Hospital Phase III Development*, Report of Comptroller and Auditor General, HC 761, Session 1997–98 (London: The Stationery Office).

—— (1999a), *The Private Finance Initiative: The Contract to Complete and Operate the A74(M)/M74 in Scotland*, Report of Comptroller and Auditor General, HC 356, Session 1998–99 (London: The Stationery Office).

—— (1999b), *The PFI Contract for the New Dartford and Gravesham Hospital*, Report of Comptroller and Auditor General, HC 423, Session 1998–99 (London: The Stationery Office).

—— (1999c), *Examining the Value for Money of Deals under PFI*, Report of Comptroller and Auditor General, HC 739, Session 1998–99 (London: The Stationery Office).

—— (1999d), *The Passport Delays of Summer 1999*, Report of Comptroller and Auditor General, HC 812, Session 1998–99 (London: The Stationery Office).

—— (2000a), *Public Health Laboratory Service Board Accounts 1998–1999*, Report of Comptroller and Auditor General, HC 874, Session 1998–99 (London: The Stationery Office).

—— (2000b), *The Refinancing of the Fazakerley PFI Prison Contract*, Report of Comptroller and Auditor General, HC 584, Session 1999–2000 (London: The Stationery Office).

—— (2000c), *Supporting Innovation: Managing Risk in Government Departments,* Report of Comptroller and Auditor General, HC 864, Session 1999–2000 (London: The Stationery Office).

—— (2000d), *The Radiocommunications Agency's Joint Venture with CMG*, Report of Comptroller and Auditor General, HC 21, Session 2000–01 (London: The Stationery Office).

—— (2000e), *The Financial Analysis for the London Underground Public Private Partnership*, Report of Comptroller and Auditor General, HC 54, Session 2000–01 (London: The Stationery Office).

—— (2001a), *The Department of Media, Culture and Sport: The Renegotiation of the PFI-type Deal for the Royal Armouries Museum in Leeds*, Report of Comptroller and Auditor General, HC 103, Session 2001–02 (London: The Stationery Office).

—— (2001b), *Modern Policy-Making: Ensuring Policies Deliver Value For Money,* Report by the Comptroller and Auditor General, HC 289, Session 2001–02 (London: The Stationery Office).

—— (2001c), *Channel Tunnel Rail Link*, Report of Comptroller and Auditor General, HC 302, Session 2001–02 (London: The Stationery Office).

—— (2001d), *NIRS2 Contract Extension*, Report of Comptroller and Auditor General, HC 355, Session 2001–02 (London: The Stationery Office).

—— (2001e), *Managing the Relationship to Secure a Successful Partnership in PFI Projects*, Report of Comptroller and Auditor General, HC 375, Session 2001–02 (London: The Stationery Office).

—— (2002a), *The Joint Services Command and Staff College,* HC 537, Report of Comptroller and Auditor General, Session 2001–02 (London: The Stationery Office).

—— (2002b), *Public Private Partnerships: Airwave*, Report of Comptroller and Auditor General, HC 730, Session 2001–02 (London: The Stationery Office).

—— (2002c), *MOD: Redevelopment of MOD Main Building*, Report of Comptroller and Auditor General, HC 748, Session 2001–02 (London: The Stationery Office).

—— (2002d), *The Public Private Partnership for the National Air Traffic Services Ltd*, Report of Comptroller and Auditor General, HC 1096, Session 2001–02 (London: The Stationery Office).

—— (2002e), *PFI Refinancing Update*, Report of Comptroller and Auditor General, HC 1288, Session 2001–02 (London: The Stationery Office).

—— (2002f), *The PFI Contract for the redevelopment of the West Middlesex University Hospital*, Report of Comptroller and Auditor General, HC 49, Session 2002–03 (London: The Stationery Office).

—— (2003a), *New IT Systems for Magistrates' Courts: the LIBRA project*, Report of Comptroller and Auditor General, HC 327, Session 2002–03 (London: The Stationery Office).

—— (2003b), *PFI: Construction Performance*, Report of Comptroller and Auditor General, HC 371, Session 2002–03 (London: The Stationery Office).

—— (2003c), *Maintaining England's Motorways and Trunk Roads*, Report of Comptroller and Auditor General, HC 431, Session 2002–03 (London: The Stationery Office).

—— (2003d), *NHS (England) Summarised Accounts 2001–2002*, Report of Comptroller and Auditor General, HC 493, Session 2002–03 (London: The Stationery Office).

—— (2003e), *PPP in Practice: National Savings and Investments' Deal with Siemens Business Services, Four Years On*, Report of Comptroller and Auditor General, HC 626, Session 2002–03 (London: The Stationery Office).

—— (2003f), *Northern Ireland Court Service – PFI: The Laganside Courts*, Report of Comptroller and Auditor General, HC 649, Session 2002–03 (London: The Stationery Office).

—— (2003g), *The Operational Performance of Prisons*, Report of Comptroller and Auditor General, HC 700, Session 2002–03 (London: The Stationery Office).

—— (2003h), *Managing resources to Deliver Better Public Services*, HC 61-1, Session 2003–04 (London: The Stationery Office).

—— (2004), *NHS (England) Summarised Accounts 2002–2003*, Report of Comptroller and Auditor General, HC 505-II, Session 2003–04 (London: The Stationery Office).

New South Wales Auditor General (1996), *'Report for 1996: Volume I'* (Sydney: NSW Parliament).

NHS (2003), *Benchmarking and Performance Management*, [online text] <http://www.nhs-procure21.gov.uk/aims/benchmarking.html>, accessed 26 August 2003.

NHS Estates (2003a), *Estates Return Information Collection (ERIC) – 2003*, [online text] <http://www.nhsestates.gov.uk/property_management/content/eric.html>, accessed 26 August 2003.

—— (2003b), 'NHS Estates Data Collection & Analysis System (NEDCAS)', [online text] <http://www.doh.gov.uk/nedcas/index.htm> accessed 26 August 2003.

—— (2003c), *NHS Estates' Annual Report and Accounts 2002/03*, HC 828, Session 2002–03 (London: The Stationery Office)

NHS Executive (1994), *Capital Investment Manual* (Leeds: NHS Executive).

—— (1999a), 'Public Private Partnerships in the National Health Service: The Private Finance Initiative Overview', *Good Practice Manual* (London: The Stationery Office)

—— (1999b), *Public Private Partnerships in the National Health Service: Private Finance Initiative* (London: Department of Health).

—— (1999c), *NHS Trust Manual of Accounts* (Leeds: NHS Executive).

Office of Government Commerce (2001), *Best Practice Gateway Review 5: Benefits Evaluation* (London).

—— (2002a), *Standardisation of PFI Contracts*, July (London).

—— (2002b), *Refinancing of Early PFI Transactions: Code of Conduct*, October (London).

—— (2003a), *Post-Implementation Review*, Successful Delivery Toolkit Version 3.91, May (London).

—— (2003b), *Achieving Excellence in Construction Procurement Guide 8: Improving Performance* (London).

—— (2003c), *Delivering Your Agenda, 2003/4* (London).

—— (2003d), *Gateway Frequently Asked Questions*, [online text] <http://www.ogc.gov.uk/index.asp?docid=1001004>, accessed 4 September 2003.

—— (2004), *Overview of OGC*, [online text]<http://www.ogc.gov.uk/index.asp?id=1000312>, accessed 28 January 2004.

Osborne, D. and Gaebler, T. (1993), *Reinventing Government: How the Entrepreneurial Spirit is Transforming the Public Sector From Schoolhouse to State House, City Hall to Pentagon* (New York: Plume Books).

Owens, J. (1999), 'Why PFI Performs in Practice', *Public Finance*, April 23–29, pp. 26–7.

Partnerships UK (2003), *What is Partnerships UK?*, [online text] <http://www.partnershipsuk.org.uk/puk/index.htm> accessed 17 April 2003.

Pike, R.H. and Wolfe, M.B. (1988), *Capital Budgeting in the 1990s* (London: Chartered Institute of Management Accountants).

Pilling, J.R. (2002), 'Establishing a Contract for a PACS Managed Service', *Clinical Radiology*, Vol. 57, pp. 178–83.

Pollock, A., Price, D. and Dunnigan, M. (2000), *Deficits Before Patients: A Report on the Worcestershire Royal Infirmary PFI and Worcestershire Hospital Configuration* (London: University College).

—— Shaoul, J., Rowland, D. and Player, S. (2001), *Public Services and the Private Sector: A Response to the IPPR* (London: Catalyst working paper).

—— —— Vickers, V. (2002), 'Private Finance and "Value for Money" in NHS Hospitals: A Policy in Search of a Rationale?' *British Medical Journal*, Vol. 324, pp. 1205–8.

PPF (2001), *Focus: Health* (London).

PPP Forum (2003a), *Project Interviews*, [online text] <http://www.pppforum.com/interviews/ interview_alanperkins.html>, accessed 1 September 2003.

—— (2003b), *Project Interviews*, [online text] <http:// www.pppforum.com/interviews/ interview_malcolm.html>, accessed 1 September 2003.

—— (2003c), *Signed Projects*, [online text] <http:// www.pppforum.com/signed.html>, accessed 1 November 2003.

Price, D., Gaffney, D. and Pollock, A. (1999), *The Only Game in Town: A Report on the Cumberland Infirmary Carlisle PFI*, Report, Unison Northern Region (London: Unison).

Public Accounts Committee (1998a), *The Skye Bridge*, HC 348, Session 1997–98 (London: The Stationery Office).

—— (1998b), *Contract to Develop and Operate the Replacement National Insurance Recording System*, HC 472, Session 1997–98 (London: The Stationery Office).

—— (1998c), *The PFI Contracts for Bridgend and Fazakerley Prisons*, HC 499, Session 1997–98 (London: The Stationery Office).

—— (1998d), *The Private Finance Initiative: The First Four Design, Build, Finance and Operate Roads Contracts*, HC 580, Session 1997–98 (London: The Stationery Office).

—— (1999a), *Delays to the New National Insurance Recording System*, HC 182, Session 1998–99 (London: The Stationery Office).

—— (1999b), *The PRIME Project: The Transfer of the Department of Social Security Estate to the Private Sector*, HC 548, Session 1998–99 (London: The Stationery Office).

—— (1999c), *Department of Health: Cost Over-runs, Funding Problems and Delays on Guy's Hospital Phase III Development*, Twenty-Eighth Report, HC 289, Session 1998–99 (London: The Stationery Office).

—— (2000a), *The Contributions Agency: The Newcastle Estate Development Project*, HC 104, Session 1999–2000 (London: The Stationery Office).

—— (2000b), *Home Office: The Immigration and Nationality Directorate's Casework Programme*, HC 130, Session 1999–2000 (London: The Stationery Office).

—— (2000c), *The PFI Contract for the new Dartford and Gravesham Hospital*, HC 131, Session 1999–2000 (London: The Stationery Office).

—— (2000d), *The Passport Delays of Summer 1999*, HC 208, Session 1999–2000 (London: The Stationery Office).

—— (2000e), *Inland Revenue/EDS Strategic Partnership: The Award of New Work*, HC 431, Session 1999–2000 (London: The Stationery Office).

—— (2001a), *The Cancellation of the Benefits Payment Card Project*, HC 358, Session 2001–02 (London: The Stationery Office).

—— (2001b), *The Refinancing of the Fazakerley PFI Prison Contract*, HC 372, Session 2000–01 (London: The Stationery Office).

—— (2002a), *Managing the Relationship to Secure a Successful Partnership in PFI Projects*, HC 460, Session 2001–02 (London: The Stationery Office).

—— (2002b), *The Channel Tunnel Rail Link*, HC 630, Session 2001–02 (London: The Stationery Office).

—— (2002c), *PPP: Airwave*, HC 783, Session 2001–02 (London: The Stationery Office).

—— (2003a), *The PFI Contract for the Redevelopment of the West Middlesex University Hospital*, HC 155, Session 2002–03 (London: The Stationery Office).

—— (2003b), *PFI Refinancing Update*, HC 203, Session 2002–03 (London: The Stationery Office).

—— (2003c), *The Highways Agency: Maintaining England's Motorways and Trunk Roads*, Thirty-Second Report, HC 556, Session 2002–03 (London: The Stationery Office).

—— (2003d), *PFI: Construction Performance*, HC 567, Session 2002–03 (London: The Stationery Office).

—— (2003e), *Delivering Better Value for Money from the Private Finance Initiative*, HC 764, Session 2002–03 (London: The Stationery Office).

Queen Elizabeth Hospital NHS Trust (2003), *Queen Elizabeth Hospital PFI Project: post-project evaluation report* (Woolwich).

Rhodes, R.A.W. (1994), 'The Hollowing Out of the State', *Political Quarterly*, Vol. 65, pp. 138–51.

Ricketts, M. (1994), *The Economics of Business Enterprise: An Introduction to Economic Organisation and the Theory of the Firm*, 2nd edn. (Brighton: Wheatsheaf).

Ridley, A. (1997), 'Infrastructure – Private Finance without Privatisation', in *Privatisation of Utilities and Infrastructure: Methods and Constraints*, OECD Proceedings, Centre for Co-operation with the Economies in Transition (Paris: OECD).

Rosenau, P.V. (2000), 'The Strengths and Weaknesses of Public-Private Policy Partnerships'. In P.V. Rosenau (ed.), *Public-Private Policy Partnerships* (London: MIT Press).

Rowsell, S. (2001), 'The Partnering Approach to Procurement', *Private Finance Initiative Journal*, Vol. 6, No. 5, November–December 2001.

Royal Infirmary of Edinburgh (1997), *Royal Infirmary of Edinburgh Full Business Case* (Edinburgh).

Seal, W. (1999), 'Accounting and Competitive Tendering in UK Local Government: An Institutionalist Interpretation of the New Public Management', *Financial Accountability & Management*, Vol. 15, Nos. 3 and 4, August/November, pp. 309–27.

Senate Community Affairs References Committee (2000), *Healing our Hospitals* (Canberra).

Shaoul J. (1998), 'Charging for Capital in the NHS: To Improve Efficiency?' *Management Accounting Research*, March 1998, Vol. 9, pp. 95–112.

—— (2004a), '*Railpolitik*: The Financial Realities of Operating Britain's National Railways', *Public Money and Management*, Vol. 24, No. 1, pp. 27-36.

—— (2005), 'A Critical Financial Analysis of the Private Finance Initiative: Selecting a Financing Method or Reallocating Economic Wealth?' *Critical Perspectives on Accounting* (forthcoming).

Silva, G. F. (2000), *Toll Roads: Recent Trends in Private Participation*, Private Sector and Infrastructure Network, Note Number 224 (Washington DC: World Bank).

Sinfield, A. (2000), 'Tax Benefits in Non-State Pensions', *European Journal of Social Security*, Vol. 2, No. 2 pp. 137–67.

Spackman, M. (2002), 'Public-Private Partnerships: Lessons from the British Approach', *Economic Systems*, Vol. 26, pp. 283–301.

Standard and Poor's (2002), 'How is the UK Private Finance Initiative Risk Changing?' *Ratings Direct*, October 14 (London).

Standard and Poor's (2003), *Public Finance/ Infrastructure Finance: Credit Survey of the UK Private Finance Initiative and Public-Private Partnerships* (London).

Sussex , J. (2001), *The Economics of the Private Finance Initiative in the NHS* (London: Office of Health Economics).

—— (2003), 'Public-Private Partnerships in Hospital Development: Lessons from the UK's "Private Finance Initiative"', *Research in Health Care Financial Management*, Vol. 8, No. 1, pp. 59–76.

Taylor, P. and Cooper, C. (2002), *Privatised Prisons and Detention Centres in Scotland, An Independent Report* (Universities of Stirling and Strathclyde: Mimeo).

The Cabinet Office (1997), *Your Right to Know: The Government's Proposals for a Freedom of Information*, presented to Parliament by the Chancellor of the Duchy of Lancaster, Cmnd 3818 (London: The Stationery Office).

Timms, S. (2001), *Public Private Partnership, Private Finance Initiative*, Keynote Address by the Financial Secretary to the Treasury to Global Summit, Cape Town, 6 December.

Transport Select Committee (2003), *The Work of the Highways Agency, Select Committee on Transport: Eighth Report*, HC 453, Session 2002–03 (London: The Stationery Office).

Travers, M. (1996), 'Banks call for less talk and more action', *Project Scotland*, June 20, pp. 16–17.

HM Treasury (1991), *Appraisal and Evaluation in Central Government: The Green Book* (London: The Stationery Office).

—— (1997a), *Appraisal and Evaluation in Central Government: The Green Book* (London: The Stationery Office).

—— (1997b), *A Step-By-Step Guide to the PFI Procurement Process* (London: HM Treasury).

—— (1998), *Modern Public Services for Britain: Investing in Reform. Comprehensive Spending Review: New Public Sector Spending Plans 1999–2002*, Cmnd 4011 (London: The Stationery Office).

—— (2000), *Guide to the Centre of Government* (London: HM Treasury).

—— (2002), Minute in response to PAC Report *Managing the Relationship to Secure a Successful Partnership in PFI Projects*, Cmnd 5600, Session 2001–02 (London: HM Treasury).

—— (2003a), *Appraisal and Evaluation in Central Government: The Green Book* (London: The Stationery Office).

—— (2003b), *Budget Report: Red Book* (London: The Stationery Office).

—— (2003c), *PFI: Meeting the Investment Challenge* (London: HM Treasury).

—— (2003d), *Draft Value for Money Appraisal Guidance* (London: HM Treasury).

—— (2003e), *PFI Construction Performance, Treasury Minutes*, Cmnd 5984 (London: HM Treasury).

Treasury Taskforce (1999a), *How to Account for PFI*, Technical Note No. 1 (Revised) (London: HM Treasury).

—— (1999b), *How to Construct a Public Sector Comparator*, Technical Note No. 5 (London: HM Treasury).

Walker, B. and Con Walker, B. (2000), *Privatisation: Sell Off or Sell Out? The Australian Experience* (Sydney: ABC Books).

Whorley, D. (2001), 'The Andersen-Comsoc Affair: Partnerships and the Public Interest', *Canadian Public Administration-Administration Publique du Canada*, Vol. 44, No. 3, pp. 320–345.

World Bank (1994), *World Development Report 1994: Infrastructure for Development* (Washington DC).

Worthington, J. (2002), *2020 Vision: Our Future Healthcare Environments*, Report of the Building Futures Group (London: The Stationery Office).